W9-CCX-619

SCHOOL,
CURRICULUM,
AND THE INDIVIDUAL

A Blaisdell Book in Education

School,

Curriculum,

and the Individual

John I. Goodlad

UNIVERSITY OF CALIFORNIA, LOS ANGELES
INSTITUTE FOR THE DEVELOPMENT
OF EDUCATIONAL ACTIVITIES

69750

BLAISDELL PUBLISHING COMPANY
A DIVISION OF GINN AND COMPANY
Waltham, Massachusetts · Toronto · London

Copyright © 1966 by BLAISDELL PUBLISHING COMPANY
A Division of Ginn and Company
All rights reserved

Library of Congress Catalog Card Number: 66–17796
Printed in the United States of America

LB
2806
.G58

Preface

Teachers are surrounded by educational structures which influence their thinking, planning, and teaching, for better or for worse. Significant among these are the existing patterns of school and curriculum organization. These patterns assist teachers or they get in the way. They assist by emphasizing the significant and relevant; they restrict by emphasizing, or even imposing, the insignificant and irrelevant. It is conceivable that, as the organization of the school and of the curriculum influences teaching, so does it, to a considerable extent, influence learning.

Patterns of school and curriculum organization cannot be eluded, but they can be changed. And new, alternative patterns can be created — alternatives to provide choices for teachers and opportunities for research. Human variability and potentiality demand them.

For more than a quarter of a century, I have observed the facilitating-restricting character of school and curriculum organization, from early teaching experience in a one-room, eight-grade rural school, through years of consulting in many kinds and sizes of schools. These experiences have in part been guided by, but have more been productive of, a set of beliefs and assumptions about the aims of education, the role of schools in our society, human potentiality and variability, what is worth knowing and teaching, and the nature of certain conditions pertinent to effective learning. From these beliefs and assumptions, honed by modified trial-and-error experimentation, I have formulated some implications for organizing schools and for selecting and arranging what is to be taught in them. These implications, in turn, have been expressed in argument, criteria, and actual school practices.

Since the mid-1950's, I have formulated in writing some of these ideas and their meaning for school practice. This volume consists of more than two dozen papers selected from a larger number because of their relevance to the central topic of school and curriculum organization and arranged so as to bring assumptions and implications into close physical

v

as well as, hopefully, logical relationship. Three of the papers were written in collaboration with others. In one instance, the paper was written entirely by others but grew directly out of my activities as curriculum consultant to the Montgomery County (Maryland) Public Schools. These papers have been modified and trimmed in various ways since original publication in order to align them closely with the central themes. Assumptions tend to be implicit rather than explicit, except in the single chapter comprising Part I, which sets the theme regarding school function and the individual. This theme is developed further and applied to school organization and curriculum organization, respectively, in Parts II and III. Part IV concludes with some observations and recommendations concerning the utilization and education of teachers and concerning tomorrow's schools.

Dr. Lois Nelson, with consummate insight, compiled and arranged the initial selection of papers, and to her I am most grateful. My thanks go also to Mrs. Elsa Gilbert, Mrs. Jean Moore, and Miss Ann Edwards for their assistance in preparing the manuscript; to Professor Robert H. Anderson of Harvard University who is co-author of two papers; to Professor Kenneth J. Rehage of the University of Chicago who is co-author of another; and to those members of the Curriculum Office, Montgomery County Public Schools, Rockville, Maryland, who wrote a fourth.

Finally, I acknowledge with thanks the following publishers who so readily granted permission to reproduce the selections comprising this volume: Department of Elementary School Principals (National Education Association); Harcourt, Brace and World, Inc.; National Education Association of the United States; Journal of the National Education Association; University of Chicago Press; Association for Childhood Education International; The Macmillan Company; American Educational Research Association; Kappa Delta Pi; Association for Supervision and Curriculum Development (National Education Association); Saturday Review, Inc.; Bureau of Educational Research and Service, The Ohio State University; National Science Teachers Association (National Education Association); National Commission on Teacher Education and Professional Standards (National Education Association); University of Pennsylvania Press.

January, 1966   JOHN I. GOODLAD

Contents

SCHOOL,
CURRICULUM,
AND THE INDIVIDUAL

PART I Introduction

What are schools for? Traditionally, we have viewed schools as society's crucibles for molding the talents needed by that society. But predicting the talents likely to be needed by a given society a generation hence and, therefore, to be developed in the young today is a difficult, if not impossible, task. We cannot predict what society will be like, but only that a dynamic, self-renewing society will require self-renewing individuals.

Schools, if they are to contribute to the production of such individuals and such a society, must identify and foster human abilities not always cherished by schools of today and yesterday. Furthermore, in the process, they must take into account the vast differences in background, aptitude, and present attainment of students in each and every trait to be developed. Increasing insight into the nature of these differences makes the problems of schooling no less easy.

Part I of this volume consists of a single chapter which, in turn, is a composite of three previously published papers on school function, individual differences, and other educational matters. Chapter One, then, is an introduction to much of what follows, serving particularly to show the relationships among a particular conception of school function, individual differences, new patterns of school organization, and a longitudinal or vertical view of the curriculum.

1

▶1

School Function and the Individual

The tasks of education are profoundly complex. Man has rocketed his kind into space. He has brought back into pulsating life a human being already pronounced dead. He has fashioned in his own likeness robots that remember, file, and sort and then answer in moments problems that would tax a hundred men for a thousand days. But men still cheat and steal and kill as they did a thousand years ago and thousands of years before that.

These are not always trapped men or hungry men or threatened men who cheat and steal and kill. Some men pronounced learned cheat because they are vain. Some men pronounced holy steal because they are greedy. Some men pronounced wise kill because they have established no identity with their fellow men. The people who soon may bring down upon themselves a holocaust are — or will have been — the *most* educated of all time.

The central task of education and, therefore, of schools, is to develop men of good will who do not cheat or steal or kill — universal individuals who value as one both self and all mankind, sensing immortality as the idea of mankind and not the fact of man. What is the nature of such men and what goes into their making?

SOURCE: John I. Goodlad: *Some Propositions in Search of Schools* (Washington: Department of Elementary School Principals, 1962), pp. 7–28; "Elementary Education," *Education and the Idea of Mankind,* Robert Ulich (ed.) (New York: Harcourt, Brace & World, Inc., 1964), pp. 97–119, copyright 1964 by Council for the Study of Mankind; "Values and Data," *Planning and Organizing for Teaching* (Washington: National Education Association, Project on the Instructional Program of the Public Schools, 1963), pp. 11–16. All reprinted by permission of the publishers.

3

Goal

The central aim of education, then, is to develop rational men who do not sin against themselves and their kind. To specify *rational,* rather than simply *men,* is to appear to state a redundancy, for men who neither cheat because of their vanity nor steal because of their greed nor kill because of their malice *are* rational men. Nonetheless, so as not to mistake the intellectual man or the much-schooled man for the rational man, we must specify what rational men do and do not do.

The intellectual man thinks about the problems before him but he is not necessarily committed to the conclusions to which his intellectuality brings him. The much-schooled man is more likely to come face to face with the drama of mankind's triumphs and tragedies and to be committed to the tentative conclusions of his inquiry. But he does not necessarily act or see the need for acting upon these conclusions. Some "educated" men regard action as beneath them, as unsuited to their learned state.

The rational man not only is committed to the rich fruits of inquiry but also is prepared to act and, indeed, acts upon insight rendered compelling by commitment. He knows, as perhaps the most vital ingredient of his rationality, that only through action following understanding and commitment does man forge the links in the chains of his own humanity and of mankind's immortality. He senses his place in time and space and his individual responsibility to that place, time, and space.

The intellectual man standing disdainfully uncommitted, the educated man standing impeccably uninvolved, these are the living symbols of imperfection in education and schooling. For all nations that approach universal elementary and secondary schooling, these — not the stumbling reader, the guessing speller, the by-chance figurer — are the challenge to educational reform. For those nations where adult illiteracy prevails, the challenge is to assure rationality in that large segment of the childhood population fast becoming literate. For both, lethal danger lies in equating literacy with rationality.

Literate nations, in seeking to assist pre-literate nations, should remind themselves that their own universal schooling has not assured development of the universal individual.

What are the qualities of "the rational man"? Ulich has elaborated three closely interconnected human characteristics: "The first is the quality of faith, the second the quality of self-transcendence, and the third the quality of vision — all three disciplined and purified by reason and self-criticism [1].* In the words of Phenix:

---

* Refer to end of article for chronological list of references.

. . . the rationalist faith is that there is one standpoint — that of disciplined reason — which comprehends all the others, making it possible to escape the relativities of time and culture and the illusions of provincialism. This is the peculiar property of reason, that it enables man to achieve a degree of universality, to rise to some extent above the limitations of circumstance and history. . . . [2]

"To develop disciplined reason" is a compelling, overarching goal for all levels of education. It needs no restatement for each step in the vertical structure of schooling. But disciplined reason is a condition neither found full-blown nor produced by magic formula. Nor is it assured in the much schooled and necessarily absent in the near-illiterate. Schooling, we think, contributes to its attainment.

Individual Differences

Viewing man as a class of creatures, one is struck with the overriding common features shared by all members of the species. Viewing a group of men brought together for a common purpose, one is struck by the startling person-to-person differences that make agreement on even the nature of that purpose difficult. These are the differences that complicate the problems of school-keeping.

In the sense of these differences, men are born different and unequal. The socialization process in which school plays a part smoothes out some of these differences so that the individual achieves a sense of identity with his kind and of contributing to a common welfare. In the process, however, there is always danger that the cutting edges of individuality will be blunted and shaped to the contours of whatever mold is currently popular. The school is challenged to find firm ground combining the discipline of conformity with the exciting, often dangerous, appeal of other possibilities. The school finds such ground too infrequently. It tends to play it safe — perhaps necessarily — toward the side of conformity.

Body chemistry provides the differences brought into a world of people and things. Nutrition — physical, mental, social — favors or deprives initial tendencies. One child is lusty from the beginning in his cries and movements, another is lethargic. One sits still almost in pain, another moves reluctantly. How does the school provide for these differences? At first glance, it would appear that the school provides well for the lethargic one, with long periods of sitting and tasks that minimize physical movement. The active one has some additional lessons to learn.

One child learns about the way things are — or, at least, about the way adults believe things to be. Another child wonders why. Still another seems almost to resent the way adults see things and insists that they are different. The school shoulders no easy task in seeking to point out that not all is known or agreed upon and yet that differing interpretations are not equally valid.

Researchers are finding out what artists have long sensed: that creativity is a human trait which does not correlate perfectly, or even nearly perfectly, with what we have chosen to define and measure as intelligence. Humans possess this trait (or these traits) in widely varying degrees and express it in innumerable ways. But schools often do not recognize the trait behind the many unconventional ways in which it is expressed. In condemning the expressions, schools often condemn the human beings responsible for them to lives of partial fulfillment. Whenever schools too narrowly define that which is to be approved, they tend to deny expression of tendencies for want of which society soon may be crippled. Mankind suffers from denial of that which is innately man.

Young children around the world are more alike than different. The very young in China, Brazil, Nigeria, Nicaragua, Newfoundland, and the United States are surprisingly similar in their spontaneity, their joy in laughter, their abandon in play. But culture soon begins its relentless work, and toddlers capable of communicating with toddlers everywhere are molded into children scarcely capable of communicating with anyone anywhere. The range of effective interaction is reduced to ethnic group, social class, or even geographic neighborhood.

In any segment of population, closely circumscribed as it is by uniformity in tradition, religion, caste, or socio-economic status, children's native abilities conspire, nonetheless, with environmental opportunity and happenstance to produce profound differences in their readiness for school fare.

The mental age range in a group of six-year-olds entering the first grade is more than three years. The spread between the quick and the slow increases with time, just as a fast car steadily increases its lead on a slow one. Thus, by the time youngsters coming into school together enter the fifth grade, a few of them compare favorably in mental age with high school freshmen. And, alas, a few have developed no further in their ability to use language and manipulate number symbols than have most children still in the first grade.

Learners vary widely in their school achievement. The spread in *average* achievement in an elementary-school class slightly exceeds the number of the grade level. Hence, this spread in achievement is more than three years in a third-grade class, four in a fourth-grade, five in a fifth-grade, and so on. By the junior high school years, this overall spread is estimated to be approximately two-thirds the mean age of the grade-group. A group entering the seventh grade is approximately twelve years of age. Two-thirds of this figure is eight. Consequently, the spread in achievement is from the third grade to the eleventh.

At least part of the variability picture in a class group is found within the individual. Youngsters of average intelligence often out-class their genius-level peers in posing novel solutions to problems. Children and youth who break with tradition in the way they view phenomena or manipulate art media sometimes are indifferent scholars.

Class data revealing both intelligence and achievement test scores show that the correlation between the two is far from perfect. The student at the top of the list in achievement often is a third of the way down in IQ. And one often finds children with the highest IQs ranking down to the midpoint in achievement.

Differences from subject-field to subject-field in a single learner are even more striking. Few children are at grade-level in all subjects. In fact, mid-year achievement test scores reveal that only three or four youngsters in an elementary-school class of thirty are at grade-level in all subjects, even when one defines grade-level to allow a full-year spread. Thus, only three or four fourth-graders are at fourth-grade level in all subjects at the end of January, with grade-level defined as the range from 4.0 to 4.9. The remaining eighty or ninety per cent of the children range from several grades below to several grades above present grade placement. A teacher who says, "I teach the fourth grade," is talking about only three or four children in the class!

Students with high or low averages often deviate markedly from these averages in one or more fields. A slow-learning child in the fourth grade with average achievement of 2.9 may score 4.1 in arithmetic computation but only 1.4 in paragraph meaning. Another child in the fourth grade with average achievement of 5.2 may score 3.9 in arithmetic computation and 7.4 in paragraph meaning. In the usual heterogeneous class group, one finds children who range from subject area to subject area by as much as the grade level. Thus, the range from some aspect of reading to some aspect of arithmetic for a child in the third grade may be three or more years.

In what grades do the above individuals belong? The obvious answer is that each child belongs in several grades; the first one, above, in the second for reading and the fourth for arithmetic; the second child in the third for arithmetic and the seventh for reading. But where does one place the limits? The first child is about to move into the third and the second child into the fourth for arithmetic. Should they be transferred if it is only mid-year? And if all children are moved subject-by-subject, should ten-year-olds who read at the second-grade level be placed with six-year-olds who read at the second-grade level? Obviously, their reading problems, to say nothing of their interests, are likely to be markedly different. And what about the fourth-grader reading at the seventh-grade level? Is he to be transported to the junior high school? The obvious answer to the question of appropriate grade placement slips into obscurity — except for those many inexperienced would-be school reformers who have not thought the problems through in the light of appropriate data. There are no panaceas but there are some promising alternatives, as we shall see.

The problem of trait variability in relation to school and curriculum organization is complicated by the fact that youngsters advance irregularly. This fact is significant at all levels of education and is particularly compelling in high school. We know very little about students' perceptions of their learning environment. Some students, for reasons that are not at all clear, become fascinated with aspects of certain subject matters. The attraction may be because of or in spite of how the subject is taught at school. Nonetheless, a child or youth starts reading everything he can about snakes or rocks or Indians or sea life. Perhaps of more importance than the fact that he is fascinated by these phenomena, he becomes suddenly aware of his fascination. The desire to know more dominates his present life and shapes his life goals. Every real teacher looks for this great awakening in a student and, when he finds it, cultivates it with painstaking care. When the pursuit of happiness becomes indistinguishably enmeshed with finding happiness in the pursuit of knowing, there are few learning problems.

Some Implications for Schooling

What should and can the school do to modify human traits? Philosophers and psychologists have long pondered the two questions implied. Their answers, at best, have provided an illuminating picture of part of an elusive whole: schools must teach "the method of intelligence"; or, the what, why, and when of schooling are found "in the potential of the individual learner"; or, the tasks of learning must be organized around "the significant problems of a changing world society"; or, the learner must be introduced to "the central concepts and methods of inquiry" of the several disciplines.

Child, culture, subject-matter discipline, method — these and more are the stuff of schooling. Schoolmen must not wait for more compelling statements of goal, essential though it be that men of wisdom persist in the quest for them. Likewise, schoolmen must not wait for more precise clarifications of means, for the grand synthesis of method, essential though it be that men of science intensify their researches into them. Schoolmen must act daily upon the fruits of these insights and inquiries, depending upon judgment refined by schooling and by experience in the trial-and-error process of improving education [3].

We now turn to four significant aspects of schooling — facilities, expectations, curriculum, and method — which lend themselves to being "disciplined and purified by reason and self-criticism." All four are means toward the ultimate development of rational men, men who respect self but who are capable of transcending self in achieving a meaningful identity with their fellow men.

Educators may disagree with the proposals that follow but they dare not ignore the issues and problems posed by them.

Facilities ▪ For most of the world, the first significant step in educational improvement is to get children into schools and keep them there long enough for some permanent value to result. Approximately 45 per cent (250 of more than 550 million) of the world's boys and girls between the ages of five and fourteen is yet to be enrolled in any school, public or private [4]. And large numbers of the 55 per cent currently enrolled do not remain long enough to become functionally literate.

It is difficult for persons living in countries where universal elementary education is established to comprehend the magnitude of the world task that lies before us. The future of mankind no doubt depends on ideas, but the spread of those ideas that are to prevail awaits the construction of millions of classrooms and the preparation of millions of teachers for them. The children who will enter these classrooms await in their turn humanizing reform in the conduct of schooling if significant ideas ever are to reach them.

The provision of these facilities and teachers must be guided by an awareness of the fact that tomorrow's schools can and must provide a bastion for individuality in a world of increasing anonymity. A population tidal wave is threatening to engulf a world-wide awakening of the human spirit and its accompanying striving for education. In every large city and in most of the world where poverty prevails, children share such dingy quarters and have so little opportunity to be alone that anything other than a struggle-for-survival concept of self is hard to come by. Certainly, opportunity to contemplate the state of man and his world is missing.

The opportunity to fashion one's own dwelling according to a personal conception of what is pleasing is available to and used by only a small fraction of the human race. The need to provide endless numbers of roofs and walls, cheaply and quickly, threatens to extinguish man's quest for the beautiful and the utilitarian merged compatibly into his buildings.

One remaining chance to blend form, line, color, and material in useful works of lasting architectural beauty is in the construction of public buildings.

Regrettably, the earth's surface already is strewn with stark, prison-like monstrosities, clearly identifiable the world around as "schools." Forward-looking citizens who seek to change this stereotype through bringing the best in architectural talent to the problems of school construction encounter rough going. Taxpayers equate beauty with cost, even though handsome schools usually cost less per square foot than commercial buildings constructed close by. School design is only beginning to break out of the traditional mold. As a consequence, the "egg-crate" concept is stubbornly yielding to the fascinating possibilities of what architects call "malleable space."

Colorful, airy, spacious schools, with nooks for the individual as well as assembly halls for the many, provide yet another opportunity for children to catch a glimpse both of the infinite and of personal potentialities not previously perceived. Schools should be anything but a reminder of the squalid, fear-ridden existence many children live outside of school.

A little thing — this concern for building design? Perhaps. But just as there *is* an overarching concept of goal sufficiently motivating to give direction to the whole of education, so there is *no* sweeping panacea for attaining it. The character of the education needed is made up of complex, interlocking parts.

Expectations ▪ The schools of the world must provide a reasonable balance of success and failure for *all* children. In many countries, 25 per cent of each class group receives 75 per cent of the failing marks and up to 40 per cent fails and is required to repeat the work of the grade. A steady diet of failure for even hardy personalities is destructive of self-esteem. But these failing youngsters tend to be the least hardy and least advantaged of the child population. What repeated failure does to them must be damaging beyond belief.

The facts of individual differences among learners and their possible implications for schooling are perceived only dimly by educators and scarcely at all by the lay public. The schools we know are geared to adult expectations for childhood education that have been frozen into the grades and persist in spite of the repeated failure of some children to meet them. Nonpromotion serves as the adjustment mechanism for children who do not come up to "grade standard." Such evidence as is available suggests that grade repetition does not produce the benefits assumed for it. Nonpromoted children achieve no more during their year of repetition than their promoted, equally slow-learning age mates. In fact, such children often show up less well on achievement tests *after* a year of repeating the grade than before doing so. As an alternative to nonpromotion, "social promotion" is less than satisfactory, too, because this practice often moves the slow-learner into a classroom environment of still greater demand [5]. Children either labelled "failure" or faced continuously with little or no prospect of success come to regard themselves as failures. Such children cannot be expected to develop a wholesome regard for self and fellow man.

This is no plea for rewarding any or all effort, however puny. Nor is this an argument for relative standards in judging human products. Rather, the writer envisions schooling that probes beneath the surface of immediate accomplishments to find and guide the processes rapidly becoming characteristic of the person. How is each child perceiving himself, his world, and his place in that world? If he perceives each day in school as failure, the school fails the child and the child, in all probability, will fail mankind.

School expectations are an aspect of culture. Controlling agencies for schools and professional educators translate general expectations into specific content or skills to be acquired at each grade level. Thus, in the United States, learning to read is a task for the first grade and manipulating common and decimal fractions a task for the fifth and sixth. Expectations that have been translated into specific requirements are not easily changed: this topic for the second grade and that one for the fourth. However, there is little evidence to support the grade placement of subject matter. Much of what is taught at one level could be interchanged with what is taught at another, or even eliminated. Sequences of learning tasks as they are prescribed provide inadequate assurance that all children will be challenged appropriately.

Three prongs in the advancement of modern education offer promise for modifying the arbitrariness of school expectations and for devising curricular sequences likely to be reasonable, realistic, and conducive to the development of divergent as well as convergent thinking. These are teaching machines, modification of graded school structure, and increasing attention to the nature and cultivation of creative talent in children.

TEACHING MACHINES — Teaching machines force attention to the programming of subject-matter sequences according to the syntax of that subject matter, where it has been defined, and an awareness of problems and rates of pupil progress through it. The absence of such syntax quickly becomes clear in the process and thus focuses attention on the pedagogical requirements of subject-matter organization. Consequently, the programming process always must be closely aligned with realities of both subject-matter structure and differences in children's learning rates. The teaching machine clearly shifts emphasis away from the normative expectations of school grades to the more absolute expectations set by experimentally ordered subject-matter sequences.

Several other virtues in teaching machines become apparent. Limitations in budget and personnel frequently restrict school offerings to a narrow range of subjects. Children's burgeoning talents go begging because the diverse array of teaching talents necessary to their cultivation is not available. But a dozen teaching machines programed for foreign languages, advanced mathematics, or aspects of music could very well assure the "branching" needed by an eager group of learners but beyond the grasp of a single, human teacher. Teachers are burdened, too, by marking countless "exercises" performed by children in the name of drill. The self-correcting teaching machine removes this arduous burden, freeing the teacher for more creative pedagogical activities.

The potential positive contributions of the teaching machine, as well as the limits of its usefulness, have yet to be fully determined. Continued attention needs to be given to the identification of areas of learning to which the teaching machine may be particularly adapted; to the identification of areas of learning less likely to be well handled by a teaching machine; and to the apt combination of principles of learning with the realities of subject-matter structure.

NONGRADED SCHOOL — A nongraded school is one in which the grade labels (first grade, second grade, third grade, and so on) have been entirely removed from a minimum of two grade levels.

> The nongraded school is designed to implement a theory of continuous pupil progress: since the differences among children are great and since these differences cannot be substantially modified, school structure must facilitate the continuous educational progress of each pupil. Some pupils, therefore, will require a longer period of time than others for achieving certain learnings and attaining certain developmental levels [6].

Such a scheme of school organization does not in itself improve curricular sequences. But it does turn one's attention to differences among learners and the need to differentiate expectancies for them. Instead of rewarding the bright child for his easy attainment of a common requirement, the teacher directs him to next tasks, *even if they are tasks normally reserved for the next grade* in the graded pattern of school organization. A child may work at several different levels in as many subjects; it is not necessary for him to be in a single "grade." In brief, the nongraded school represents another attempt to recognize the hard facts of pupil individuality in relation to subject-matter sequences.

DEVELOPING CREATIVE TALENT — Studies into the characteristics of creative scientists and artists suggest that the schools may need to encourage traits not always valued — and sometimes not even tolerated — in the classroom, if an increasingly large proportion of tomorrow's adults are to be capable of molding better cultures for mankind instead of merely adjusting well to existing cultures. Schools tend to approve a rather narrow range of behavior, just as they tend to set rather arbitrary, graded expectations of accomplishment. Children are rewarded for "right" answer recall of material taught, and for relatively low-level cognitive skills. Most children seek to become proficient in that which is likely to be rewarded. Consequently, the schools may be inculcating what psychologists call "convergent" behavior at the expense of developing perhaps more important "divergent" behavior.

Curriculum

The problem of curriculum is to economize scarce learning potential by making the most judicious and appropriate selection of study content. Human intelligence is too rare and precious a thing to squander on a haphazard program of instruction [7].

For what and from what shall content be selected? These are not decisions for teachers alone to make. And, clearly, these decisions are in large measure made before teachers step into the classroom. Society tends to allocate to schools the preservation of certain tendencies considered essential to survival. Ideally, these are tendencies thought essential for the survival of mankind. But when nations are locked in physical or ideological combat, the schools become instruments for inculcating those tendencies thought essential only to the survival of national interests. The struggle for national survival around the world is now being felt by children who are engaged in school activities brought to them because of world crisis and conflict.

Nations make predictions about the future that have grave consequences not only for the future of that nation but also for the future of millions of young people living and yet to be born. As a consequence of the predictions made at least by major powers, school time devoted to science and mathematics expands; school time devoted to the humanities and the social studies shrinks. Clearly, then, this science and mathematics must be humanized by a unifying concept of goal, or the attributes needed for a world still surviving decades hence will be missing.

Subjects stand in competition with each other for a place in the curriculum. Which should take priority in the resolution of highly critical human problems? Sometimes, we like to believe that subjects which take for study the very nature of man are themselves more virtuous than others in promoting man's humanity to man. But we have no highly viable evidence as to the prior virtue of one field over another.

> I have never been able to regard seriously any partisan arguments that the study of any particular aspects of man's folly-ridden history will determine whether the scholar ends up with mature wisdom or with the pseudo-erudition of an idiot-savant. The conflict between education as we have known it and maturity as we can envisage it depends upon something more profound than whether we master the history of an art-form called painting or of an art-form called science. There is no educator who does not know scholars who lack the least quality of human maturity and wisdom, yet who are true masters of their own fields, whether this field is the humanities, art, music, philosophy, religion, law, science, the history of ideas or the language by which men communicate ideas [8].

The problem of content selection is further complicated by the fact that the products and methods of man's inquiries far outstrip the capacity of a single man to know them. At the theoretical level, men fashion ideas by which only a few scholars communicate. The layman's facts are facts no more. The new facts, pouring out from the empiricists' testing of the new theory, confound the layman and compound the work of teacher and curriculum maker. The resulting pedagogical problems are not merely problems of encompassing fresh accumulations of knowledge — awesome though these tasks may be — but of making instructional order out of quantitative chaos. Utmost simplicity is called for. But superficiality is only a short step from simplicity.

Four kinds of curricular disciplining are called for, remembering that ". . . the starting point is to make provision for developing those capacities which are fundamental to man as man" [9]. The first calls for precise clarification of goal; the second for comprehensive selection of content from all major realms of human experience; the third for utilization of truly fundamental processes and principles for organizing content; and the fourth for adequate breadth in evaluating pupil behavior. We shall attempt to illustrate briefly each of these disciplining processes, beginning with a well-publicized statement of school purpose.

CLARIFYING EDUCATIONAL GOAL

> The purpose which runs through and strengthens all other educational purposes — the common thread of education — is the development of the ability to think. . . . To say that it is central is not to say that it is the sole purpose or in all circumstances the most impor-

tant purpose, but that it must be a pervasive concern in the work of the school [10].

Now, thinking is a complex process. We know surprisingly little about it, or about what subverts it, or even whether it *can* be taught. However, in order to think, a child must possess information. This is so clearly evident that schools too often begin and end here. And so the school day becomes a deadly recitation of inert facts — which, ironically, may be fact no longer.

Inquiry into the knowledge possessed by children reveals startling distortions in their comprehension of what they so glibly recite. What they appear to comprehend they frequently do not draw upon in confronting problems calling for application or situations demanding judgment. In short, they do not or cannot think. If tomorrow's adults are to possess the "power of rational self-transcendence," thought essential to the preservation and cultivation of mankind, then the curriculum of today's elementary schools must assure development of the full range of processes involved in the mother process, thinking.

SELECTING CURRICULAR CONTENT — About what are children to think in today's schools? The early years of schooling must begin with things close to the child: sounds and colors, trees and rocks, winds and rains, peers and adults. To become aware of and sensitive to immediate surroundings is to take a first step toward identifying with mankind.

> It is difficult to realize how much of our diurnal experience is what William James called it, "a big blooming buzzing confusion." It is hard to realize how much of it is a semi-stupor. Life has often enough been described as a waking dream. But not much of it has the vividness, though a great deal of it may have the incoherence of the horror of a dream. For most people most of the time it is a heavy lethargy. They have eyes, yet they do not, in any keen and clear sense, see. They have ears, yet they do not finely and variously hear. They have a thousand provocations to feeling and to thought, but out of their torpor comes no response. Only the pressure of some animal excitement, instant and voluminous, rouses them for a moment to an impulsive clouded answer. Life is for most of us what someone described music to be for the uninitiate, "a drowsy reverie, interrupted by nervous thrills" [11].

The second step for the child is to learn the use of tools and symbols which, first, give man power beyond that of his unaided hands and, second, bind him to time and space. Beyond all other creatures, man has the inherent capacity to bind himself to all cultures; to experience the joys, tragedies, heartaches, and accomplishments of all mankind. To fail to develop these capacities is to become something less than a man ought to be.

The third phase in childhood schooling brings the learner face to face with things that his primary senses of sight, vision, touch, hearing, and smell do not reveal and yet are very real. Molecular structure, the Bill of Rights, a man's hatred for his enemy — what are these, if not real? And so, through the study of art form, cellular behavior, man's quest for freedom, and linguistic patterns, the child learns that "culture is not nature, but nature cultivated" [12]. Because no single ordering of man's experience clearly is superior in developing the rational man, the curriculum must assure balance among the major fields of knowledge and their methods: the humanities, the social sciences, and the physical and biological sciences.

These curricular progressions are spiral rather than serial in character. They are encompassed as in an envelope by a learning-teaching process of rational inquiry about which we shall have more to say. This is a process involving choices and the moral responsibility for making them wisely.

ORGANIZING CURRICULUM CONTENT — A third kind of curricular disciplining requires the utilization of fundamental processes and principles in organizing specific content for instruction. The school curriculum should be planned to reveal continuing threads — ideas, generalizations, principles, concepts, methods — by means of which specific learnings might be related effectively one to another. These threads are derived from at least three sources: the developing characteristics of children, the subject-matter disciplines, and the nature of society. We shall illustrate a central problem of order in the curriculum by discussing the second of these sources.

From the subject-matter disciplines come both the methods by which the fields have advanced and the generalizations or observations deemed significant for general dissemination. These methods and generalizations tend to be more lasting and more broadly applicable than the specific data which they utilize or explain. Consequently, they are of more permanent value for curriculum planning, especially in a time of rapid accumulation of knowledge.

However, schools have tended to stress specific bits and pieces of knowledge, in part because these can be packaged attractively for instructional occasions and in part because more basic methods and principles were thought to be beyond the grasp of the young. Research into the alarming rate at which youngsters forget information they have not organized or related and recent experimentation with children's ability to comprehend fundamental methods and principles force a new look at the variables and constants of the elementary school curriculum. In the past, specific content has tended to be the constant. Teachers and pupils alike have been left to find unifying principles where and when they could — often at the expense of truth. In the future, specific content must be recognized as dispensable data in the effort to understand things more fundamental and constant.

EVALUATING PUPIL BEHAVIOR — Schools embrace a narrow range of pupil behavior, just as they tend to provide learning activities designed for only limited aspects of the goals they seek to attain. Too often, schools reward only that which is most easily measured. And what is easily measured may be inconsequential in the conduct of human affairs. Children, like adults, see a certain expediency in doing that which is to be rewarded. Consequently, the world's children spend shocking proportions of valuable time on that which is of little importance.

Worse, pressure to succeed in school, increasing the world over, encourages behavior that is antithetical to goals of rational self-transcendence. Children steal answer booklets, copy each other's work, and falsify records in order to appear to have attained minimum standards set by the system. Education, the individual, and mankind are corrupted. Little wonder, then, that we have much-schooled men devoid of self-understanding and good will toward humanity.

To be effective, reform in evaluation of behavior must take place simultaneously in classrooms, in schools, and in society's provision of educational opportunity. The intimate setting of the classroom provides the daily cues which tell the child whether he is valued for what he is and can become or for appearing to be what he is not. The narrower the range of approved behavior, the greater the pressure to deceive the teacher and, in time, one's self.

The school, in turn, determines the variety of academic races that are to be run and, to a degree, the rates at which they are to be run. The school must not be all things to all people; it is not the sole educational agency. Nonetheless, a narrow prescription of races to be run under school auspices, together with a sharply defined time span for completing them, limit dangerously both the talents that will flourish in tomorrow's world and the number of persons who will possess them.

Societal concept of school function determines *who* will be educated. Some societies appraise the quality of their school system by evaluating the academic competence of those who complete it. Through rigorous testing, all who do not measure up are weeded out; only the most hardy — not necessarily the most able — survive. If the quality of a school system were to be determined by evaluating children both retained *and eliminated* by that system, schooling around the world would experience a purifying enlightenment.

Method ▪ Teaching seeks to develop that which is already waiting. The first principle of method, then, is to find out what is in the person. This is not where most teaching begins.

Most teaching begins with determination of what is to be brought to the learner. But how can this step be taken with confidence and precision when we know not where the learner is? How many lessons are wasted, how many hours spent in boredom or frustration because the teacher failed to determine first how much or how little of what he sought to offer already was possessed by the class!

There is little agreement on the kind or amount of scholarship required in the teacher. The debate over requirements for teacher certification continues to be largely a political one, inconsequential data on what makes for good teaching being used only to camouflage this fact. Certainly, however, excellence in the teaching of children requires a transcendence of scholarship. The scholar who also teaches often wears his scholarship as a mantle. This may be desirable for the teacher of adults, persons who now should have some insight into what they want to know and so be attracted by the brightest mantles. But the teacher of children who is also a scholar must wear his scholarship as a vest, half-hidden under his jacket. That vest should give him patience and understanding but not dazzle and confound the children as he moves into their lives.

The good teacher comes into the situation looking for clues to the child's drives. What is this child seeking? How can he be helped toward his goals and the envisioning of new goals, instead of converted to the goals that adults have for him? How can the teacher, seeking to close a gap between what he sees in the child and what he wants the child to become, be helped to remember that under what he sees and may not like are the forces of man as man? To be unable to accept these forces is to be poorly qualified to teach.

Children seek to be respected and worthy of respect, to relate themselves constructively to others, and to identify with what lies outside of their own immediate being. But these good ends often become hidden under layers of corrupted human interpretation, both self-interpretation and the interpretation of others, each layer like a coat of too-thick paint. In time, the searching teacher has to scrape off a formidable amount of paint to discover what lies waiting: the clear, fine, beautifully grained wood that is underneath. In the scraping process, conscientious teachers become angered that human beings should have so corrupted what is basically first-rate, forgetting that the corrupting process probably was effected by persons whose ends were good. In their anger, however, they must not give up the search for what lies beneath, thus yielding to the easy temptation to brush on still another, perhaps brighter, coat of paint.

Teaching seeks to stir that which is already waiting into a fresh becoming — and an awareness of that becoming. A second principle of method, then, is to provide a setting in which children's goals and what stands in the way of movement toward those goals may be perceived, examined, and perhaps articulated. With these goals at the conscious level, there is a rallying point for educational endeavor and progress is rapid. Children begin to perceive personal potentialities not previously imagined or believed possible. They begin to accomplish things that belie their own previous, limited expectations. They should — and sometimes do — thrust out their chests proudly and proclaim, "Look, look what I have done — and I did it all by myself!"

Too often, sadly, they do not feel this way or dare not say so. Teachers, regrettably, because of their own needs to be wanted and to be identified with others, do not always understand the true basis of self-fulfillment through teaching. Knowing that he *has been* a force in a child's becoming, it is not easy for a teacher to stand by complacently while the child crows like a cocky little bantam rooster. Shocked and abused, the teacher retires to lick his wounds. "Did it all by himself, did he? The ingrate! Doesn't he see how much of what he has now become is because of me?"

But what is the goal of teaching? Is it not to bring forth just such becoming? If so, then the process of education is corrupted once again when the child must credit the teacher just before tasting the fruits of success. In so doing, the child is denied his moment of self-fulfillment and, ironically, the teacher is denied his. The child's passage to freedom is blocked. The hand, grasping the teacher as it would a crutch, grows weak and withers; the person is consumed in self-gratification and, ultimately, by self-hatred. Heavy-laden with mankind's guilt is the teacher who must exact "thank you" from his pupils.

Just as education has been impoverished through neglect of its first pedagogical principles, so has education been corrupted through misinterpretation of them. Good teaching does not *both* begin and end with the learner, for fear that he come not to love but to idolize himself, turning in upon such little knowledge as he already possesses. In the same way that the child must be helped to envision the potentialities of his becoming and his own role in that becoming, so must he be helped to develop the wholesome relativism that stems from awareness of the world's history, mankind, and the universe.

With the sense of timing that no amount of curriculum planning can assure, the teacher capitalizes on what the child begins to see in himself and, in so doing, reveals to the teacher. Aware now of where the child is, and of how the child's awareness of success aids and abets the teaching effort, the teacher brings the child to what he has not yet learned. Love of self is the beginning, not the end. But without that beginning, the end comes not into view.

REFERENCES

1. ROBERT ULICH (ed.). *Education and the Idea of Mankind.* New York: Harcourt, Brace & World, Inc., 1964, p. 26.
2. PHILIP H. PHENIX. "Education and the Concept of Man," *Views and Ideas on Mankind,* Bulletin No. 9. Chicago: Committee for the Study of Mankind, 1961, p. 10.
3. JAMES B. CONANT. *Trial and Error in the Improvement of Education.* Washington: National Education Association, Association for Supervision and Curriculum Development, 1961.
4. *World Survey of Education.* Vol. 2, Primary Education. Paris: United Nations Educational, Scientific and Cultural Organization, 1958, p. 15.
5. Effects of promotion and nonpromotion are reviewed by Henry J. Otto and Dwain M. Estes, "Accelerated and Retarded Progress," *Encyclopedia of Educational Research.* (Edited by Chester W. Harris) New York: The Macmillan Company, 1960, pp. 4–11.
6. JOHN I. GOODLAD and ROBERT H. ANDERSON. *The Nongraded Elementary School.* New York: Harcourt, Brace & World, Inc., 1959, pp. 62–63.
7. PHILIP H. PHENIX. *Philosophy of Education.* New York: Henry Holt and Company, Inc., 1958, p. 59.
8. LAWRENCE S. KUBIE. *Neurotic Distortion of the Creative Process.* Lawrence, Kansas: The University of Kansas Press, 1958, p. 128.
9. PHILIP H. PHENIX, *op. cit.,* p. 60.
10. *The Central Purpose of American Education.* Washington: National Education Association, Educational Policies Commission, 1961, p. 12.
11. IRWIN EDMAN. *Arts and the Man.* New York: W. W. Norton and Co., 1928, p. 15.
12. ROBERT ULICH. *Education and the Idea of Mankind, op. cit.,* from the first draft, prior to editing for publication.

Organizing School and Classroom

PART II

Part II presents ten papers organized into three chapters. The title of the first paper in Chapter 2, "Unscrambling the Vocabulary of School Organization," is self-explanatory. It proposes a vocabulary of school organization which, if used consistently, might clear up the present semantic jungle. The next two papers analyze the differences between vertical and horizontal organization of the school, describe some alternative patterns under each type, and end with recommendations for breaking the teacher-per-class-per-grade school and classroom organization.

The two papers of Chapter 3 reveal clearly that nonpromotion, an adjustment mechanism designed to improve the effectiveness of the graded structure of school organization, simply does not achieve what is intended for it. They also reveal that to promote or not to promote is really a secondary problem. The primary problem is whether our schools should be organized vertically by grades, or by some other alternatives.

The first paper of Chapter 4 begins with an identification of some of the factors thought to be productive of recent changes in our schools and briefly describes some of the more visible changes. It concludes with a brief analysis of the relationship between changing schools and a changing culture. The second paper in Chapter 4 documents the efforts of one school faculty to effect the changes they envisioned as a consequence of identifying incompatibilities between their knowledge of children and certain traditional ways of conducting schools. The third and fourth papers report the results of an investigation into the perceptions of selected administrators in 89 communities seeking to replace graded schools with nongraded alternatives. Chapter 4 concludes with a review of research pertaining to school and classroom organization.

21

2

Dimensions of School Organization

Is team teaching more effective than nongrading in providing for individual differences? Is ability grouping superior to grading in fostering academic achievement? Is heterogeneous grouping preferable to departmentalizing?

Such questions frequently are asked about the variety of procedures available for organizing schools. These questions would be asked less often if there were general agreement on a common understanding of the terms describing school organization. Team teaching, for instance, is not an alternative to nongrading. These terms describe different ways to fulfill two separate functions of school organization. Ability grouping can be used whether or not a school is graded, and a departmentalized school can have either heterogeneous or homogeneous grouping.

Sources of Confusion

Schools are organized to serve specific functions. They must classify students and move them upward from a point of admission to a point of departure. *Vertical* organization serves this function. Schools also must divide the student body among available teachers. *Horizontal* organization serves this second function.

SOURCE: John I. Goodlad and Kenneth J. Rehage, "Unscrambling the Vocabulary of School Organization," *NEA Journal,* 51 (November 1962), pp. 34–36. Reprinted by permission of the publisher.

Confusion arises from a failure to differentiate between vertical and horizontal aspects of school organization. Grading, multigrading and non-grading are the vertical organization plans from which to choose. The horizontal pattern may be determined by grouping children homogeneously or heterogeneously, by organizing the curriculum so as to emphasize the separateness of subjects or the interrelationships among them, by having self-contained or departmentalized classrooms, or by using any one of many possible patterns of interclass grouping.

The remainder of this article will look further into the differences between vertical and horizontal plans of school organization.

Vertical School Organization

Grading has been the traditional way of organizing schools for the vertical progression of students. For example, an elementary school enrolling children aged five to twelve, is divided into seven year-long steps, starting with kindergarten and going successively through grades one to six. A rather specific body of subject matter is assigned to each grade level; textbooks are prepared for the grade; teachers are categorized as "first-grade" or "fifth-grade" teachers; and children refer to themselves as being in the "second grade" or going into the "sixth grade." The pieces fit together in an orderly fashion with a year of work for a grade of vertical progress through the school as the common denominator.

The graded system, long the predominant scheme of vertical school organization, is often criticized for ignoring individual differences among learners by demanding that all children cover the same material at approximately the same rate of speed. Those children who fail to keep up with a predetermined rate of progress for their grade are not promoted and are required to repeat the work of that grade.

Periodically, attempts are made to modify or depart from graded structure. In multigrading, for example, each class contains two or more grades simultaneously. Although grade labels are retained, children are permitted to work in several grades at once, depending on their progress in each subject. In a multigraded class containing grades three, four, and five, a child could be in grade three for arithmetic, grade four for social studies, and grade five for reading.

Nongrading is an arrangement in which grade labels are removed from some or all classes. When grade labels are removed from kindergarten and the first three grades, the arrangement is known as a nongraded primary unit. A similar vertical arrangement for the customary grades four, five, and six is a nongraded intermediate unit.

Theoretically, grading and nongrading are the polar opposites among alternatives available for organizing a school vertically. In *pure* grading, the content of the instructional program and its sequential arrangement are determined by assignment of subject matter to various grade levels, by designation of instructional materials suitable for particular grade levels, and by promotion of pupils upon satisfactory completion of the work specified for each grade level. In *pure* nongrading, the sequence of content is determined by the inherent difficulty of the subject matter and the children's demonstrated ability to cope with it; materials are selected to match the spread of individual differences existing within the instructional group; and the children move upward according to their readiness to proceed. Promotion or nonpromotion does not exist as such. An important goal is to provide continuous progress for each child.

Nongrading and virtually all modifications of grading are intended to facilitate curricular and instructional provisions for the individual differences always present in a class group. However, no scheme of vertical school organization automatically makes the provisions. The removal of grade labels, for example, is no guarantee that teachers will take advantage of the opportunities nongrading is supposed to provide. A nongraded school with only grade labels removed remains a graded school, nonetheless.

Exponents of nongraded schools claim benefits with respect to pupil well-being and achievement which have not been proven conclusively. Critics of the nongraded plan claim that what nongrading purports to do can be accomplished as readily in graded schools. To date, research — most of it comparing pupil achievement in graded and nongraded schools — is inadequate and inconclusive. Some studies favor graded schools, some favor nongraded schools, and some show no significant differences between the two.

The crucial inadequacy of most such studies is the failure to identify two sets of characteristics by means of which nongraded and graded schools may be clearly differentiated. Consequently, the researchers often are not making a valid comparison. Several of the studies, for instance, report the use of ability or achievement grouping in the sample of nongraded schools selected but not in graded schools used for comparison. Are differences between pupils in these schools and in the sample of graded schools the product of graded or nongraded practices or are they the product of ability grouping?

Nongrading is a vertical plan of school organization. It cannot be compared with ability grouping or any other scheme of horizontal organization. Failure to understand this difference frequently leads to meaningless comparisons of organizational plans and, ultimately, to misleading conclusions.

Horizontal School Organization

As stated earlier, a pattern of horizontal organization results when an identifiable cluster of students (e.g., all first-graders or all high school juniors) is divided into class groups and assigned to available teachers. Whereas vertical organization allows only two major alternatives — grading and nongrading — horizontal organization permits literally dozens of alternatives. In setting up horizontal class groups, priority considerations may be given to children, to the curriculum, or to teacher qualifications.

If the primary consideration in establishing a pattern of horizontal organization is children, then a choice must be made between homogeneity (likeness) and heterogeneity (difference) in pupils comprising each class group. If the choice is for homogeneity, the criterion of likeness may be age, size, interest, ability, achievement, or a combination of these and other factors. If the primary consideration is the curriculum, a choice may be made between separate subjects and various combinations of subjects as the basis for setting up class groups. If the primary consideration is teacher qualification, one choice is between the self-contained classroom (one teacher for all subjects) and departmentalization (a different teacher for each subject).

Thus simplified, horizontal organization begins to be comprehensible. However, schools often combine the results of several kinds of choices, which complicates understanding of the organization. A high school, for instance, might be semidepartmentalized, with a different teacher for each subject except for English and social studies, which are combined in a core curriculum and taught by one teacher. All except core classes might be set up according to pupil homogeneity in achievement. The over-all pattern of school organization might then be further complicated by introducing vertical variety — nongraded classes in the core but graded classes in all other subjects.

Team teaching is one horizontal scheme that combines considerations of children, curriculum, and teacher qualifications in establishing class groups. It is a significant departure from the variety of horizontal plans existing up to the present, just as nongrading in vertical organization represents a significant departure from grading.

Unfortunately, the term *team teaching* is applied to so many different ventures in cooperative teaching that it has come to have many meanings. Communication would be enhanced if the term were used only in referring to ventures embracing all three of the following characteristics: (1) a hierarchy of personnel — team leader, master teacher, auxiliary teacher, teacher aide, intern teacher, clerk, and so forth; (2) a delineation of staff function based on differences in preparation, personal interests, and so on, or on the kinds of learning activities planned; (3) flexibility in grouping embracing all the students under supervision of a team.

Such a definition excludes all those cooperative teaching efforts in which there is no attempt to define a hierarchy of personnel. These efforts might better be called associated teaching.

Schools utilizing team teaching can be graded or nongraded. Since team teaching is a form of horizontal organization, and grading or nongrading is a form of vertical organization, these forms are not interchangeable devices for achieving common organizational functions. A school may practice nongrading and team teaching simultaneously.

Toward a Common Vocabulary

Given all this variety and complexity in the organization of American schools, we may expect to find confusion in discourse, practice, and research. Moreover, the mere existence of complexity is a compelling argument for a more precise vocabulary.

Vertically, schools may be graded or nongraded or fall somewhere in between. Horizontally, schools may be organized into any one of many alternative patterns. But all these horizontal patterns are derived from only three essentially different kinds of considerations: considerations of children, of the curriculum, or of teacher characteristics.

Any meaningful description of a school's over-all organizational pattern includes both vertical and horizontal aspects. Such description may be "nongrading (vertical) and ability grouping (horizontal)" or "grading (vertical) and team teaching (horizontal)" or "nongraded (vertical) and departmentalized (horizontal)." To describe a school as nongraded is to describe only half its organization. Likewise, to describe a school as practicing achievement grouping and departmentalization is to be quite descriptive of horizontal organization but to say nothing of vertical.

The use of a common vocabulary for analyzing and describing school organization is long overdue.

VERTICAL ORGANIZATION OF THE SCHOOL

Introduction

A total educational system is segmented into organizational units. Vertically, units are stacked one upon the other, providing for the upward progression of students through a time sequence. Horizontally, segments of these vertical units are arranged side by side, providing both a pupil-to-teacher ratio and a basis for assigning students and teachers to available space.

The attempt to organize schools effectively (with respect to individual differences, for example) along the horizontal axis produces problems of grouping and devices such as team-teaching. The attempt to organize schools effectively along the vertical axis produces problems of promotion and nonpromotion if the schools are graded and leads to proposals for modifying grade structure. These pages discuss aspects of organizing schools vertically in relation to what we know about individual differences and deal in some depth with nongraded plans as alternatives to the graded plans in common use.

In the United States of America, the major vertical structural units are elementary schools, secondary schools, colleges and universities. Occasionally, as in demonstration or experimental schools, a nursery-school unit precedes the elementary school. Frequently, junior high schools exist between the elementary and higher secondary units, and junior colleges parallel but do not necessarily duplicate the first two years of college. With few exceptions, each of these major units is subdivided into grades representing segments of time to be spent and subject-matter content to be covered.

These major structural units, with their graded subdivisions, tend to persist, flurries of interest in modifying them appearing and reappearing at intervals of several years or decades. Teachers give relatively little attention to the desirability or efficacy of the unit within which they teach, concentrating their energies upon curricular and instructional matters. Nonetheless, the structure of this unit profoundly affects circumstances with which teachers must deal: age and academic sophistication of the

SOURCE: John I. Goodlad. "Individual Differences and Vertical Organization of the School," *Individualizing Instruction*. Sixty-first Yearbook of the National Society for the Study of Education, Part I. (Chicago: University of Chicago Press, 1962), pp. 209–238. Reprinted by permission of the publisher.

student group, time available for effecting changes in pupil behavior, anticipated norms and standards for judging student accomplishment, and range and types of subject matter deemed appropriate. In effect, school organization profoundly influences the answers which will be given to classic educational questions of who shall be educated, what shall be taught, and when specified learnings shall be introduced. Determining school structure appropriate to the educational processes deemed desirable is a pressing problem for educators.

Individual Differences, School Function, and Organizational Form

The realities of individual differences among learners raise a perplexing array of educational issues and problems for society and its schools. The complexity of this picture of human variability is such that educators cannot frame it comfortably within the school structure.

The first lesson for school people seeking "to do something" about individual differences is that *no scheme of school organization, however elaborately worked out, provides for the types and ranges of learner variability encompassed by the school.* Thorough acceptance of this idea is some assurance that educators will not relinquish their educational responsibilities to limiting classificatory contrivances and practices, such as ability groups, achievement levels, grade skipping, and nonpromotion. We've been around the clock several times before in our zeal to "organize away" the stark realities of individual differences. Let us not go around again without first learning to tell the time. In the matter of dealing educationally with individual differences, there are no organizational panaceas.

However, differing school structures are not equally supportive in the pursuit of selected educational ends. Some educators, understandably preoccupied with instructional techniques, maintain that structure is immaterial, "good teachers overcome any obstacle in doing right by the unique individuals in the class." The phraseology so often used in extolling "the good teacher" is symbolic. Good teachers should not have to overcome structural obstacles standing unnecessarily in the way of what they seek to do. Furthermore, school organization should help the many average teachers to do an acceptable, satisfying job.

Somewhere, then, between advocacy of a structural scheme to account for individual differences and the discounting of school organization as irrelevant, there lies a regard for structure as one of several influential factors to be dealt with in encompassing recognition of and concern for individual differences in the total educational enterprise. If the school's organization harmonizes with desired educational objectives, these objectives are likely to be better realized. *It is futile and even dangerous to weigh the merits of this or that organizational scheme without respect to what the educational enterprise is or should be for.*

The past century has witnessed considerable debate over the emphasis to be placed upon learners and subject matter, respectively, in making a variety of curricular and instructional decisions. Often, participants in the debate, listening poorly and not expressing their own positions adequately, have reduced the complex problems of balance and relationship in the curriculum to empty dichotomies. They have created the impression that it is possible (even desirable) to use learners *or* subject matter as the only bases for program-planning and teaching, whereas *both* learners *and* subject matter are integral parts of a larger whole, with one or the other receiving priority attention in practice according to the nature of the decision and the values of the decision-maker.

The ideal function of the school, as viewed from the subject-centered perspective, is to impart a body of most important facts, principles, and ways of doing. These "minimum essentials," for the first unit of school structure, constitute an elementary education. On mastering, covering, or internalizing them, one "has an elementary education." The first function of the school, as viewed from the child-centered perspective, is to develop the unique potentialities of the young human beings encompassed within it. There are no "minimum essentials" of subject matter laid out in advance and to be "covered," although bodies of knowledge are to be examined for their usefulness in promoting optimal development of the learners. Because these two views are not really discrete, but might be described more accurately as polar extremes of deviance within a class of phenomena, the practical consequences stemming from them have not been and cannot be sharply differentiated.

At the level of intellectual commitment, the learner-centered view has gained at the expense of the subject-centered view, although there have been sharp swings from one to the other over the past sixty years. But the actual function of anything is what it is used for, regardless of what humans may intend it to be at any given time. Schools have been used for the provision of dental care (child-centered?) when their function was proclaimed as subject-matter mastery. Schools have been used for intense competition in learning to spell a selected group of words (subject-centered?) when their function was proclaimed to be development of the unique potentialities of the child at his own rate of speed (child-centered?). Teachers who passionately extol the school's obligation to promote human variability (child-centered?) protest the lack of readiness for grade-level work (subject-centered?) in the entering group. Teachers who see the school's function as developing the 3 R's (subject-centered?) engineer reading programs wherein every child advances at his own rate of speed (child-centered?). Obviously, there is much inconsistency between intellectual commitment to the ideal and the variety of functions which a school serves at any given moment.

Human beings create tools, instruments, and other devices to achieve their ends. For example, a huge scaffold-like frame serves as part of the instrumentation for bringing oil from deep within the earth. But, as soon as the oil gushes forth, this framework no longer functions for the production of oil, although it may serve residual functions, such as the provision of roosting places for birds or subject matter for artists. Justification for retaining the framework no longer rests on criteria pertaining to the pumping of oil.

Educators create machinery to serve their educational ends. At the outset, the relationship between the end in view and the tool or form created to serve it may be clear. In time, however, the quality of the "fit" often deteriorates. The ends change without accompanying modification of the means. Or, the means are refined over and over without respect to the character of the ends until modification or perpetuation of the machinery becomes an end in itself. The ultimate separation occurs when the machinery is operated by technicians who know nothing of the purposes it was intended to serve. And the ultimate sterility occurs when these same technicians extol perpetuation of the machinery in the name of a creator who would recoil at the sight of what he purportedly wrought. Justification for retaining the machinery no longer rests on criteria pertaining to educational ends. (Witness the story of various organizational devices in the history of American education: the Pueblo Plan, the Gary Plan, the platoon plan, the Winnetka Plan, and others.)

School architects make much of the form-follows-function concept. Leading architects seek to comprehend the functions a school serves or is intended to serve in order that the form of the building — the arrangement of space, for example — will be appropriate. The concept is no less significant in designing the organizational arrangement whereby learners move upward from *entry into* until *departure from* the program. In the next section of this chapter, the writer applies the form-follows-function concept to problems of vertical school organization.

Form and Function in Vertical School Organization

The dominant view of school function during the middle decades of the nineteenth century was the mastery of minimum essentials, especially in reading, writing, and arithmetic. At that time, too, accompanying the emerging concept of education being a state responsibility and not the privilege of a favored few, enrollment rates were increasing rapidly. The

Quincy (Massachusetts) Grammar School, opening its doors in 1848, was organized into grades, each representing a quantity of material to be covered. The graded form offered promise for serving perceived school function on a mass basis. Form followed function.

By the 1860's, most city schools were graded. In order that these schools might operate efficiently, certain refinements were effected: content was divided into manageable chunks, each to be covered in a year's time; this content was taught to the teachers who were to teach it to children; and content was "packaged" between the covers of books. These activities, although compatible with over-all school procedures, served the function of efficient operation of the graded school. Thus, grading created functions of its own: the classification of content, the classification of materials, the classification of teachers, the classification of children, and the classification of parent expectations. Function followed form.

In seeking to reorganize vertical school structure, it is necessary to remember that the graded school served rather well the concept of school function prevailing at the time the graded form crystallized. It is necessary to remember, too, that forms always create certain functions of their own which, in their turn, are maintained and promoted in the name of economy, efficiency, aesthetic qualities, and so on. When one seeks to substitute one form for another, he must exercise great care in appraising *both* form *and* function. To seek a better fit between perceived ends and means is one thing. To seek refinement of means when ends are no longer perceived is quite another. Service to forms that are not seen to follow function is a pernicious kind of pedagogical idolatry.

To date, two major types of vertical school organization have been devised, namely, grading and nongrading or, simply, the presence or absence of grades. Between these polar types is an array of variations such as multigrade or multiage plans, the discussion of which is temporarily postponed. The first replacement of the graded plan (which had emerged in the United States during the nineteenth century) by a nongraded plan occurred in the late 1930's.* It is significant that this pioneering effort occurred at the time educators (George S. Counts, for example, in *Dare the Schools Build a New School Order?*) were questioning the long-standing role of the school in promoting subject-matter coverage and schools (notably those of the Eight-Year Study) were seeking to achieve a very wide range of educational aims (such as those formulated by the Educational Policies Commission in its 1938 statement). Is there some possibil-

---

* Available data indicate that Milwaukee, Wisconsin, has the oldest nongraded plan in continuous existence since inception. Experimental and demonstration-type plans of school reorganization introduced before that time appear to have been designed primarily to modify horizontal structure or only an aspect of vertical structure.

ity, then, that the nongraded plan, rather than the graded plan, was seen as the appropriate organizational form to follow fresh pronouncements of school function?

The first really significant movement toward replacing grading by non-grading methods occurred during the last half of the 1950–59 decade and is accelerating today. It is of perhaps more than incidental import that this surge of interest coincides with confusing and often contradicting cries for more rapid advancement of the gifted, return to the 3 R's, more attention to individual differences among learners, and more concern for the individual. Endorsement in practice of nongrading as a device for moving children at varying rates of speed through a common set of sub-ject-matter requirements led one writer to protest the implied narrow con-cept of school function and to appeal for the rescue of the nongraded school from some of its advocates [1]. Is there some possibility, then, that the nongraded plan is being seen by some educators as more appropriate than the graded for fulfilling either or both of the two "ideal perceptions" of school function described earlier in this chapter?

A survey of practices in nongraded schools conducted in 1960 by An-derson and Goodlad [2] reveals that nongrading as an organization plan is supported by persons with differing conceptions of what a school is for. Some of its advocates see it as structure for more efficiently regulating the progress of learners through a relatively common set of subject-matter prescriptions. Others see it as a structure within which individual needs, interests, and abilities may be identified and used in fulfilling a more child-centered concept of school function. Analysis of practice also reveals much confusion in the minds of those conducting nongraded schools re-garding the school function they seek to serve.

The writer concludes that the nongraded scheme of school organization can be designed to serve either of the two "ideal" perceptions of school function which have struggled for clarification and implementation in American education. Failure to clarify the function to be served by a non-graded form leads, however, to confused and confusing practices under the name of nongrading and, sometimes, disillusionment and subsequent return to grading. To sort out and describe some of these practices and to attempt to explain the bases of confusion are major goals for the last half of this chapter.

The major provocation for current interest in nongrading appears to be the compilation of evidence about individual differences. Consequently, persons with widely differing philosophies of education are equally will-ing to examine a scheme promising ready adaptability to the peculiar shade of coloring cast upon the data by their particular philosophical orientation. Nonetheless, it appears desirable to summarize certain aspects that daily confront educators and lead them to consider alternative schemes of vertical school organization.

Individual Differences and Vertical School Organization

Circumstances surrounding human birth and subsequent existence set individuals off on widely varying pursuits and condition their success in these pursuits. Human beings differ in their under-the-skin functioning, in their perception of and readiness for any given task, in their manner of approaching a situation, and in their ways of responding to the exigencies of that situation.

The total picture of human variability (a picture which is as yet only roughly sketched in) is too complex for most of us to begin to grasp. Consequently, most parents and teachers consider individual differences in relation to specific, identifiable children and a rather confined set of traditional school learnings, usually expressed as subjects and subject matter. Limited though such perceptions and concerns may appear to some biologists, anthropologists, sociologists, and educationists, they express the best reality picture we have of local school expectations.

Unfortunately, parents and teachers bring a very narrow view of even this limited concept of individual differences to the consideration of practical educational matters confronting them. For example, the slow readers in a third-grade class typically use, at the end of the year, the readers used by the best readers at the beginning of the year, as if the spread in reading accomplishment from top to bottom were only one year. And when teachers seek to differentiate reading materials for children on an individualized basis, Susie's parents complain because Joan, in the same class, has a different, presumably more advanced (and, therefore, more prestigious), book.

The writer has asked more than ten thousand parents and teachers in eleven states to indicate their knowledge of academic variability among fourth-graders. A fourth-grade child is defined as one enrolled in a fourth-grade class and who scores between grade 4.0 and 4.9 in *each* subject on a standardized achievement test taken at the end of January (the midpoint in the school year). In answer to the question, "What percentage of a fourth-grade class is at grade-level?" respondents select from five choices: less than 20 per cent, 20 to 40 per cent, 40 to 60 per cent, 60 to 80 per cent, 80 to 100 per cent. Although the first is the correct response, the answers for all groups queried spread out in a bell-shaped curve peaking slightly to left of center. Obviously, there is much to do in merely teaching the facts of individual differences to persons who deal with individuals every day.

We are prone to say, in educational circles, that the possession of knowledge related to a decision to be made is no guarantee that the decision-maker will see the knowledge as relevant or that he will use it even if he sees its relevance. However, the circumstances that lead us to so observe may be rather different from what we assume. Because teachers have long mouthed clichés pertaining to individual differences does not necessarily mean that they grasp the concept adequately. Perhaps more effective organization and presentation of *pertinent* data concerning individual differences would lead to the fundamental understandings needed by those who teach groups of learners.

For example, the standardized tests used in most schools are for group, not individual, appraisal. And yet, the method of compiling class results alphabetically focuses attention on individual scores and disguises the distribution of the group on whatever is being measured. Rearranging the results from an achievement test so that the highest average achiever is at the top of the distribution and the lowest average achiever is at the bottom, permits some observations that should be of rather immediate utility to any reasonably creative teacher. The compilation of class profiles, so arranged, for a sample of classrooms across the country permits generalizations that are useful in considering vertical school organization.*

1. The broad spread from high to low achiever steadily increases with the upward movement of heterogeneous classes (relatively homogeneous by chronological age) through the school. In the intermediate grades, this spread is approximately the number of years designated by the number of the grade-level: that is, by the third grade, three years; by the fourth grade, four years; by the fifth grade, five years. However, since the spread in achievement accelerates slightly faster than a year-per-year of schooling, the overall range in junior high school classes is approximately two-thirds the median chronological age of the groups.

2. In subject areas, such as reading and language arts, where children can readily proceed on their own in a variety of out-of-school situations, the spread from high to low achiever frequently is one and one-half to twice the number of the grade-level. Hence, in the fifth grade, there frequently is an eight-year spread in reading achievement between the best and poorest readers. Differentiation in classroom group stimuli to provide for varying levels of accomplishment does not encompass this range, but the encouragement of self-selection of materials for supplementary reading at home and school facilitates highly individualized rates of progress. In arithmetic, the over-all spread in achievement is rarely greater than the

---

* These are expressed here as rather conservative understatements for the sake of simplicity and easy application.

number of the grade-level. Instruction in arithmetic, as generally carried on, makes relatively little provision for individual progress. Often, common stimuli are provided for an entire class, differentiation being simply the completion of more problems or exercises by the more gifted. Individual exploration of mathematics as a spare-time activity is a rare phenomenon among elementary-school children. Clearly, however, adequate school opportunity accentuates student differences in this field, too, as evidenced by the profound differences between sixteen-year-olds taking college-level courses and those taking standard tenth-grade mathematics. Ready access to individual as well as group stimuli for independent study appears to be a significant factor conditioning the size of the achievement spread in any given subject for a class group.*

3. There are very few fourth-grade children in a so-called fourth-grade class when a fourth-grade child is defined as one who achieves at fourth-grade level in *all* subjects at approximately the mid-point of the school year. (Fourth-grade level, in turn, is defined as between 4.0 and 4.9 on a standardized achievement test.) Actually, only three or four such children are found in the heterogeneous classes of today's elementary schools, according to the results of preliminary analyses. Certainly, the number is safely within the 0-to-20 per cent bracket of choice which, according to the writer's inventory, very few parents, teachers, principals, or supervisors select when asked to choose among five alternative responses. A teacher, then, who considers himself a fourth-grade teacher is addressing himself to only three or four youngsters!

4. The relative absence of fourth-graders in a fourth-grade class is a corollary of the irregular progress of a single child in the several fields of school study. Most children in the intermediate grades vary in achievement from subject to subject by at least a full grade. That is, a sixth-grader may achieve at 8.1 in reading, 6.9 in arithmetic, 7.7 in spelling, 6.3 in science, 7.8 in social studies, for an over-all range of 1.8 grades. But some students vary from subject-field to subject-field by as many years as the number of the grade-level. Thus, a fifth grader may score at 9.6 in reading, 5.8 in science, 8.4 in spelling, 6.7 in social studies, 4.8 in arithmetic for an over-all range of 4.8 or just short of 5.0 full grades. Most so-called heterogeneous classes contain at least two or three children whose achievement profiles represent such diversity and many others who approach it.

*Studies such as those conducted by Herbert A. Thelen reveal that we are far from clear on the relative usefulness of various instructional techniques — lecture, group discussion, "paired" or small-team study, self-direction, and so forth — in promoting maximum student learning. See Herbert A. Thelen, "Classroom Grouping of Students," *School Review*, XLVII (Spring, 1959), 60–78.

In any attempt to see what these realities mean for vertical school organization, the matter of educational values enters upon the scene once again. Many people, over the years, have endorsed subject matter accomplishment for school students and the graded system as an organizational form for promoting pupil progress. Retention of those students falling seriously short of grade-level expectations has long been used as a device for maintaining standards and assuring reasonably acceptable "fit" between actual progress and grade-level expectations. But twentieth-century research casts doubt upon nonpromotion as a device for furthering the efficient functioning of the graded system as a form for expediting subject matter accomplishment or for effectively relating the range of pupil accomplishment to grade norms. Nonetheless, nonpromotion continues as a major corollary of graded schools.

It could be that these research findings are not known to those who set promotion policies and make decisions on pupil promotion and nonpromotion. If this be true, then the professional education of our teachers and administrators is in a sorry state, indeed. These studies have been recounted for decades in the textbook literature on both educational psychology and general elementary education.

Another explanation for the continued practice of nonpromotion in the face of evidence questioning its usefulness in serving graded functions is the sheer illogic of the alternative. In the graded system of school organization, students are either retained in their present grade or passed along to the next one. These two choices exhaust the possibilities. The fact that research casts doubt upon retention does little to improve the attractiveness of the promotion alternative *for persons who place high value on subject matter accomplishment as defined by grade-level prescriptions.* For them, continued, upward progression through the graded hierarchy for students who obviously have not mastered the work of their present grade (perhaps even their previous grade and the grade before that) is sheer nonsense, not to be tolerated for a moment, research notwithstanding!

And, of course, the notion of moving students upward through a graded system when the achievement distribution of each "graded" class so little resembles anything that might reasonably be defined as a grade *is* sheer nonsense. Grades, to have meaning, denote graded subject matter, graded textbooks, graded teachers, graded students, and graded expectations. But students in today's "graded schools" are not graded, as the data presented in this yearbook clearly reveal. If the students still aren't graded after more than one hundred years of perfecting a system of graded subject matter, graded textbooks, graded expectations, and nonpromotion designed to thoroughly grade them, then perhaps it's about time to quit trying!

At this point, one hears that quiet voice of protest, "Good teachers don't try to fit children to the grade. They ignore grade-level expectations in seeking to deal with individuals." What better argument against the graded system than that good teachers seek to (in fact, *must*) ignore it? We seem to have entered into a strange never-never land. The form created to serve certain functions appears not to serve those functions well. We then suggest justification of the form on the grounds that creative people develop ingenious ways of circumventing it!

Why not, instead, get rid of the form?

Modifying Grade Structure: The Search for Continuous Progress Plans

Most educators, whatever their priorities regarding school function, want continuous, unbroken progress for students. Those who emphasize subject matter coverage look for a progression from easier to more difficult tasks in the material presented. Those who emphasize the unfolding of human potentiality look for a psychological progression based on readiness of the learner, as implied, for example, in so-called developmental reading programs.

The difficulty with this laudable goal of providing for continuous progress is that there must be an identifiable "something" that progresses. Each item of subject matter must add depth to the concept of number in mathematics. Or, each new experience must increase the learner's competence in organizing relative data from which to draw appropriate conclusions. The importance of identifying concepts, principles, or other structural elements of subject matter to serve as longitudinal threads for the systematic provision of continuous pupil progress was emphasized in the 1930's by Judd [3], in the 1940's by Tyler [4], in chapters of a 1958 yearbook of the National Society for the Study of Education [5], and in other writings [6] of these decades. Bruner's [7] articulation of the idea in 1960 and current efforts to program automated teaching devices attest further to the importance of finding both the "something" to be continuously developed and the specific learnings that promise to develop this something sequentially. Efforts to translate the idea into program specifics are likely to be the dominant curriculum-making activity of the 1960's. These efforts are paralleled by a search for forms of school organization that facilitate continuous pupil progress through these programs.

But programs of study based on structural analyses of subject matter do not constitute adequate curricula in the minds of those educators who are concerned primarily with the wholesome development of human potentiality. Furthermore, for many of these educators, moving students through such programs at individual rates of speed does not constitute adequate (or even, for some, appropriate) attention to the significance of individual differences. They raise questions about whether learnings arranged according to adult perceptions of difficulty correspond to students' perceptions of difficulty; whether what can be learned by some students should be learned by all, even at differentiated rates of speed; and whether learnings that *can* be accomplished by very young children are necessarily the most appropriate learnings for these early stages of human development. A small kernel of present interest in finding answers to these questions may well stimulate and ultimately guide curriculum-making activity of the 1970's. This activity, in turn, will be accompanied by the search for appropriate plans of organizing the school vertically to encompass resulting curricula and facilitate continuous pupil progress.

In graded-school structure, grade-level subdivisions and the classification of content, instructional materials, and various expectations in accord with these subdivisions combine to stress a horizontal, crosswise view of the curriculum. Grade demarcations wall off what is being studied now from what was studied last year and what will be studied next year. Normally, children in the third grade cover material laid out for that grade; they tend not to explore new topics with a deliberate view to deepening concepts or insights opened up in the first and second grades and to be extended in the fourth. Grades are barriers to continuous pupil progress. These grade-level barriers are likely to prove increasingly irksome in intensified efforts to translate structural sequences in subject matter into longitudinal curricula for elementary and secondary education.

Concern for individual differences (expressed particularly in efforts to encourage varying rates of speed in learning), for new subject-matter sequences (dramatized through the need to program automated learning devices), and for continuous pupil progress are educational phenomena of our time. The graded form of school organization serves none of these concerns well. It is not at all surprising, then, that schools and school systems across the country are in search of structural plans better suited to serving one or more of these predominant concerns. Personnel in some of these schools and school systems know not why or what they search. They seek only to be going with the tide, to be on the band-wagon, or to emulate an aggressive neighbor. It is heartening to note, however, that those local school leaders who appear to be setting the pace, rather than blindly following, describe their new structural forms as devices for facilitating continuous, individual pupil progress. This is a legitimate expectation for structure. An organizational scheme cannot teach, cannot provide the substance of a curriculum, cannot place materials in a classroom. But it can, should, and does affect the progression of students from *entry into* until *departure from* the major unit (elementary, secondary, or higher) of vertical school organization. The appraisal of any plan should be directed at what organization can do — no more and no less.

Schools and school systems which have moved to somewhat similar but interestingly unique patterns of school structure emphasizing concern for individual, continuous pupil progress are Englewood, Florida, and Torrance, California.* Torrance developed a multigrade plan in which each class group was made of up three different grade-levels, one third of each group being new each year [8]. Within each group, actual grade-level classifications were largely ignored for instructional purposes. Thus, a child classified in the third grade but achieving at the fifth in reading and the third in arithmetic, placed in a multigrade room of grades three, four, and five, would move freely from a fifth-grade (multiage) group in reading to a third-grade (multiage) group in arithmetic. Thus, the framework provides certain "legal" degrees of freedom for dealing with both inter-individual and intraindividual differences. The teacher does not have to defy the system, so to speak, in stretching somewhat further up and further down the graded curriculum in accounting for individual differences. A longitudinal view of the curriculum by the teacher and continuous progress for the pupils are encouraged through the instructional modification of grade-lines within a three-year unit. Administrative personnel in Torrance see considerable virtue in not casting children, teachers, and parents completely adrift from at least some of the classificatory meaning of conventional grades.

Principal and teachers of the Englewood Elementary School in Sarasota County, Florida, became interested in modifying grade structure through observing gross differences among children at each grade-level. The need to "do something" about differentiating educational opportunity became glaringly apparent in faculty study of the progression of two children, one academically talented and the other academically retarded, through the grade hierarchy of the school. Valuing recognition and encouragement rather than suppression of individuality, the group was shocked by the similarity of the two progressions.

They decided to modify existing grade structure for the following year by creating a system of overlapping multigraded classrooms. Figure 2.1 depicts one variation of the overlapping multigrade plan. The letters refer to a single class group; the numbers to the grades encompassed within a

* The brief descriptions that follow represent conditions that existed in the 1959–60 academic year. The author cannot testify to what exists now. Dynamic school systems change.

class group. Each class contains approximately 30 pupils; deviation in block size for groups E and J is an artifact of depicting overlap rather than symbolic of differing class sizes. Note the alternative placements available for a child classified at any given grade-level. Note, also, the opportunities for holding a group together for two years or for three (class E) as in Torrance, with half or a third of the group being added each year, according to teacher preference.

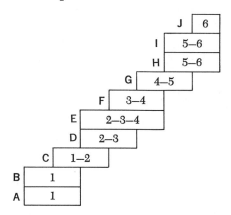

FIGURE 2.1 One of several possible variations in a
plan of overlapping, multigrade classes.

Toward the end of a year's trial with a multigrade plan, the Englewood group effected a further modification. They sought to pay less attention to grade classifications of children which, from their year's experience, caused them to think still in terms of what a child classified in the third grade *ought* to be capable of doing rather than what he actually could do. In an attempt to rid themselves of grade-mindedness, they set up a scheme of overlapping multiage groups, still conscious initially of overlapping, multigrade groups but hopeful that this consciousness would evaporate. The addition of two kindergarten sections encouraged some further modification of what had been the first- and first-and-second-grade groups of the preceding year. (See Figure 2.2 in which letters — with the exception of kindergarten designations — once again represent classes; the numbers now represent pupil ages.)

During the succeeding year, consciousness of grade classifications disappeared sooner than anticipated; the word "grade" disappeared from the teacher's vocabularies before they were aware of this fact. For example, they referred to children as eight-year-olds rather than third-graders and to classes as eight- and nine-year-old groups rather than third- and fourth-grade groups. At the end of this year (less than three years after faculty studies had aroused initial discontent over existing grade structure), the faculty became aware of the fact that a nongraded plan had evolved. They found themselves not with a modification of but, rather, a replacement for grade structure [9].

Educational leaders in school systems across the United States are modifying grade structure for many of the reasons that motivated professional personnel in Torrance and Englewood to set up multigrade, multiage, or

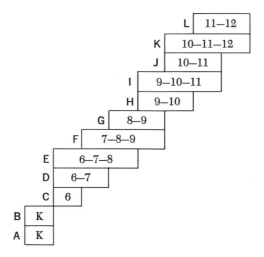

FIGURE 2.2   One of several possible variations in a plan of overlapping, multiage classes.

nongraded plans of vertical school organization. In the nongraded plan, now found in several variations, grade labels are entirely removed from a minimum of two grade-levels. Nongraded form of structure serves well the function of moving students of varying abilities and present accomplishments at differentiated rates of speed upward through the specified subject-matter requirements of a school unit. But this form also serves well the core and so-called "emerging" types of curriculum organization more characteristic of society-oriented and learner-centered approaches to education.

From the beginning, efforts to break graded lock-step have sought to provide greater flexibility in expectations for any given class. This has been done by placing several grade-levels (multiaging) in a single class or by simply recognizing spread of attainments in any class group and then eliminating the grade as a classificatory device (nongrading). In the European reform movement of the twenties and thirties, there were several examples of multigrading. The Montessori elementary schools and the Jenaplan schools are of particular interest. The latter plan embracing a three-grade homeroom, was introduced in the Jena University (Germany) elementary school in 1924. Peter Petersen, a guiding force in the Jenaplan, lectured in the United States during the twenties and, because of his visit to Milwaukee in 1928, may have contributed to the later introduction of nongrading in that city.

The primary-unit plan initiated in Western Springs, Illinois, in 1934 (now discontinued) and in Milwaukee, Wisconsin, in 1942 (apparently the oldest such plan in continuous existence from inception to the present) is an attempt to create flexibility through complete removal of grade-level designations in a three-year or four-year (when kindergarten is included) unit. This type of plan has been extended upward in some school systems to embrace the upper years of the elementary school and is being considered as an alternative to the grades of the junior and senior high schools. Description and appraisal of nongraded plans are reserved for Chapter Four.

In Conclusion

Preoccupation with organizational form as an end in itself is attention misplaced. Attention to form as aid or hindrance in achieving school function is appropriate concern. Logically, school structure stands or falls on the basis of its perceived relationship to school function. Empirically, school structure stands or falls according to the extent to which it fosters curricular and instructional practices which, in turn, correlate with the educational objectives sought. Rigorous evaluation of the effectiveness of school structure is not easily accomplished. It requires, as a beginning, the separation of logical from empirical enquiry.

The concept of school function emphasized here is that of mastering certain fundamentals of knowledge, often defined as "minimum essentials." The rationale for so doing is that this is the school function perceived by most lay citizens and a substantial proportion of educators. But increased insight into individual differences suggests that grade-levels and what they stand for, by definition — graded content, graded materials, graded teachers, graded children, and graded expectations — do not logically serve this school function. The removal of grades, resulting in some form of nongraded plan, promises to free teachers, children, and parents from certain symbols, and, presumably, to open doors to freedom from these symbols and the restrictive educational practices they suggest.

Take grades away, then; have done with them. The result is nongraded structure. All of this appears rather simple, but it is only the beginning.

Since school structure is but a shell, dropping the grades and adding or changing nothing else leaves curriculum and instruction — the heart of the educative process — as they were before. *Nongrading is a significant factor in school improvement only as it is seen and used by teachers as means to significant ends they wish to achieve.* If educators depend on school structure alone for basic educational reform, they will be disillusioned, and potentially unshackling devices such as nongrading will be discredited for failing to do what they cannot do and, therefore, should not be expected to do.

Some educational reformers would hold in abeyance comparison of new and old organizational procedures while perfecting and exploring the full potential of the former. They fear that inconclusive results or initial findings favoring an old pattern will abort innovations before they are much more than a gleam in the eyes of their creators. The problem of experimentally comparing graded and nongraded schools and of interpreting the findings thereof will be simplified with the clear-cut delineation of school practices differentiating these schools.

To compare the respective effectiveness of graded and nongraded schools using as data instances of differing instructional practices as measured *product* is to put the cart before the horse. One must first differentiate between graded and nongraded schools by describing ongoing practices which, in effect, define the differences between the two. Without such a model, one knows not whether he is comparing graded schools with graded schools which are labelled "nongraded," or nongraded schools with nongraded schools labelled "graded," or a piece of each with another piece of the same. Without such models, comparative studies of any aspect of school or classroom organization are largely specious.

To seek more effective means of serving present perceptions of school function is not necessarily to accept them as ideal. The writer, for example, believes that upon the world's schools depend the health, sanity, moral behavior, safety and, in fact, survival of the world's peoples. Contrary to the views of many, exposure to the most noble, sanguine, and elevating ideas of man does not necessarily ennoble his deeds, raise his vision, or purify his thoughts. The generation that plunged the world's peoples into the bloodiest war in all history and the generation that may do so again was and may be the *most* educated of all time.

The more effective coverage of subject-matter sequences is not likely to produce generations significantly different from previous generations in matters of brotherly love, honesty, integrity, and the other virtues. The advent of automated learning, according to its advocates, already permits the coverage of twice as much in half the time — and we are only at the beginning, they say, Are we to conclude, then, that elementary and secondary schooling are to be reduced to perhaps a tenth of their present time-span? Or, are we to conclude that they will cover ten times as much in the present time-span?

For the writer, an appealing alternative is to allocate to automated devices whatever fundamental learnings appear not to require interposing the human teacher between learner and robot. Teaching machines might be housed in schools but it is conceivable that they could be provided to homes by the state and used by entire families in a process of self-education. Schools, freed from routine burdens, would now be forced to create programs scarcely imagined today.

What would these programs be like? The vocabulary for describing them is hard to come by; we have for too long thought in the grade-minded vocabularies handed down from generation to generation. There would be, perhaps, broad cultural studies carried on, conceivably, in the locale of the peoples studied. There would be explorations of mountain-sides, creek beds, lava flows, eroded gullies, the seashore. There would be art and music studios; trips to museums; attendance at lectures, debates, colloquies; no bells or periods or Carnegie units; no "assignments," examinations, or term papers. Goals of mere possession of facts would be replaced by goals of human value and valuing.

Would such educational programs be graded or not?

REFERENCES

1. ALEXANDER FRAZIER. "Needed: A New Vocabulary for Individual Differences," *Elementary School Journal,* 61 (February 1961), pp. 260–268.
2. Reported in "Self-Appraisal in Nongraded Schools: A Survey of Findings and Perceptions," *Elementary School Journal,* 62 (February 1962), pp. 261–269; and "Educational Practices in Nongraded Schools: A Survey of Perceptions," *Elementary School Journal,* 63 (October 1962), pp. 33–44.
3. CHARLES H. JUDD. *Education as Cultivation of the Higher Mental Processes.* New York: The Macmillan Company, 1936.
4. RALPH W. TYLER. *Basic Principles of Curriculum and Instruction.* Chicago: University of Chicago Press, 1950.
5. *The Integration of Educational Experiences.* Fifty-seventh Yearbook of the National Society for the Study of Education, Part III. Chicago: University of Chicago Press, 1958.
6. See, for example, OLE P. SAND, "Continuity and Sequence in Social Studies Curriculums." Unpublished doctoral dissertation (University of Chicago, 1948); JOHN I. GOODLAD, "Three Dimensions in Organizing the Curriculum for Learning and Teaching," *Frontiers of Elementary Education,* Vol. III (Edited by Vincent J. Glennon), pp. 11–22. Syracuse: Syracuse University Press, 1956.

7. Jerome S. Bruner. *The Process of Education.* Cambridge: Harvard University Press, 1960.
8. Warren Hamilton and Walter Rewoldt. "By Their Differences They Learn," *National Elementary Principle,* 37 (December 1957), pp. 27–29; J. H. Hull. "Multigrade Teaching," *Nation's Schools,* 62 (July 1958), pp. 33–36.
9. For further information, see reports of the principal, John M. Bahner, "An Analysis of an Elementary School Faculty at Work: A Case Study." Unpublished doctoral dissertation (University of Chicago, 1960); "Grouping within a School," *Childhood Education,* 36 (April 1960), pp. 354–356.

HORIZONTAL ORGANIZATION OF THE SCHOOL

A pattern of horizontal school organization results from dividing the school population into groups and assigning the students to classes. The process is often referred to as interclass grouping. Intraclass grouping is a process of dividing single classes into instructional groups, after the school pattern of horizontal organization has been determined through interclass grouping.

For analytical purposes, problems of organizing schools horizontally must be differentiated sharply from problems of organizing schools vertically. *Vertical organization provides a system for classifying students and moving them upward from entry to departure from the school unit.* As pointed out earlier, the choice for vertical organization is graded structure, nongraded structure, or some modification of the two. *Horizontal structure provides a system for dividing students into instructional groups and allocating them to teachers.* The over-all school structure is a product of decisions on both vertical and horizontal organization of the school.

There may be literally dozens of possible patterns of school organization. Students in a school that uses a graded vertical structure may be grouped horizontally according to their presumed homogeneity in ability, achievement, interests, or study habits — or they may be grouped quite heterogeneously. Students in a school that uses a nongraded vertical pattern likewise may be grouped horizontally according to some criterion of

SOURCE: John I. Goodlad, "Toward Improved Horizontal Organization," *Planning and Organizing for Teaching* (Washington: National Education Association, Project on the Instructional Program of the Public Schools, 1963), pp. 70–91. Reprinted by permission of the publisher.

homogeneity, or they may be grouped quite heterogeneously. Furthermore, a school that is either graded or nongraded in its vertical pattern of organization may utilize some type of team teaching arrangement for horizontal interclass grouping.

Interclass grouping is a practical necessity, if only to utilize effectively both available teachers and available space. Educational values are brought into play in deciding the basis on which learners are to be allocated to groups. Educators and lay citizens tend to hold rather strong views about whether or not to separate the sexes, whether or not to group by ability, whether or not classes should be consistently small, and so on. Research into the merits of various patterns of interclass grouping is inconclusive, controversial, and misleading, in part because the range of evaluative instruments available for measuring outcomes is much narrower than the range of benefits claimed by advocates of the various positions.

There is so much chaos and confusion in regard to the whole problem of interclass grouping that anyone seeking to make sense out of it must reduce the various alternatives to a very limited number of patterns. One way of doing this is to focus on the fact that in setting up instructional groups one must focus on learners, curriculum, and teachers. In choosing learners as a focal point, one decides between heterogeneous and homogeneous class groups. If the decision is made for homogeneous groups, then one must choose among a great many alternatives for homogeneous grouping. In interclass grouping based on curricular priorities, one chooses between departmentalization and some means of combining subjects. In considering teachers, one decides whether to have one or several teachers responsible for any given group of students.

A comprehensive pattern of horizontal school organization, therefore, embraces decisions on whether students are to be grouped homogeneously or heterogeneously, whether the program is or is not to be departmentalized, and whether classes are to be taught by one teacher or by several. The emerging pattern usually bears some relationship to assumptions about desirable class size. Several of the major alternatives in determining the horizontal organization of the school are analyzed here.

Homogeneous and Heterogeneous Interclass Grouping

The issues involving homogeneous and heterogeneous interclass grouping frequently are reduced to the question of whether or not to practice "ability" grouping. This is a gross oversimplification. The frequency with which this term is applied to grouping practices that have little or nothing to do with criteria of student ability points to the necessity for clarifying some terms.

Homogeneous grouping is a practice wherein the total student population is divided into instructional groups according to some criterion of likeness. As pointed out earlier, this criterion of likeness could be almost anything: height, weight, sex, IQ, achievement, interests, study habits, hair color, socioeconomic class, occupation of fathers, marital status of parents, and on and on. Heterogeneous grouping constitutes an attempt to bring students together according to dissimilarity rather than similarity.

Very few thorough-going attempts at heterogeneous grouping exist in our schools, in spite of the fact that many advocates of such grouping are quite vociferous in expounding its merits. Most of the classes in most of our schools are quite homogeneous in regard to chronological age and socioeconomic status. Many of our most vexing educational problems grow out of the fact that two schools within the same system may be poles apart in respect to the socioeconomic level of the student population and the relative appropriateness of the prevailing programs.

A recurring controversy pits the advocates of homogeneous grouping based on achievement or ability against the advocates of more heterogeneous arrangements. The research-minded individual, faced with this controversy, asks himself, "What happens when students are grouped into this or that pattern according to some criterion of homogeneity?"

There are at least three different ways of answering the question. The first way, and the one that can most easily be tested, is to provide data regarding the character of the groups after they have been put together on some criterion of homogeneity. The second kind of answer constitutes an appraisal of outcomes: "What happens to the learners in this or that homogeneous pattern?" The third raises questions about values: "What outcomes are desired for the school? What kinds of intergroup relationships should prevail in a democracy?" Questions like these bring us back to the matter of school function.

The criterion most commonly used in seeking to establish homogeneous *ability* groups is IQ. As pointed out earlier in this chapter, groups that are relatively homogeneous on IQ are not at all homogeneous on achievement. Ability is a better predictor of educational potential of students than it is an indicator of present achievement. For example, in a fifth grade class in which the IQ spread of 60 or more points normally found in heterogeneous classes is cut in half by removing all pupils having an IQ over 120 or under 90, the spread in achievement in this group differs very little from the spread usually found in classes where no such modification is made.

Most teachers are aware of the gross discrepancies between IQ distributions and achievement distributions in the classes they teach. Many pupils who rank toward the top in achievement are in the middle range on IQ distributions, and many students with genius IQ are mediocre in their school accomplishments. In his excellent review of the literature on ability grouping, Otto concludes that the separation of students into two groups according to ability reduces the variability in achievement to about 93 per cent of what it was before. When three groups are formed, the range in achievement becomes approximately 83 per cent of what it was before such selection is made [1].

There are two major bases for achievement grouping. The first is an average achievement score computed by compiling the results from all sections of an achievement test. This is a score combining all subscores in arithmetic reasoning, arithmetic computation, paragraph meaning, word recognition, spelling, and so on. The data on individual differences presented earlier in this chapter reveal that students are not consistent in their scores. A student in the seventh grade, for example, may be at the seventh grade level in *average* achievement but at the eleventh in an aspect of reading such as paragraph meaning and at the fifth in an aspect of arithmetic such as computation. These intraindividual differences cannot be organized away through interclass grouping.

A much more precise basis for achievement grouping is one wherein students are grouped according to their achievement in specific subjects. This is fairly common practice at the secondary school level where there are often several sections of mathematics, English, social studies, and so on. These sections sometimes are set up to provide a narrower range of pupil accomplishment in the group than would be provided through random assignment of students to classes. If there are 90 students enrolled for algebra, the range of achievement in the usual heterogeneous class is reduced 66.67 per cent by dividing the 90 into three homogeneous classes *using the criterion of achievement in algebra.* A given student might move during the day from Section I in English to Section III in algebra and then to Section II in social studies. In this arrangement, the pattern of horizontal organization is homogeneous according to pupil achievement and departmentalized according to curriculum design.

Critics of interclass grouping on the basis of achievement in each subject cite three practical objections applying primarily to elementary education. First, they object to the amount of class-to-class movement that is required as children go from one class to another. Second, they maintain that the accomplishments of children in the early age brackets change quickly, with the result that a group that is relatively homogeneous at the beginning of instruction rapidly becomes more and more heterogenous. Third, they point out that children of very different chronological ages would be brought together because of similarity in accomplishment in a given subject. A ten-year-old who is reading at the second grade level is very different from a six-year-old reading at the second grade level. Consequently, problems of dealing with individual differences are compounded rather than simplified.

No single measure provides an adequate basis for grouping. Some school systems use elaborate bases combining achievement test scores, intelligence test results, teacher judgment, and observations of children in a variety of educational settings. Some educators conclude that the results simply are not worth the effort, particularly in the elementary school, and recommend pure random interclass grouping in which teachers accept variability as inevitable and do the best they can with it instructionally. Still other educators have been known to advocate a kind of self-selection process. It is in this particular process that youngsters gravitate to the educational environment suited to their personality needs and study habits.

What is the character of groups after students have been brought together on some criterion of homogeneity? Ability grouping based on IQ reduces achievement variability in a group only slightly. Likewise, achievement grouping based on average achievement falls far short of providing group homogeneity in one subject since students vary so in their attainments. Grouping in specific subjects on the basis of student homogeneity in achievement reduces group variability. This homogeneity can be refined more and more to the extent that there are many students from whom to select in grouping and to the degree that very precise areas of learning are selected. Thus, 200 students of the same age can be grouped rather precisely when the criterion used is arithmetic computation. Of course, the groups will remain very heterogeneous in regard to all other attainments.

Should children be grouped on a criterion of homogeneity? The answer to this question depends in large measure upon what one values. If one values subject matter achievement, then the outcomes of such groupings in regard to achievement become important. The research findings regarding this question are inconclusive. Reviews of the literature reveal that the number of studies reporting statistically significant results favoring homogeneous grouping are about equaled by the number of studies reporting statistically significant results favoring heterogeneous grouping [2]. Students of the grouping problem raise serious questions about patterns that simply divide a student population into groups and then require each group to pursue the same studies. Achievement results favoring homogeneous grouping tend to emerge when the group is a gifted group following an accelerated curriculum. Unless such provisions are made, it is extremely doubtful that any pattern of general achievement or any pattern of ability grouping is worth the effort made by those involved in organizing patterns of achievement or grouping.

Interclass Grouping and Horizontal Curriculum Organization

The central issue to be considered here is whether the horizontal pattern of curriculum organization is to be separate subjects, combinations of subjects, or some kind of problem-centered arrangement that tends to ignore subject field designations.

The matter certainly is not settled at the secondary school level, but the situation there is more stable than the one prevailing at the elementary school level. The prevailing high school pattern is separate subjects with some combination of subjects into broad fields such as general science, social studies, and so on. Occasionally, there is a core pattern, usually combining English and the social studies. The result of this curriculum organization is that students tend to be grouped according to subjects and combinations of subjects at the secondary school level.

On criteria pertaining to learners, the students are grouped both homogeneously and heterogeneously in this departmentalized curriculum. The decision to assign students heterogeneously to the various subject fields frequently is based as much on administrative considerations as on other values. Scheduling problems are simplified when students are left free to choose among several sections of a given course according to absence of conflict with other classes. Increasingly, however, as students advance through the secondary school, a selection process occurs whereby more able students are assigned to the advanced section of a course.

There are periodic upsurges of dissatisfaction over the departmentalized approach of secondary schools. The common criticism is that the departmentalized organization limits the range of problems with which students can deal. As a result, significant human problems that cut across several subject fields are passed by in favor of topics inherent in the character of the field itself.

At the elementary school level, grouping practices as related to horizontal curriculum organization frequently have been reduced to debate over the virtues of departmentalization as contrasted with the self-contained classroom. This is an oversimplification. The curriculum may be departmentalized, the classroom self-contained. The practice of moving students from room to room in a system of departmentalization or semidepartmentalization is known as *platooning*. Consequently, the grouping issue is whether to platoon or not to platoon.

The *curriculum* of the elementary school, like the curriculum of the secondary school, is largely compartmentalized. Teachers tend to teach reading, spelling, arithmetic, social studies, science, art, music, and physical education as separate subjects in separate blocks of time. There may be no bells during the day as there are in most high schools, but pupils frequently move from activity to activity according to a schedule and the clock, nonetheless. It is really amazing that elementary schools have adhered so closely to such an arrangement in the self-contained classroom where the teacher is largely free from school-wide divisions in the instructional day. Readers will protest at this point that many self-contained classrooms are not organized in this fashion, and the writer agrees. Nevertheless, this is the prevailing pattern.

A major criticism of the departmentalized curriculum, whether or not it is conducted in a self-contained classroom, is that meaningful interrelationshps among the various parts of the curriculum tend to be ignored or denied. Therefore, exponents of correlation among the various subjects protest platooning because they see this practice as destroying any prospect for such correlation. They argue that the self-contained classroom at least creates a setting wherein the teacher may ignore subject matter divisions in order to deal with major instructional problems, even if the curriculum is departmentalized.

The extreme of self-containment is present when a single teacher personally handles all aspects of the instructional program throughout the entire day. Such practices are more prevalent in rural areas than in large urban and suburban districts where the class often is taken over at some time during the day by a specialist in physical education, music, art, speech therapy, or something else. The extreme of platooning is present when the class moves to a new room and a new teacher for each of 10 or more separate subjects. The alternative to platooning, which is still the antithesis of the self-contained classroom, is to have the class remain at a single station throughout the day but to have a steady stream of different teachers for each subject. Perhaps the most complex arrangement is one whereby platooning is coupled with some kind of ability or achievement grouping. A class of 30 pupils coming together briefly for a homeroom period in the morning is unlikely to be together again throughout the balance of the day. Few, if any, specialists in elementary education endorse such a practice.

The main argument advanced for a departmentalized curriculum taught by different teachers is that subject matter specialists bring richer teaching and learning into the classroom. The main arguments for the self-contained classroom, whether or not departmentalized in curriculum organization, stress the importance of correlation among the component parts of the curriculum and the importance of the group tone emerging from the long-term association of one teacher with a single group of students. Over a half-century or more, there has been a long stream of organizational innovations designed to capture some advantages of the two procedures and avoid the disadvantages. A recent one is the dual progress plan proposed by Stoddard [3]: In it, a home teacher is placed in charge of two rooms on a half-day basis for each. This teacher is responsible for registration and counseling and for teaching reading and the social studies (the cultural imperatives) in what is essentially a graded plan in its scheme of vertical organization. The other half-day is assigned to special teachers who teach mathematics and science, music, arts and crafts, recreation and health (the cultural electives) in what is essentially a nongraded vertical scheme of organization. Stoddard stresses the importance of all-round maturity as a central goal of the homeroom and rapid advancement on a highly individualized basis through the cultural electives in the second half of the day.

Surveys conducted between 1910 and 1950 reveal shifting enthusiasm for departmentalization accompanied by platooning. Interest in platooning and in separate teachers for separate subjects in the elementary school grew during the first of these decades, even though the one-teacher-per-class plan became more widely used. The debate over the respective virtues of platooning and self-contained classrooms grew intense during the third decade with equivalent virtues being claimed for these two essentially different practices. In the fourth decade, 1940–49, more schools reported departmentalization on the way out than on the way in. Toward the end of the 1950–59 decade, the plan of different teachers for different subjects in the elementary school was picking up its advocates again. Practice of such plans was found most frequently in the upper elementary grades, particularly in those schools having the eight-four pattern of vertical organization.

Research into the effects of these differing plans is too inconclusive to give much guidance, and outcomes satisfying all participants in the debate are unlikely to emerge soon. At the secondary school level, the present system of departmentalization and platooning is likely to prevail. At the elementary school level, the modified self-contained classroom is likely to be the dominant pattern for some time to come, especially at the primary level. Woodring [4], for example, advocates a nongraded and largely self-contained arrangement for the primary unit. For the upper elementary level he advocates a graded departmentalized arrangement with several teachers rather than a single teacher per class. The constant experimental search is for patterns embracing the virtues of both self-containment and the several-teachers-per-class alternatives.

Interclass Grouping Based on Teacher Utilization

The long-standing, over-all organizational design of American schools is a teacher-per-class-per-grade at the elementary school level and a teacher-per-class-per-subject-per-grade at the secondary school level. In other words, the vertical pattern is graded; the horizontal pattern is self-contained in the elementary school, especially at the primary level and platooned by separate subjects at the secondary school level. Modifications of anything, by definition, are away from existing patterns. Consequently, the anticipated direction of change at the elementary school level is away from self-containment as generally practiced in the past or toward patterns that more precisely reflect the advantages sought in self-containment. The direction of change at the high school level is toward patterns that overcome segmentation in the curriculum and the daily life of the student or toward patterns that more precisely implement concern for either individualized advancement or subject matter rigor.

Modifications of horizontal organization in the past have tended to begin with consideration of learners or subject matter. Some recent modifications, however, have begun with questioning the teacher-per-class-of-25-or-30-students arrangements so central to the design of American education. One such modification gaining nationwide attention is cooperative teaching.

Some varieties of cooperative teaching are labeled *team teaching*. This term is used here to refer only to cooperative teaching ventures embracing all three of the following characteristics. First, there is a hierarchy of personnel: team leader, master teacher, auxiliary teacher, teacher aide, intern teacher, clerk, or some other array of resources. Second, there is a delineation of staff function based on differences in preparation, personal interests, and so on, or on the kinds of learning activities planned. Third, there is flexibility in grouping that embraces *all* students under supervision of the team. Most so-called team teaching projects possess only the second and third characteristics; some, only the third. Consequently, they do not meet the demands of our definition. Efforts wherein two teachers simply divide the curriculum into two halves — "You take my arithmetic, and I'll take your reading" — are not team teaching. They are merely examples of departmentalization.

Just as there are several patterns of cooperative teaching, there is also a wide range of assumptions underlying current innovations. Some arrangements are designed simply to maintain as many as possible of the virtues of the self-contained classroom while providing students with the benefits of some teacher specialization. Other plans emphasize the role of experienced teachers in the induction and education of new teachers. Still others emphasize a hierarchy of classroom tasks and differentiated responsibility for them [5].

A simple model of cooperative teaching is that developed in the Englewood (Florida) Project. The teachers were studying the virtues of various cooperative efforts at the time they were presented with the opportunity to make some modifications in the plans for a new school building. They proposed classrooms ranging in size from 750 to 1,500 square feet. They then proposed movable partitions between pairs of rooms, leaving the 1,500-square-foot room as a single, undivided space. Doors were then cut between all rooms where a movable partition had not been provided. Teachers who wished to cooperate in various ways were then placed side by side in adjoining rooms separated by the partitions.

At the beginning, teachers in these partitioned rooms planned only a small segment of the day to be taught in a cooperative fashion. Gradually, however, with growing confidence, they extended their collaborative efforts until the partitions rarely were closed. Thus, 50 to 80 children, depending on the current enrollment, normally divided into two separate classrooms, became a single self-contained group taught by two teachers. The entire group divided and redivided throughout the day into groups varying in size from two or three youngsters to the entire two-room population, depending on the particular activity called for. Each teacher recognized approximately half the student group as his homeroom, so to speak, but both teachers worked throughout the day with all children and came to know them well. In recent years, cooperative teaching efforts have been extended to include three or four class groups, with varying degrees of success. The teachers do not see the lack of three- and four-room clusters as an insurmountable obstacle to cooperative teaching, but they admit that more flexible space arrangements would constitute a considerable asset.

Much refinement of practices such as these will be required before controlled research studies will be meaningful. Teachers who tried this teaching arrangement at Englewood claim several advantages. First, they maintain that it is possible to secure more precise groupings of children when homogeneity is called for without the disruptions caused by shifting from class to class. All grouping occurs in a fluid fashion within the confines of this larger self-contained classroom made up of two conventional classes. Further, they claim that there is much less wasted time. One teacher is able to concentrate fully on the instruction of a single group while the other teacher manages various activities underway with the remaining pupils. Third, and perhaps surprising to many readers, the teachers claims that they get to know the students better than in the conventional self-contained classroom. The reason for this, they say, is that they have more time to observe children at work without being personally involved, and then to compare observations with a colleague who has been observing the same child. There appear to be several concomitant aspects here. Two teachers are able to confer on a student presenting unique problems and to agree on specific instructional steps. They find, furthermore, that this dual knowledge of the child facilitates parent conferences. One teacher takes responsibility for conferring with parents in regard to half the class, but the other teacher is called in as a consultant and an additional observer whenever this appears to be desirable. Teachers claim many additional benefits having to do with opportunity to get away from class supervision in order to select materials, to plan, and just to rest. One major advantage claimed by all teachers who have participated is the opportunity to discuss truly professional matters with a colleague throughout the day as occasions arise to do so. They feel that they have the advantages of continuous communication with at least one other adult as well as with the students.

Emphasis on developing a special field of teaching competence in the elementary school has varied from teacher group to teacher group in the Englewood setting. Both teachers of a primary pair take about equal responsibility for all aspects of the curriculum. In another pair, both assume most responsibilities equally but one tends to dominate during music activities and the other for art. In still another teaching cluster, there is a considerable division of subject matter responsibility throughout the day with one member of the group stressing arithmetic, another social studies, and another physical education. However, all teachers participate in all planning and most teaching, frequently assisting the others even when some differentiation of responsibility has been worked out.

One important aspect of the Englewood situation is the freedom to choose whether or not to form or to participate in a cooperative teaching group. One teacher who had been a member of two different two-teacher groups for two sequential years decided to return to a completely self-contained situation. He took over a different classroom, giving up his space in the partitioned room to someone else who wished to work with a colleague. Following a year of being in a completely self-contained class involving full-time responsibility for 30 students, this teacher had worked out certain problems and chose to go back into a cooperative teaching situation. The constant availability of this kind of flexibility may be a crucial element in cooperative teaching. This is a factor well worth studying in the future appraisal of all such efforts.

Team teaching models are complex in that they utilize a hierarchy of personnel. Much stimulation for existing projects has come from a commission of the National Association of Secondary-School Principals; Educational Facilities Laboratories and the Fund for the Advancement of Education of the Ford Foundation; and universities such as Chicago, Harvard, Wisconsin, and Claremont Graduate School. Many of these have clusters of up to a half-dozen rooms and employ a hierarchy of personnel such as the following: team leader, master teacher, intern teacher, student teacher, teacher aide, and clerk. Activities range from completely individualized learning to instructional activities embracing the entire student population supervised by the team.

Team teaching, as defined here, is a recent innovation. In 1957, the Franklin School in Lexington, Massachusetts, introduced team teaching and became the prototype for several other team teaching projects, most of which possess their own unique characteristics in addition to some of the basic elements introduced at Franklin. Usually, a team leader coordinates the work of several other persons responsible for the instruction and guidance of perhaps as few as 50 or as many as 200 pupils. Commonly, too, the team leader does some teaching, but much of his time goes to curriculum planning, staff leadership, pupil evaluation, and so on. The intent is to make the post attractive, professionally and financially, in order to keep good teachers in the classroom. Master and auxiliary teachers assume most of the teaching duties and are relieved of many chores by teacher aides and clerks. The opportunity to move upward in the hierarchy is available to most members of the team, depending on their ability and willingness to assume responsibility and secure additional preparation.

Planning is crucial in seeking to provide individual and group instruction, smooth movement from activity to activity, and careful appraisal of pupil learning in all areas. Early in its efforts, the team confronts the difficult problem of deciding on the kinds of learning best suited to individual, small-group, and large-group instruction. Most elementary school teachers are not accustomed to teaching large groups. Whether or not many elementary school activities lend themselves to large group organization remains a much debated issue. Clearly, the intelligent planning of tomorrow's school buildings depends heavily on early resolution of this issue.

At the secondary school level, Ridgewood High School in Norridge, Illinois, and Wayland Senior High School in Wayland, Massachusetts, are interesting prototypes likely to have an impact on other school facilities contemplating team teaching. In the former, there are no conventional classes of 30 or 35. In the latter, students spend approximately half their time in conventional-sized classes and the other half in large lecture groups and in seminar groups of only 15 members. With its description of these schools, Educational Facilities Laboratories includes a revealing sketch of the conventional plan of high school organization as contrasted with a team organization modeled after Ridgewood High School [6]. Both the Wayland and Ridgewood plans stress flexibility in size of group and length of instructional period, together with opportunity for teachers to engage in a variety of teaching tasks and to develop special teaching talents.

In the foregoing discussion of horizontal school organization based heavily on considerations of teacher utilization, little has been said about interclass grouping. This is because each team or cluster of teachers and students is, initially, a *single* group. All subdivisions within this group are

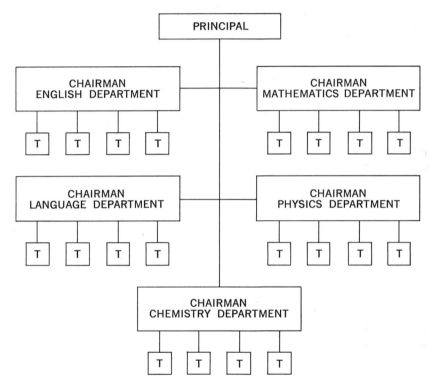

FIGURE 2.3   A Conventional Plan of Personnel Organization

essentially intraclass rather than interclass groups, if one considers clusters of pupils rather than classrooms as the core element in any consideration of grouping. In cooperative teaching, staff members begin their thinking about grouping by examining an initial, self-contained cluster of, for example, 90, 150, or 200 students — all those to be taught by an identifiable cluster of personnel. *They do not begin by spinning off, in their minds, or in actual practice, three or five or seven class groups of 30 each.* It is this initial conceptualization of cooperative teaching that is so crucial and, frequently, so difficult to grasp.

The moment one opens up his thinking from closure on the self-con-

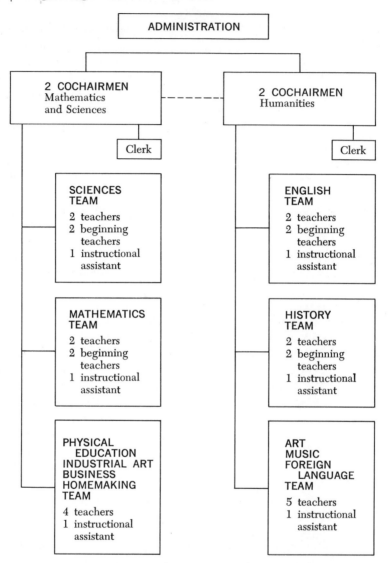

FIGURE 2.4 A Team Teaching Plan of Personnel Organization

tained *classroom* of 30 pupils to focus on the possibilities of the self-contained *group* of 90 or 150 pupils, much of the debate over self-contained
versus platooned, departmentalized arrangements fades into insignifi-
cance. Admittedly, a fully self-contained class of 30 pupils taught by one
teacher is quite different from a self-contained group of 120 pupils managed by six persons of differing talents. But is the latter arrangement

farther away from the ideal of self-containment proposed by some educators than, say, a so-called self-contained classroom taught most of the time by one person but interrupted several times per day by various special teachers?

This debate is really quite fruitless. Discussants rarely argue their case from clear-cut models. Consequently, they employ slogans rather than facts. Much more to the point is inquiry into questions such as the following: What is the tolerance level of children of different ages and temperaments for identifying with several teachers during a school day? (Interestingly enough, some educators have made much of the single-teacher-per-group idea on the grounds that children, particularly in the early school years, need this for security. And yet, most people hold to the idea that two parents are to be preferred over one! Further, reputable nursery schools recommended two or more adults for each group of children.) What happens to the learning skills and interests of pupils who have access to several specialists rather than a single generalist? Are there maximum and minimum group sizes for various kinds of learning activities? Do teachers teach any better or with greater enjoyment when they are relieved of routine chores? Can teaching be divided into a hierarchy of tasks and subdivided meaningfully for differentiated teaching roles?

We have not been successful in finding answers to these and other related educational questions while using the relatively monolithic school structures of the past. Innovations of the present serve at least to reveal the significance of such questions and to create fresh opportunities for studying them. The search for evidence will not be aided, however, by educators who hold tenaciously to unexamined patterns of the past or who stubbornly defend their new but untried brain children.

Conclusions and Implications Regarding the Dimensions of School Organization

A two-fold set of decisions about how to move students upward through the school (vertical organization) and how to assign them in groups to available teachers (horizontal organization) determines the over-all pattern of organization that will exist in a school at any given moment. Vertically, the choice is between graded or nongraded organization or some adaptation of the two. Horizontally, the choice is among many alternatives or combinations of alternatives: ability grouping, achievement grouping, the self-contained classroom, departmentalization, team teaching, and so on.

Vertical school structure should provide for the continuous, upward progression of all learners, with due recognition of the wide variations among learners in every aspect of their development. School organization, then, should be flexible enough to permit differentiated rates of pupil progress. Further, the pattern of vertical school organization should provide several alternative classroom placements for a given learner, the final choice of a placement being dependent upon careful teacher diagnosis of the individual.

The graded plan does not appear to be readily adaptable to these demands of flexibility. *Nongrading and multigrading are promising alternatives to the traditional graded school and should be given careful consideration in seeking to provide flexible progress plans geared to human variability.*

The respective advantages of various patterns of horizontal school organization often have been argued or investigated quite apart from the functions a given school was intended to serve. Increasingly, we are coming to see that considerations of the specific learners to be served, of curriculum, and of teacher interests and abilities must be taken care of simultaneously in assigning students to classroom groups. There are no panaceas that resolve instructional problems, however, even when all of these factors are taken into account in determining a pattern of horizontal organization.

So-called ability grouping or some other plan of interclass homogeneous grouping often is recommended, especially by laymen, as a cure for all sorts of educational ills. *Efforts to set up interclass groups on the basis of ability or achievement do little to reduce the over-all range of pupil variability with which teachers must deal.* Such efforts, therefore, are *not* recommended as general practice. Selective grouping and regrouping by achievement sometimes is useful, especially at the secondary school level. However, such practices as the aforementioned grouping and regrouping do not materially reduce teachers' problems of dealing educationally with individual differences.

Many efforts to reorganize schools appear to have been directed toward "organizing away" individual differences. This is futile. Further, such efforts can be damaging in that they may lead teachers, particularly beginners, away from teaching efforts designed to cope with individuality. School organization can perform a highly valuable service by revealing individual differences and through directing teacher attention toward the need to provide for them instructionally.

School organization does not exist for its own sake, but to serve the educational welfare of individuals. Organizational form must follow, not mold, school function.

REFERENCES

1. See HENRY J. OTTO, "Elementary Education: III. Organization and Administration," *Encyclopedia of Educational Research,* rev. ed. (Edited by W. S. Monroe) New York: The Macmillan Company, 1950, pp. 377–378.
2. See RUTH B. EKSTROM, *Experimental Studies of Homogeneous Grouping: A Review of the Literature.* Office of Naval Research Contract Nonr-2214(00), Project Designation NR 151–174. Princeton, N.J.: Educational Testing Service, April, 1959.
3. GEORGE D. STODDARD. *The Dual Progress Plan.* New York: Harper and Row, 1961.
4. PAUL WOODRING. *A Fourth of a Nation.* New York: McGraw-Hill, 1957, p. 225.
5. See JOHN A. BROWNELL and HARRIS A. TAYLOR, "Theoretical Perspectives for Team Teaching," *Phi Delta Kappan,* 43 (January 1962), pp. 150–157.
6. *Profiles of Significant Schools: High Schools 1962.* New York: Educational Facilities Laboratories, Inc., 1961, p. 15.

▶3

The Promotion - Nonpromotion Dilemma

RESEARCH AND THEORY REGARDING PROMOTION AND NONPROMOTION

Bring together a number of elementary-school teachers from anywhere in the country and ask them the question: "What are your ten most vexing educational problems?" The problem of grade-to-grade promotion is likely to be included in all their lists. There are no panaceas for taking care of the problem. Blanket promotions for all children are not the answer. Promotion on the basis of fixed minimum standards is not adequate. What to do with the slow-learning child after he has been retained or sent along to the next grade is a problem that is at least as complex as the problem of whether to promote. Present-day educators, in seeking solutions to such problems, pose the question: "What is best for the total development of this child?" In answer, there are many opinions, some well-conceived theory, and also a considerable body of research worth examining. This research and representative theory are the subjects treated here.

SOURCE: John I. Goodlad, "Research and Theory Regarding Promotion and Non-promotion," *Elementary School Journal* 53 (November 1952), pp. 150–155. Copyright, 1952, by the University of Chicago. Reprinted by permission of the University of Chicago Press.

Promotion Practices and Achievement

Studies into the achievement of repeaters indicate that these children do no better than children of like ability who are promoted. This was suggested by Keyes more than fifty years ago, when he reported that only 21 per cent of a large group of repeaters did better after repeating a grade than before and that 39 per cent actually did worse [1]. Of course it is impossible to estimate how well the same children might have done had they been promoted. Arthur sought to answer this question when she matched a group of repeaters with a group of nonrepeaters on the basis of mental age and discovered that the former learned no more than the latter over a two-year period [2]. She put forward the thought, however, that failure to eliminate the causes of retention, rather than the repeating experience itself, may have been the more potent factor in determining subsequent achievement of the pupils.

The cause-and-effect relationship of a given factor can be clarified only by holding constant other factors likely to be influential. Klene and Branson took cognizance of this fact when they equated children, all of whom were to have been retained in the grade, on the basis of chronological age, mental age, and sex [3]. Half were then promoted, and half were retained. Klene and Branson concluded that, on the whole, potential repeaters profited more from promotion than did the repeaters from nonpromotion, so far as achievement was concerned. In this connection, Cheyney and Boyer observed that lack of readiness for the work of a given grade is largely due to a slow learning rate, which will not be improved by repeating a grade section [4].

Saunders summed up an extensive survey of studies into the effects of nonpromotion upon school achievement as follows:

> It may be concluded that nonpromotion of pupils in elementary schools in order to assure mastery of subject matter does not often accomplish its objective. Children do not appear to learn more by repeating a grade but experience less growth in subject-matter achievement than they do when promoted. Therefore a practice of nonpromotion because a pupil does not learn sufficient subject matter in the course of a school year, or for the purpose of learning subject matter, is not justifiable [5].

Promotion Practices and Homogeneous Grouping

For most teachers, to secure a class of children closely approximating one another in all areas of development would be the realization of a teaching utopia. However, Keliher questions the social desirability [6] and Elsbree doubts the feasibility [7] of obtaining any such condition of general homogeneity. Burr points out that, when groups are made non-overlapping in achievement for one subject, or even for a phase of a subject, they overlap greatly in other subjects or other phases of the same subject [8]. From a study of forty-six schools with varying rates of slow progress, Caswell [9] concluded that variability in pupil achievement is no less for schools with high rates of nonpromotion than for schools with lower rates of nonpromotion — findings that are substantially in agreement with those of Akridge [10]. Whether or not homogeneous grouping be desirable or attainable, nonpromotion does not appear to reduce the range of specific abilities with which the teacher has to cope.

Promotion Practices, Habits and Attitudes

Viele, arguing for the abandonment of no-failure programs, claimed that children will not put forth their best efforts when they know from the start that they are to be promoted [11]. However, studies into the relative effects of various incentives upon school work tend to discredit this line of reasoning.

Both Hurlock [12] and Gilchrist [13] found that groups of pupils who had been praised for their work showed greater improvement over a period of time than did pupils who had been reproved for the quality of their work. Sandin found that the attitude of slow-progress pupils toward school was not commendable. He reported that approximately 40 per cent of these children wished to quit school as soon as possible and that a like per cent — as against 14 per cent of regular-progress pupils — indicated that they disliked school and school work [14a]. Of course, these children might have felt the same had they been promoted; Sandin set up no control factors, such as matched groups. However, the findings support Farley's conclusions that the failing child, receiving less satisfaction from his work, tends to become discouraged and frequently antagonistic [15].

Promotion Practices and Behavior

The question of the effects of promotion practices upon behavior has provoked considerable controversy. Robinson, for example, maintains that pupils' failure replaces their interest in school work with feelings of resentment that may be expressed in aggression [16]. Jablow, on the contrary, maintains that the frustration produced by inability to perform the work of the higher grade leads promoted slow-learning pupils to become disciplinary problems [17]. Research studies conducted by McElwee [18] and by Sandin [14b] revealed a greater incidence of behavior considered troublesome among retarded children than among regular-progress pupils. Although these findings favor promotion over nonpromotion, further experiments with carefully controlled situations need to be conducted.

Promotion Practices and Personal-Social Adjustment

In the field of promotion practices, the area involving personal-social adjustment probably is the area most barren of research. A study by Farley, Frey, and Garland indicated a significant correlation between retardation and a low score on a five-point character-rating scale, but left open the question of whether this was a cause or an effect relationship [19]. Anfinson sought to determine the nature of this relationship by setting up controls [20]. He matched 116 pairs of junior high school pupils on the basis of school attendance, chronological age, sex, intelligence, and socioeconomic status, one member of each pair having been promoted regularly and the other having repeated some previous grade. His findings showed a significant advantage for nonrepeaters over repeaters in social and personal adjustment as revealed by the Symonds-Block Student Questionnaire. As Anfinson pointed out, it would have been better to have tested these irregular-progress pupils soon after the failure occurred — in some cases several years had elapsed. In addition, the range of measuring techniques was very limited. The results of such questionnaires, when used without other sorts of evidence, must be handled with considerable reservation.

Sandin used sociometrics, rating scales, check lists, observations, and interviews to study aspects of social and personal adjustment [14]. In general, he found that nonpromoted children tended to choose companions from grades higher than their own, to be pointed out by classmates as children who associated with pupils from grades other than their own, and to be discriminated against in the selection of study companions. This last findings did not hold true for the first grade, where nonpromoted children received significantly more than their expected share of choices. Sandin's findings concerning attitudes and feelings, described previously, disclosed a general outlook indicative of a less happy adjustment among slow-progress pupils than among normal-progress pupils. Since he made no attempt to equate the groups studied on other factors likely to affect social and personal adjustment, it is impossible to weigh the contributing influence of the promotion factor. Sandin put his finger on this problem when he concluded:

> It is necessary to conduct further study to discover to what extent children who might have been nonpromoted according to grade

standards, but who actually were promoted, show a better picture of adjustment than those who were held back [14c].

The writer conducted an investigation in an attempt to throw some light on the question raised by Sandin. He equated a group of fifty-five promoted second-grade pupils with a group containing a like number of nonpromoted first-grade pupils on the basis of chronological age, mental age, and achievement. Considerable preliminary research was done in order to secure equivalent conditions in regard to such matters as enrolment, urban-rural location of schools, physical normality of the selected children, and socioeconomic status of their families. Two major hypotheses, tested as null hypotheses, gave direction to the study

1. There are no differences in social adjustment between school children who repeat grades and those who do not.
2. There are no differences in personal adjustment between school children who repeat grades and those who do not [21].

The instruments for evaluating adjustment were chosen with three purposes in view: (1) to give the selected children an opportunity of rating themselves, (2) to give all children an opportunity to rate one another, and (3) to give the teachers an opportunity to rate the subjects selected. These three purposes were fulfilled, in the order given, by administration of the California Test of Personality (Primary Series), utilization of sociometric "best-friend" questions, and administration of the Haggerty-Olson-Wickman Behavior Rating Schedules. The California Test of Personality and sociometric questions were administered both at the beginning and at the end of the school year. The Haggerty-Olson-Wickman Schedules were administered only at the end of the school year.

Since twenty-nine instances of significant difference were identified, the two hypotheses were clearly rejected. Eighteen of the significant differences favored the promoted group, and eight favored the nonpromoted group. The remaining three instances were not clearly to the advantage of either group. A heavy concentration of those differences favoring the promoted group had to do with peer-group relationships. All three sources of data pointed to the general difficulty of the nonpromoted children in making satisfactory social adjustments. The promoted children, on the other hand, tended to be more disturbed personally over their school progress and their home security — concerns that appear to be closely related.

Conclusions

Throughout the body of evidence runs a consistent pattern: Undesirable growth characteristics and unsatisfactory school progress are more closely associated with nonpromoted children than with promoted slow-learning children. Conversely, slow-learning children who have been promoted tend to make more satisfactory progress and adjustment than do their peers who have been kept back. Equally obvious, however, is the conclusion that not all the differences identified favor the promoted groups. The greater incidence of differences favoring the promoted groups is counterbalanced, in part, by certain significant differences favoring nonpromoted groups or individual children. It becomes clear that blanket promotion policies are not justified by the evidence. Nevertheless, the evidence supports promotion over nonpromotion as the more defensible educational practice.

Recommendations

The findings of these studies suggest the following recommendations related to the classification of pupils in graded elementary schools.

1. Each child should be considered individually rather than in the light of system-wide policy. When an affirmative answer, based on fact rather than opinion, cannot be given to the question, "Is nonpromotion likely to favor the all-round development of these children?" then children about whom there is doubt should be promoted to the next grade.

2. Teachers should adopt a broad, factual basis for making their decisions. Facts related only to achievement and intelligence are not sufficient; nor is the division of a limited body of information into more categories adequate. Needed are facts related to all phases of human growth and development, collected from a wide range of sources throughout the year rather than during the last few weeks of the school term, and analyzed in relation to sound principles of child growth and development.

3. Instructional needs of the pupil should take precedence over matters of administrative expediency in dealing with questions involving promotion and nonpromotion. Determining and dealing with cause and effect are infinitely more important educational matters than making decisions regarding the immediate act of retaining or promoting. School personnel must examine the curriculum out of which failure grows and is being perpetuated. Then, matters of pupil classification are likely to emerge as by-products rather than as ends in themselves.

REFERENCES

1. CHARLES H. KEYES. *Progress through the Grades of City Schools.* Teachers College Contributions to Education, No. 42. New York: Bureau of Publications, Teachers College, Columbia University, 1911, p. 63.
2. GRACE ARTHUR. "A Study of the Achievement of Sixty Grade I Repeaters as Compared with That of Nonrepeaters of the Same Mental Age," *Journal of Experimental Education,* 5 (December 1936), pp. 203–205.
3. VIVIAN KLENE and ERNEST P. BRANSON. "Trial Promotion versus Failure," *Educational Research Bulletin* (Los Angeles City Schools), 8 (January 1929), pp. 6–11.
4. W. WALKER CHEYNEY and PHILIP A. BOYER. Division of Educational Research, Philadelphia. A study reported in mimeographed form. Extracts quoted in *Elementary School Journal,* 33 (May 1933), pp. 647–651.
5. CARLETON M. SAUNDERS. *Promotion or Failure for the Elementary School Pupil?* New York: Bureau of Publications, Teachers College, Columbia University, 1941, p. 29.
6. ALICE V. KELIHER. *A Critical Study of Homogeneous Grouping in Elementary Schools.* New York: Alice V. Keliher, 1950, p. 22.
7. WILLARD S. ELSBREE. *Pupil Progress in the Elementary School.* Practical Suggestions for Teaching, No. 5. New York: Bureau of Publications, Teachers College, Columbia University, 1943, p. 44.
8. MARVIN Y. BURR. *A Study of Homogeneous Grouping in Terms of Individual Variations and the Teaching Problem.* Teachers College Contributions to Education, No. 457. New York: Bureau of Publications, Teachers College, Columbia University, 1931, p. 55.
9. HOLLIS L. CASWELL. *Non-promotion in Elementary Schools.* Field Studies No. 4. Tennessee: Division of Surveys and Field Studies, George Peabody College for Teachers, 1933, pp. 44–46.
10. GARTH H. AKRIDGE. *Pupil Progress Policies and Practices.* Teachers College Contributions to Education, No. 691. New York: Bureau of Publications, Teachers College, Columbia University, 1937, p. 54.
11. JOHN A. VIELE. "Does the No-Failure Plan Work?" *Grade Teacher,* 65 (June 1948), pp. 19, 66.
12. ELIZABETH B. HURLOCK. "An Evaluation of Certain Incentives Used in School Work," *Journal of Educational Psychology,* 16 (March 1925), pp. 145–159.
13. EDWARD P. GILCHRIST. "The Extent to Which Praise and Reproof Affect a Pupil's Work," *School and Society,* 4 (December 2, 1916), pp. 872–874.
14. ADOLPH A. SANDIN. *Social and Emotional Adjustments of Regularly Promoted and Non-promoted Pupils.* Child Development Monographs, No. 32. New York: Bureau of Publications, Teachers College, Columbia University, 1944. (a) 123; (b) 97; (c) 136.

15. EUGENE S. FARLEY. "Regarding Repeaters: Sad Effect of Failure upon the Child," *Nation's Schools, 18* (October 1936), pp. 37–39.

16. B. B. ROBINSON. "Failure Is Too Costly for the School Child," *Parents' Magazine, 11* (January 1936), pp. 22–23, 55–57.

17. LILLIAN JABLOW. "Deferred Promotions in Grade One," *Baltimore Bulletin of Education, 25* (December 1947), pp. 146–147.

18. E. W. McELWEE. "A Comparison of Personality Traits of 300 Accelerated, Normal, and Retarded Children," *Journal of Educational Research, 26* (September 1932), pp. 31–34.

19. EUGENE S. FARLEY, ALBIN J. FREY, and GERTRUDE GARLAND. "Factors Related to the Grade Progress of Pupils," *Elementary School Journal, 34* (November 1933), pp. 186–193.

20. R. D. ANFINSON. "School Progress and Pupil Adjustment," *Elementary School Journal, 41* (March 1941), pp. 507–514.

21. JOHN I. GOODLAD. "Some Effects of Promotion and Nonpromotion upon the Social and Personal Adjustment of Children," *Journal of Experimental Education, 22* (June 1954), pp. 301–328.

TO PROMOTE OR NOT TO PROMOTE?

To promote or not to promote . . . that is the question that will plague teachers — several hundred thousand teachers — this coming June. And it is a question that has plagued them each year for decades. Had Rip Van Winkle been a teacher and had he dozed off twenty years ago while deliberating the fate of thirty youngsters, he might have resumed his deliberations quite naturally on awakening today. Not a soul would laugh; not a soul would consider his activities bizarre. Only the thankful thirty, spared through Rip's somnolent sojourn, might rejoice that the belated decisions would now have no bearing upon their lives.

Some claim that promotion no longer can be considered a significant educational problem. "Why, I seldom find it necessary to retain more than three children," they may add. Three children out of, say, thirty? That's ten per cent. And ten per cent amounts to three million elementary school children in all of America. But it must be recognized that many schools

SOURCE: John I. Goodlad, "To Promote or Not To Promote?" *Toward Effective Grouping*, Bulletin No. 5-A, pp. 34–38. Reprinted by permission of the Association for Childhood Education International, 3615 Wisconsin Avenue, N.W., Washington, D.C. Copyright 1962.

promote all or nearly all pupils. Let's be very conservative, then, and say that only one million elementary school children are retained in their present grades each year. Promotion an insignificant problem? One could hardly agree.

Not To Promote

Why retain a child? Let us think through some of the reasoning that must lie behind a million decisions not to promote. We may not agree with them, but the following are some of the reasons often given to justify nonpromotion:

When promotion is assured, pupils are unconcerned about their school work, developing poor work habits and careless attitudes.

Bright children come to resent equal promotion rewards for work that is obviously inferior.

Because of the need for teachers to spend a disproportionate amount of time with slow-learners, the presence of these children in the room serves as a hindrance to progress. The range of achievement is widened and group homogeneity reduced.

Achievement levels are enhanced through the repetition of only partially learned material.

Immature children, through grade repetition, are more likely to find suitable play and work companions at the lower grade level.

The promoted slow-learner, unable to do the work of the grade, frustrated and discouraged, develops inferiority feelings which adversely affect his social relationships and personality development.

To Promote

There are many people who believe that slow-learning children should be promoted, regardless of present levels of attainment. Again, we may not agree with the arguments put forth to support this position but let's examine a few of them:

The possibility of nonpromotion is a threat that constitutes negative motivation. Children learn best under conditions of positive motivation and therefore should be promoted.

Children distribute themselves from poor to excellent on each of the many school endeavors in which they engage, usually with only slight variations from child to child on the continuum. To average these attainments is unrealistic. To determine arbitrary cutting points for passing or failing demands a refinement in judgment that defies human capacities.

The presence of older, repeating children in a classroom decreases group homogeneity.

Learning is enhanced when children move on to new endeavors instead of experiencing the dullness and boredom of repetition.

Grade repetition results in over-ageness which, in turn, produces behavior problems requiring special disciplinary action.

Promotion retains approximately equal chronological age as a common factor and results in improved personal and social relationships.

What Are the Facts?

It is vividly apparent that the two sets of arguments are virtually identical. Each claims for itself the same virtues and, for the other, the same vices. Now for both to be right, obviously, is impossible. Either there is nothing to choose from between the two practices, or one must be superior to the other on the questions in debate. What are the facts?

Fortunately, a considerable body of research is available and is summarized on preceding pages. On each of the arguments above, where there is research evidence in any acceptable form, that evidence points clearly to the fact that *slow-learning children profit significantly more from promotion than from nonpromotion.* They attain higher achievement levels when promoted, require less disciplinary action, display more positive attitudes toward school and teachers, and appear to enjoy more satisfactory social and personal lives. It should be clearly understood that promotion is no universal panacea for learning disabilities. It simply is the more defensible of two promotion alternatives.

Neither Is the Answer

The crux of the promotion issue is that there ought not be any alternatives. *There ought not be a decision to make. Promotion and nonpromotion are both inconsistent with certain significant insights into children and their learning:*

Neither promotion nor nonpromotion, in and of itself, can change a child's basic learning rate.

Very few children in a given grade approximate the grade norms for that grade in their achievement. For example, only three or four children out of a class of thirty are found to be at grade norm in all subjects at the middle of the year. And this is true even when "grade norm" is defined generously to include a one-year spread in achievement from subject to subject.

A child seldom approximates arbitrary grade norms in all areas of endeavor. He may be significantly above in one and below in another and only slightly above or below in still others.

The spread in mental age among a group of children, already as much as four years in the first grade, becomes greater as these children progress through the elementary school. The spread in academic attainment, in turn, will tend to keep pace with the broadening spread in mental age, especially under conditions of good teaching.

In the light of these facts, how can concepts either of promotion or non-promotion be applied meaningfully? Susie is at third-grade expectancy in all areas except arithmetic where she lags behind at low second-grade level. Teddy's work spreads out from the second to the fifth grade but if all his attainments were averaged, his placement would be only three months into the third grade. Mary is very advanced. She is at the fifth-grade level in all her work but is very small for her age. All three are completing their third year at school. Should Susie be promoted and Teddy retained? Should Teddy be promoted and Susie retained? Should Mary be advanced to the sixth grade? Are these really the questions to which teachers' time should be devoted?

Neither promotion nor nonpromotion materially changes the natural heterogeneity ever present in a group of six-year-olds, nine-year-olds or twelve-year-olds. This statement has been amply documented. Miss Stevens must make provision for those children who read well or poorly, are large or small, get along well with others or have difficulty sharing. Keeping back two or three children each year doesn't help her or her colleagues. It may lull her into thinking, for a few blissful moments, that she has a homogeneous group. Alas, even groups of two aren't homogeneous! Promotion and nonpromotion are merely the trappings of an educational era that should be long past. They do absolutely nothing to ease or expedite the job of the teacher. They certainly do nothing for children.

Several Answers — Not One

To promote or not to promote . . . What is the answer? There are several answers rather than one.

First, it must be recognized that most teachers in America today work in a system of grade classification requiring that children move from step to step through it. It is recognized, further, that courses of study, textbooks and even teachers are organized around the grade concept. When children are brought together in groups of thirty and more under such a grade classification system, it soon becomes apparent that some children deviate so markedly in certain characteristics that the desirability of retaining them in the group comes in for questioning.

Under such an organizational setup, retention of some children, while the group as a whole progresses to the next step, occasionally appears to be a logical solution. (The author deplores the circumstances over the act of retention itself.) In the face of ample research evidence, to the effect that nonpromotion less frequently than promotion results in favorable later adjustment of children, the teacher should be cautioned to ponder carefully each instance of doubtful promotion. When he cannot say with conviction, "Knowing this child as I do, the chances for successful school experience next year and in subsequent years are greater if he be retained," then he is advised to give the child the benefit of any existing doubt and promote him. We can ill afford to ignore the research that is before us.

But under such circumstances the act of promoting or retaining is only the beginning. The repeater must be provided for. Simply to do over work that was inadequately done before is not the answer. The year with younger classmates must be filled with exciting challenges; not dulled with the repetition of activities long since wrung dry of interest and stimulation. To promote the slow-learner to tasks far beyond his comprehension likewise is no kindness. Whether slow-progress children be regularly or irregularly promoted, adequate subsequent provision for their needs is essential.

These are short-term answers to the promotion question. In a sense, they constitute tardy treatment for a very sick horse. But now, let us go back to an earlier statement that neither nonpromotion nor promotion is the real answer. *Needed is an educational organization that facilitates continuous progress of all children in each of the various facets of their development.*

Is it not logical that children who are ready for more advanced work in reading should proceed to it, free from the artificial restrictions of grade barriers? Is it not logical that certain of these children, slow in arithmetic, should proceed slowly with appropriate work in this field?

These are the realities with which we are faced. Is it not time that we adapted organizational procedures to fit them? The time for us to abandon our Procrustean lock-step system that chops children to make them fit the norms is long past. Instruction has for too long been the handmaiden of organization.

The long-term answer, then, is the elimination of those grade barriers that have given rise to a host of fallacious notions about pupil progress, of which the fantasy that children should arrive precisely at a given "norm" each June is the most preposterous. Nongraded schools constitute a step in the right direction.

Perhaps years of experimentation with such plans will show us at long last that grade barriers are unreasonable. At any rate, thousands of schools in the United States are now being reorganized from top to bottom with a view to becoming nongraded.

The obvious result, of course, is that promotion and nonpromotion simply will disappear from school practice — yes, even from our vocabularies. With the philosophy of continuous progress (and there is a vast difference between "continuous progress" and "social promotion" or any other kind of one hundred per cent promotion) firmly entrenched and grade barriers no longer existent, to promote or not to promote no longer will be a question. Let us hope that this Utopia is so imminent that should any modern Rip Van Winkle doze off in the midst of his promotion meditations, continuation of his activities on awakening twenty years later would be absurd indeed!

4

Alternative Patterns and Practices

THE CHANGING AMERICAN SCHOOL

American education has changed since World War II and the forces of change are by no means spent. Witness, for example, curricula organized around basic concepts, programed instruction, nongrading, team teaching, innovations in school plant design, and the use of electronic data processing in education.

To what extent do these changes represent fundamental reform? Is the heart of American education beating any more vigorously? Is our educational enterprise guided by a new spirit or an old one that has become more compelling? These are the central questions we must raise in examining the postwar educational reform movement.

My purpose in this paper is threefold: first, to set forth some of the conditions and assumptions underlying instances of school change; second, to define and describe cooperative teaching and other examples of educational change; and, third, to respond to the questions raised above pertaining to the heart and spirit of the pre-collegiate educational enterprise.

The Educational Reform Movement

It is, indeed, a valid generalization to describe what has been happening to and in our schools these past dozen years as an educational reform movement. School leaders in all sections of the country have been caught

SOURCE: John I. Goodlad, "Cooperative Teaching in Educational Reform," *National Elementary Principal 44* (January 1965), pp. 8–13. Reprinted by permission of the Department of Elementary School Principals of the National Education Association.

up in the fervor; many university professors have become enthusiastically involved; and few laymen are completely unaware of the ferment in their schools. To assume that all the innovations that have been introduced are good is to be dangerously uncritical. But promising alternatives to the monolithic educational patterns and structures of the past have been introduced. Refinement and testing of new and old alternatives could keep us well occupied for decades to come.

To account for each instance of change in turn against the political and substantive fabric of our times is impossible. Nonetheless, most of the major reforms appear to have been motivated, at least in concept, by the same set of conditions or assumptions, perhaps only two or three of these conditions and assumptions applying specifically to any given reform. This retrospective observation may be quite in error. And yet, it is difficult to escape the conclusion that there is a persistent relationship between reforms in school organization and curriculum organization, for example, as well as among the several conditions that produced them.

Ten brief statements appear below without elaboration or explanatory comment. These — and others, admittedly — are the observations so frequently used in justifying or accounting for those instances of school change which concern us here. Subsequently, there is an attempt to show the relationship between several school reforms and some of these ten observations.

1. There is an intimate relationship between national welfare and security and the existence of sound educational programs for all children and youth.

2. Fast growing awareness of educational inequalities and inadequacies, particularly with respect to various disadvantaged groups, has brought unrelenting pressure upon educators to come up with fresh solutions.

3. The American school enterprise has grown to mammoth proportions, entailing the expenditure of billions of dollars annually, involving millions of teachers and students, and creating complex problems of information processing and communicating.

4. As a consequence of (1), (2), and (3) above and other factors, education has come under intense public scrutiny; education news and opinion are high priority items for press, radio, and television.

5. The bodies of knowledge available to man and the myriad ways of inquiring into the unknown surpass the capacity of any one man to encompass them.

6. Increasingly, we are becoming aware of hitherto neglected human traits which, for the sake of both society and the individual, must be identified, developed, and rewarded.

7. We are gaining increased insight into the vast differences among human beings with respect to their ability in and development of any given trait.

8. Tens of thousands of students pass through our schools without adequate diagnosis and remediation of their learning ills.

9. Widely accepted principles of learning such as, for example, reinforcement, have not been adequately implemented in school programs.

10. New cultural patterns are rapidly emerging. The new culture rejects the concept of *inevitable* progression toward an ever-better society, is oriented toward probabilities rather than certainties, and places man and his rationality at the center.

The above list represents a cross-section of both societal pressures arising outside of education and substantive pressures arising from advances in knowledge within education itself. The first four and the tenth are so all-pervasive that it is virtually impossible either to discount them or to specify their precise influence on any educational change. Consequently, in the brief ensuing discussion of reforms, the others tend to come in for more attention.

Curriculum Reform ▪ Various groups and individuals, supported primarily by the National Science Foundation, have developed new courses and instructional materials to go with them for high-school mathematics, physics, chemistry, biology, economics, geography, anthropology, English, and foreign languages, and for several subjects taught in elementary schools. Without exception, the various projects seek to identify and to organize basic concepts, generalizations, or principles considered to make up the "structure" of the field and to involve students in its methods. Many of the leaders in this reform movement have been content to produce and revise a comprehensive instructional package; several, however, have become deeply immersed in the psychological and pedagogical problems of learning and teaching [1].

The roots of this movement are found in intense dissatisfaction with the science and mathematics backgrounds of many high school graduates recruited in World War II. Planned attack upon the problem goes back at least to 1952 and was sharply accentuated by the launching of the first Russian satellite in 1957. Broad-scale curriculum reform was seen as essential to national welfare — in fact, to national survival.

The directions which the movement took were influenced by the knowledge explosion, by new insights into learning, and by increasing understanding of teaching roles. Hence, we find the curricular search for something more fundamental and lasting than the factual fruits of inquiry; the use of programed, self-instructional sequences; and the preparation of textbooks, laboratory experiments, films, supplementary materials, and teachers' manuals to assist teachers in every way possible. There has been some provision for individual differences among learners but concerted attack upon the special curricular needs of disadvantaged pupils, particularly those from harsh environments, is an agenda item for tomorrow.

The current curriculum reform movement is not a passing fad. It is having a significant impact upon millions of students and tens of thousands of teachers and already is assured of extensive analysis by historians of American education.

Programed Instruction ▪ The roots of programed instruction go back to the early search for principles of human learning and of teaching as a special instance of instruction. It joins research on learning and teaching with curricular inquiry into clarifying educational objectives, providing for scope and sequence, and evaluating outcomes. Programed instruction represents, therefore, a unique synthesis of lines of inquiry which, although related, have tended to proceed apart [2].

It is difficult to determine how much programed instruction has been influenced by the societal forces listed earlier. One's first inclination is to say "very little." And yet, ardent exponents see it as a significant answer to the problems of educating the disadvantaged, as wiping out certain kinds of individual differences which unnecessarily prejudice children's futures. Certainly, research and development in programed instruction have profited from the general visibility of educational problems in recent times.

Although a wide range of problems is brought under scrutiny through focus on programed instruction, the typical schoolman is relatively unaware of the significance of this educational reform. Few good programs for general school use are available and school administrators have no assurances that substantial numbers will be available in the near future. But many of the characteristics of programed instruction are conceptually compatible with assumptions underlying current reforms in school and curriculum organization. Consequently as these more visible reforms increasingly take hold, the demand for suitable programs is likely to increase sharply and, in all probability, to be met.

Nongrading ▪ Organizationally, a nongraded school is one in which the grade levels and grade labels representing years of vertical progress are replaced by a plan of continuous upward progress. Conceptually, it is intended to eliminate the promotion-nonpromotion adjustment mechanism of graded schools; to raise the ceilings and lower the floors of attainment expectancies for learners, thus encompassing their individual differences;

to encourage the utilization of content and materials in accordance with pupil individuality; and to force pedagogical attention to individual differences and the individual. There are very few, if any, so-called nongraded schools that have yet attained what has been built into conceptual models of nongrading.

Clearly, nongrading represents a direct response to our growing insight into individual differences. It is seen as having potential for providing appropriate learning for disadvantaged children who have not yet profited much from school, but for whom a low grade placement would be damaging. Further, the absence of grade barriers is conducive to the long-term development of basic concepts and principles inherent in the new curricula.

Perhaps of greatest potential significance, nongrading removes the system by means of which so many educational decisions are almost automatically made: promotion or nonpromotion, selection of materials, establishment of instructional groups, evaluation of children according to normative standards, and so on. With this system removed, teachers are forced to diagnose the individual, prescribe for him, and fill their prescriptions from a repertoire of available alternatives. These are professional behaviors which, when performed effectively by most teachers, will justify professional status for teaching. As teachers mature in them, there should be a marked decrease in the number of students who pass through our schools without adequate diagnosis of their learning ills.

Electronic Data Processing ▪ Electronic data processing, with the computer as the mainstay, is a newcomer among newcomers in a changing educational world. As in industry, early uses have been in the gigantic management enterprise involving budgets, payroll, accounts, property inventory, pupil personnel data, employee personnel records, and teacher certification [3]. Increasingly, it is entering into vast building programs calling for precise scheduling of tasks — and saving millions of dollars in the process.

Now we are beginning to see the possibilities of electronic data processing in instruction. The computer coupled with teaching machines, for example, enables researchers to monitor the step-by-step performances of students using programed instructional materials. This technique already has proved useful in modifying sequences in several of the current curriculum reform projects. Research studies employing electronic data processing procedures, now underway, promise to provide us with fresh insights into the learning-teaching process.

The diagnosis and remediation of learning ills calls, first, for the conceptualization, collection, and storage of data appropriate to decisions about the individual. Then, these data must be brought to bear meaning-fully in the decision-making process. The complexity of these tasks — the volume of data required together with the needed precision in recall — surpasses unaided human capacity. Perhaps only the computer will make such educational refinements possible.

We see, then, that electronic data processing today and increasingly in the future is central to managing the enterprise, to understanding educational processes, and to effecting educational decisions.

Cooperative Teaching ▪ Cooperative teaching is a process wherein two or more persons, not necessarily of the same professional status, share in planning any segment or, conceivably, all of the learning opportunities for a specified group of students and in carrying out their joint plans. The arrangement may be quite simple as when two teachers of sophomore social studies, normally teaching close physically but far apart communicatively, pool students and resources. A slightly more complex but conceptually similar situation pertains when two elementary-school teachers, normally separated in self-contained classrooms, come together for planning and teaching. Complexity can be compounded, however, until an hierarchy of personnel — leader or coordinator, master teachers, regular teachers, interns, student teachers, aides, clerks, etc. — becomes responsible for cooperatively ministering to the needs of students comprising many previously separated classes. The practice commonly is referred to as team teaching.

Cooperative teaching is a way of organizing the school horizontally — that is, of assigning students to teachers and classes. It has nothing to do with vertical organization — that is, with the graded, multigraded or nongraded scheme of moving students upward through the school. However, the horizontal flexibility of cooperative teaching and vertical flexibility of nongrading have a certain compatibility.

Customarily, in the secondary school, students are assigned to classes by subjects and acquire teachers by chance. In the elementary school, students usually are assigned by chance to one teacher for all or most subjects, depending on the ability of the school system to provide specialists. At both levels, the system is relatively inflexible. It is not self-correcting; only with considerable difficulty can adjustments be effected later.

In the view of a growing number of educators, these organizational arrangements fail to take into account the unique needs, talents, and interests of students and teachers. They are relatively impersonal mechanisms for managing a massive human enterprise with some modicum of efficiency. The fact that they fail to provide the flexibility necessary to something so highly personal as education suggests that they may be, in the long run, inefficient and wasteful of human resources. The system rather mechanically establishes instructional groups and maintains them, regardless of how unproductively they may function.

By contrast, cooperative teaching encourages flexibility not only in setting up initial groups but especially in redeploying students and teachers at any later time. Since several adults with varying backgrounds, competencies, and interests plan the total program for an expanded number of students (50 or 100 or more), there is no need to pre-determine group structure for more than short periods of time. Thus, educational purpose, group size and membership, and time allocation can be brought into appropriate relationship.

Teachers are always in close communication, and, further, sharing the same space, they can quickly readjust their plans. Increasingly, they become diagnosticians: They analyze, prescribe, and carry out plans; evaluate, prescribe, and diagnose again. Subtleties such as the "fit" of pupil personality and teacher temperament often can be provided for. Group structure is not the reflection of an inflexible, pre-determined system; it shifts according to need and purpose. In essence, cooperative teaching forces those involved to make professional decisions based on the full range of factors — subject matter, learner interest, pupil characteristics, teacher competence, and so on — entering into the learning-teaching process.

Cooperative teaching, as sketched here, is still more in the category of potentiality than reality so far as present practice is concerned. It is anticipated, however, that certain mechanistic aspects will smooth out as educators gain experience and increasingly come to see the inherent opportunities.

Cooperative teaching grew predominantly out of two conditions which became highly visible early in the 1950's: limited leadership opportunities for career teachers; the impossibility of teachers being all things to all people. With regard to the first, the prevailing monolithic structure of the teaching profession has restricted the alternatives open to the nonadministrator. Teachers, too, deserve alternatives. The hierarchial possibilities of cooperative teaching were seen by innovators as a means of offering special inducements and rewards to career teachers. Similarly, such cooperative endeavors enabled teachers, especially at the elementary-school level, to develop and use special talents in ways not possible in conventional patterns of school organization and teacher utilization.

The aspect of cooperative teaching toward which the organized teaching profession has been least disposed is the hierarchial arrangement of teaching talent characteristic of team teaching. The cry has been for a "fully qualified teacher in every classroom." With this the proponents of cooperative teaching have no quarrel. They simply wish to expand the concept of "classroom" to include several cooperating classrooms and to open up avenues for leadership and specialization in teaching.

The Changing School in a Changing Culture

The significance of current school change must be appraised, in large part, against the significance of current cultural change. Social scientists point to the emergence of a new American culture characterized by the centrality of man and his rationality. This "new" rationalism, fostered by the "new" education emphasizing inductive thinking and the methods of man's disciplined inquiry, admits no certainties and, above all, no dogmatisms. It questions the relevance of even our most revered traditions, seeing in our continued, unquestioning adherence to them blocks to the solutions that must be found in an uncertain world today and tomorrow.

The fact that the new culture concerns itself more with methodologies than with ethical principles elicits concern that life in modern America is directionless. And the schools, it is said, having lost sight of their purpose, are redoubling their efforts to get there. Interestingly, those who react negatively to what appear to be the central trends in the new culture offer no new directions of their own. Frequently, they point to the past, implying that what served well then will serve equally well or better tomorrow.

There is little point in arguing that much of the past is myth, that the American dream was *really* only a dream. Because, comes the query, if fancy is what men perceive to be real, is not fancy fact? And so, in the new culture, the American dream itself comes in for analysis. Did it become moondust? And, if so, when and why?

In the sweep of history, the period from 1850 to nearing 1950 will be viewed as an era of great American ascendancy, guided by faith in man's potentiality under God. The United States, strong in commitment to education, demonstrated the attainability of mass public schooling. At the turn of the century, our schools were opening up previously undreamed of opportunities for aspiring youth.

The essence of the educational dream was that it held the individual human being high while offering him the means to identify with and, in fact, to cope with mankind's legacy of triumph and tragedy. Oh, yes, it offered, too, better food, clothing, and habitation — even the chance to become a millionaire or president of the United States. But these last were pie in the sky to be joked about, not the motivators that gave meaning to each day and to life itself. So went the dream.

For nearly five decades of this century, our schools were seen as contributors to the development of a people who looked not to the past but to the future, not to security but to opportunity, not to opportunity for personal enhancement but to opportunity for human advancement, not to narcissistic contemplation of self but to transcendance of self. Whatever the weaknesses of these schools in action — and there were many — they were viewed as part of and contributor to a larger faith. Whether they were departmentalized or maintained self-contained classrooms, emphasized phonics or word recognition, were graded or multigraded, probably isn't terribly important. During each successive decade, more people learned to read more and better; successive classes of high school graduates knew more than their predecessors.

Then came two periods of gloom and disillusionment: the depression of the '30's and the war of the '40's. That we survived them without becoming a Fascist or Communistic nation is significant. That the schools contributed to our strength few can deny. But the dream faded, nonetheless.

The schools received the brunt of our disillusionment before we became aware of our larger concern. For a time, the most publicized solutions involved simply turning back the clock to the schools many people think we had prior to 1925, before "the invidious work of John Dewey and his disciples" was becoming revealed. Millions of Americans apparently still see in this the solution to our ills.

But careful students of the social, economic, political, and educational scenes are impatient with those who look backward or to any easy, sweeping solution. They see neither wisdom nor possibility in seeking to make an old spirit more compelling. They see, rather, a new society emerging which, in turn, demands a new kind of education, the dimensions of which are not fully clear. What seems to be clear is that the old dimensions do not suffice.

Today's schools, then, are caught up in swirling, broiling change, change which many agree is long overdue. Much of the impetus comes from outside the schools but is not accompanied by a clearly articulated, fully satisfying sense of direction. The educational philosophers have turned to analytical philosophy and existentialism and, in company with the behavioral scientists, it is charged, have come up with methodologies, not moral principles.

Are moral principles to have no place in the new culture? This writer thinks otherwise. The questions are, rather, from what are they to be derived and to what or in what applied? Education must become more introspective. Educational philosophers, in particular, must turn more of their attention from the philosophies of our time, useful as these are in educational practice, to the "stuff" of our time. Particularly, they must get thoroughly dirtied in the stuff of American education. Is this not what Dewey did and why educators have so tried to interpret and to act on what he said?

Let us stop bewailing the fact that modern educational innovators do not clearly articulate the ends to which they strive. Our new culture as a whole is strikingly inarticulate in this regard, too. Educators must not wait for the all-encompassing statement of purpose to which their efforts must contribute. They must seek, rather, to make their purposes clear and to speak for them forcefully in the market place of ideas.

We need a new *Education and Democracy* and a new *Dare the Schools Build a New Social Order?* if only as catalysts in modern man's and modern society's search for meaning. The new John Dewey and the new George Counts will be men who can free themselves from time-hardened categories of thought, as the new culture urges each of us to do. Underlying a host of modern-day educational innovations are beliefs and assumptions which, taken as a whole and screened for inconsistencies, could be built into a compelling statement of what life and schooling are for. The analysis of them may not lead to justification or perpetuation of current school inventions but could well lead to the derivation of criteria by which to judge our efforts for a productive time into the future.

REFERENCES

1. For further description and analysis, see JOHN I. GOODLAD, *School Curriculum Reform in the United States*. New York: Fund for the Advancement of Education, 1964.
2. For a concise appraisal of programed instruction, see WILBUR SCHRAMM, *Programed Instruction Today and Tomorrow*. New York: Fund for the Advancement of Education, 1962.
3. See JOHN I. GOODLAD, JOHN F. O'TOOLE, JR., and LOUISE L. TYLER, *Computers and Information Systems in Education*. New York: Harcourt, Brace & World, Inc., 1966.

IN PURSUIT OF VISIONS

Man is a discontented creature. He is forever wanting things to be different, always hoping for something better.

SOURCE: John I Goodlad, "News and Comment: in Pursuit of Visions, *Elementary School Journal* 49 (October 1958), pp. 1–17. Copyright, 1958, by the University of Chicago. Reprinted by permission of the University of Chicago Press.

In education, we know much better than we do. We have yet to create an ideal school. But fortunately we have our visions. And as soon as one vision is translated into reality, we have others, and each seems better than the last. To close the ever present gap between reality and our best visions is the great task of human engineering, the mission that challenges every educator who wants to make good schools better.

The task of improving education is a shuttling process, a weaving back and forth between envisioning and doing. Somewhere a schoolman has an idea for a new school. He may go on dreaming about his idea, or he may set to work at it. Without action, his vision cannot take form. Without vision, his action can never lead to new paths.

Schoolmen who try to bring about changes singlehandedly are carving out a huge task for themselves. Change is most likely to result when an entire faculty shares a vision and combines with that vision long-term concerted action to make the dream come true.

Will the results be desirable? That depends on the vision and on the skills and understanding enlisted to move toward the vision.

There is a past, a present, and a future to be taken into account in school improvement. Unless educators know where they have been, they cannot judge the relevance of where they are going. Unless they know where they are, they cannot properly appraise the skills required to get where they want to be.

The source of a vision is of no importance. What is highly important is that those who are responsible for transforming a vision into reality accept that vision as worthy and as their own.

The past success record of those who are responsible for providing status leadership also counts. That record makes a difference in the amount of energy and enthusiasm displayed by those engaged in making dreams and visions come true.

Schools evolve, but certain features of our educational enterprise have hardened into rock formations so formidable that we can scarcely blast them aside or visualize what may lie beyond.

Any group that is thinking seriously of school improvement soon comes face to face with the realization that its members must first be convinced of the desirability of getting to the other side of the formidable rock pile. That is not all. The group must find its way through the intervening petrified forest.

Small wonder that many educators give up and turn to other alternatives. Rationalization, for example. What's on the other side of the rock pile isn't worth the labor, some educators tell themselves, and they put aside any thought of moving an inch.

Others turn to idolatry. They enshrine the vast rock pile, pay homage to it, and build rock gardens in its shadow out of the fragments of granite scattered about the base.

Some of us wearily reconcile ourselves to something less than excellence. It's hard to teach children to think, we complain, and we settle for the consumption and regurgitation of facts. The tests we so carefully prepare to measure the queasy possession of these facts become another offering to the great granite god.

Where do we begin, we who want to improve the school? The unit for improvement is the single school with its pupils, parents, teachers, principal, and community.

To improve this unit requires first a vision of what ought to be done. We must decide what tasks are worth doing. Then we must have concerted action to accomplish those tasks.

Programs for school improvement across the country show nationwide concern with the following tasks:

The development of faculty unity to the point where productive teamwork characterizes action for school improvement.

Study and diagnosis to learn pupil realities; the evaluation of the school program in the light of those realities.

Experimentation with a variety of procedures for dealing with wide ranges of pupil abilities and for using teaching resources more effectively. This search has been stimulated by a growing national concern for the gifted and by teacher and classroom shortages that have beset our schools for more than a decade.

Comprehensive attention to the curriculum as a whole. The pattern of improving a single subject area is important and still persists, but more and more educators are relating such efforts to improve a single subject area to the entire school program.

Direct attack on the improvement of classroom instruction. The emphasis here is on creating a permissive atmosphere and a setting rich in resources for stimulating and carrying on learning.

The construction of school buildings that serve contemporary educational ends.

The establishment of appropriate school-to-school relationships, particularly in the articulation of elementary and secondary education.

The meaningful involvement of parents and the community in the development of the school program.

The development of comprehensive evaluation programs designed to determine the need for change and the effectiveness of change.

A continued search for clues to the most expeditious ways of effecting change in long-established institutions.

Many school systems across the country are acting on the problems listed. We are reporting here on the action taken to improve the school in Englewood, Florida.

The Englewood Project, 1953–1964

The little community of Englewood is located on the west coast of Florida, some thirty miles south of Sarasota. The year 1953 marks the beginning of what is now called the Englewood Project. The story since 1953 has been one of successes and failures, satisfactions and disappointments. Above all, it has been the story of a search for a common vision of what an elementary school can be, the story of a search for ways of attaining that vision. Most of what is described here occurred between 1955 and 1961.

Situated a dozen miles south of its nearest neighbor in the Sarasota County School District, the Englewood Elementary School had suffered some deprivation.

It had been hard, for example, to find teachers who would stay for more than a year or two. In spite of the scenic attractions of this subtropical retirement paradise, many teachers who accepted positions soon left the isolated community.

Then Mr. and Mrs. William H. Vanderbilt and their school-age son settled on the offshore Manasota Key. Not long afterward Mr. and Mrs. William H. Vanderbilt and Mr. Alfred G. Vanderbilt entered into an agreement with Sarasota and Charlotte counties. The Vanderbilts wanted better schools for Englewood. Under the agreement they arranged to provide funds for this purpose.

The aim of the venture is easy to state: to develop the local school so that the children would have educational opportunities equal to the best anywhere in the country. Obviously, any such aim is tremendously difficult to carry out. It requires agreement on the nature of an outstanding educational program and long-term cooperation among all who commit themselves to carry out the program.

The Englewood Project was not experimental. It did not seek to break ground in a search for new knowledge. Rather, the Project was a venture in bringing into one school the best we know about elementary education. It was a multiple-front approach to the improvement of a single school in all phases of its work.

One of the most interesting features of the Englewood Project was the pooling of tax resources and private funds for the improvement of public education.

The project was unique in that it had a director with the responsibility of representing the Sarasota county school system, the Englewood Elementary School, and the Vanderbilt families. The Englewood school operated in every way as a unit in the Sarasota educational system, but in virtually all phases of school operation the director acted as an adviser and consultant.

On budget matters, for example, he advised the Vanderbilts on the best use of their grant. He also served as the Vanderbilts' representative in county administration of the grant. At the same time, he served as consultant to the school faculty in budget-planning and to the central county administration in relating the Vanderbilt grant to regular funds.

The first two years of the Project were devoted to explorations of the curriculum and to material improvements. Special supplies were purchased and a central library was developed.

It soon became apparent, however, that competent teachers and vastly improved physical circumstances do not themselves constitute a good school.

One hallmark of the good school is a spirit of accomplishment, an aura of achievement that comes only after the staff has tried difficult things together, only after it has succeeded often enough to nullify the effects of occasional failure.

During the Project, holding power improved somewhat, but even after the Project had been underway for three years, teacher turnover was still high.

Then subtle changes appeared, changes that were first noticeable in the children. No doubt they began to sense a growing unity among the faculty members. And no doubt they learned that their teachers were spending long hours planning for their pupils.

It takes time for changes to come to the surface. Quite likely, invisible changes took place long before any sign of change could be detected.

Next, parents showed signs of change. Before 1958 they had been reluctant to accept positions of leadership in the parent-teacher association. But as the conference type of reporting brought parents and teachers together, both groups sensed a unity of purpose. Parent participation in lunchroom, playground, and classroom activities created still more interest in school affairs. By 1958 the change was unmistakable. That year every parent nominated for a post in the parent-teacher association accepted the responsibilities he was asked to assume.

Interest in the school was not confined to parents. An evening art class for adults, which met in the school and was directed by one of the teachers, attracted residents who otherwise would have known little about school activities.

One essential to school improvement was emerging: a feeling of pride, of ownership, of participation in a common enterprise worthy of attention.

Meanwhile, the faculty had been putting its house in order. Each week teachers met for two hours to study school improvement.

The year 1956–57 brought to Englewood a new way of looking at curriculum. How the change came about makes an interesting story in which geography plays no small part.

Englewood is not far from the shore. For some children, marine life is no farther away than their yards, front or back, which border on canal, bay, or beach. Naturally the children of Englewood have an intense interest in sea life. And naturally the teachers in Englewood want to nourish this interest in their science classes. Yet the faculty feared that without careful planning the use of the children's interest would result in wasteful duplication of activity and a chaotic science program. To avoid these aftereffects, the group began to explore ways of maintaining continuity while using the pupils' interest.

The staff finally worked out two approaches to a sequential curriculum. In one approach they identified basic concepts in science that elementary-school children might understand. For example, living things are interdependent and interrelated; adaptation is a characteristic of all living things; man is constantly trying to control his environment.

In the other approach, the teachers prepared a set of pupil behaviors that the study of science might foster. Among the behaviors listed were the ability to make valid generalizations; the desire to observe, explore, and question; the ability to use many sources of information.

The teachers proposed and examined activities that might be used to teach the concepts and to develop the general abilities. A longitudinal, sequential view of the curriculum replaced the previous grade-to-grade listing of topics "to be covered."

A more detailed description of this approach to curriculum-making may be found in the author's article "Illustrative Programs and Procedures in Elementary Schools," in *The Integration of Educational Experiences,* Part III of the Fifty-seventh Yearbook of the National Society for the Study of Education, distributed by the University of Chicago Press.

The weekly planning sessions led to other changes in school practice. For example, the school adopted a conference system of reporting to accompany and supplement the countywide card system. In addition, the teachers drew up a plan for involving parents more meaningfully in certain phases of the school program.

The planning sessions added to the teachers' understanding of child development. They brought a greater emphasis on pupil involvement in planning. And out of these gatherings came the beginnings of a more comprehensive evaluation system.

In a project of this kind, one thing leads to another. Faculty discussions and a series of parent-teacher study sessions raised serious questions concerning the appropriateness of conventional elementary-school organization. The opportunity for parents and teachers to take part in planning a new school building unit brought still other questions to the fore.

A faculty session on the progress records of two pupils — a very fast learner and a very slow learner — sharpened the issues on organization. A grade level tells us virtually nothing about individual differences in that grade. The range in over-all achievement may be as great as, or greater than, the grade-level designation.

For example, in a fourth-grade class, the range in academic attainment may be four years or more. In reading, the range from the highest achiever to the lowest may be twice the grade-level designation, eight years in this instance.

To the frustration of even the best teachers, a child who is advanced or retarded in arithmetic is not necessarily advanced or retarded in reading. In fact, pupils at the top or the bottom of the general-achievement scale seem to vary most from field to field. To segregate these pupils in special classes does not solve the problem of dealing with individual differences.

The problem is an old one, and old solutions are not reassuring. Homogeneous grouping of various kinds has not achieved what was expected. A group formed on the basis of any one criterion is still heterogeneous on all other criteria.

Departmentalization is one suggestion sometimes offered, but it means chopping the curriculum and the child's day into unrealistic bits, leaving unsolved the problem of meeting a wide range of individual differences within each subject.

Hypotheses derived from research on learning suggest that academic considerations may be low among the factors that contribute to an effective learning situation. Learning proceeds most effectively, some argue, when the focus is on the general climate for learning and on the way different individuals approach learning.

The Englewood faculty recognized that the conventional graded school imposes a lock-step on pupil progress. If pupil realities are to be observed, that lock-step must be ignored, the staff concluded.

Yet when the teachers considered doing away with grades, they immediately recognized obstacles, not insurmountable, but still worth attention. How does a school staff go about shifting to a nongraded school? How is a nongraded plan carried out? How does the staff interpret to parents? The teachers decided that the best course was to continue their study of the nongraded structure. Meanwhile, they agreed to take whatever steps seemed wise to meet individual differences better.

Another question was explored during the planning sessions: How should children be grouped from class to class at any given level of instruction, whether or not the school is graded?

Whatever solution was worked out, the faculty wanted to put the special talents of staff members to more effective use. How can the school make the best use of the talents of the teacher who is highly skilled in art, music, social studies, or the language arts? Some teachers are talented in one or another of these fields. Other teachers face the demands of teaching some of these subjects with considerable trepidation. The faculty was opposed to departmentalization. Would it be possible, they asked, to share teaching tasks in some kind of team arrangement?

In the fall of 1958, the Englewood faculty launched two modified plans of school organization. Both plans were exploratory, steps on the way to more thoroughgoing revisions that emerged later.

Since it was necessary to create combination grades, the teachers decided to use the arrangement, wherever possible, as a first step in breaking down grade lines. In previous years, several teachers had moved up from the lower grades with groups of children. Under this arrangement, the teachers explored practices suited to older pupils and thus acquired useful experience for teaching combination grades in 1958.

A number of considerations guided plans for changes:

The faculty decided to move slowly in grouping children of different chronological ages. In any one class, the spread was normally confined to not more than two years.

The faculty wanted the pupils, fast and slow, to move through the school at their own rate without the usual dislocations of skipping grades or nonpromotion.

The staff sought more time to explore, especially with parents, the possibility of eventually creating a nongraded school. The teachers planned to introduce the arrangement one class at a time, beginning in the primary grades. Meanwhile, they wanted to help both the very fast and the very slow move through school smoothly.

The teachers agreed to keep heterogeneous grouping, though they wanted to relieve teachers from having to work with both the extremely retarded and the extremely accelerated in the same classroom. They hoped to work out an arrangement in which a teacher might have one but not both of these groups in a heterogeneous class.

The teachers wanted to create a classroom environment compatible with pupil realities.

Acting on these considerations, the Englewood faculty changed the grade-to-grade structure for grouping pupils. The plan was worked out before the close of school in June, but by September changes had taken place that made revisions necessary. Five rooms and 147 children were affected by the new plan.

The arrangement provided for five class groupings, three of which combined two grades. In Figure 4.1, the classes are shown as A, B, C, D, and E.

Group A includes twelve children promoted from second grade; these boys and girls could not be accommodated in the third grade or in the combination second- and third-grade classes. Group A also contains five slow-moving pupils who were in the third grade the year before.

Group C includes five youngsters entering fourth grade who are very advanced and capable of doing fifth-grade work most of the time. Group C also includes twelve pupils selected at random from fifth grade.

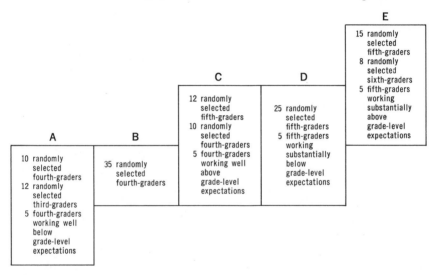

FIGURE 4.1   Sample of grouping plan used in Englewood (Florida) Elementary School for the 1958–59 school year.

Groups A, B, and C also include 55 fourth-graders, heterogeneously divided, whose general achievement is between the level of the five slow pupils in Group A and the five fast pupils in Group C.

Forty of the remaining 50 fifth-graders are distributed heterogeneously between two classes, 25 going to Group D and 15 to Group E. The five slowest join Group D and the five most advanced join Group E, where there are eight randomly selected sixth-graders.

For all practical purposes, grade lines have been abandoned. In each group, work proceeds according to the pupils' readiness. The step levels of Figure 4.1 indicate roughly the levels of activity in each class.

For the more mature youngsters, Group C is more appropriate than Group B. Therefore, the few very advanced fourth-graders are here. However, Group B still includes the variety of abilities normally associated with the term "heterogeneous" and takes on none of the characteristics normally associated with the term "homogeneous."

Obviously the teacher's problem of dealing with varying abilities has been reduced only slightly, if at all. But no entirely satisfying plan for resolving this problem has yet been devised. We may as well abandon the quest for increased teacher comfort derived from decreased pupil heterogeneity. We must focus, instead, on arrangements that foster the best possible environment for pupil learning.

The groupings described here provide more flexibility in working with the extremely retarded and the extremely accelerated. For example, depending on how well or how poorly the five retarded fourth-graders in Group A progress, several grouping alternatives will be open at the end of, or even during, the year. These children might remain where they are. Or they might move to the equivalent of Group B, thus taking an additional year to move through the six grades. Or, if these pupils do well, they might move to Group D and continue through the school program at normal speed.

The five advanced fourth-graders in Group C might remain where they are for another year. Or they might move to the equivalent of Group D, thus proceeding through school at a normal rate. Or, should they advance rapidly in the present Group C, they might move to Group E and do the work of the fourth, fifth, and sixth grades in two years without skipping.

The plan satisfied very well most of the considerations that guided the Englewood group. The arrangement modifies but does not eliminate the lock-step of graded structure. The plan gave the staff time to study the implications of nongraded structure, to which they later moved.

The Englewood faculty also worked out a grouping of pupils to develop certain teacher-team activities. Teachers pooled their talents and their pupils in a variety of ways to provide more flexibility in grouping than usually is found in the self-contained classroom.

More and more, it is becoming apparent that the traditional notion of a teacher-per-class-per-grade in the elementary school warrants serious examination. Neither departmentalization nor homogeneous grouping provides a tenable answer, though the experiments in increased flexibility described here offer hope of finding acceptable solutions.

The more flexible Englewood plans were carried out in a more flexible building unit that opened in September 1958. Figure 4.2 shows a rough floor plan of a finished nest of rooms.

Each nest provides rooms from 750 to 2,000 square feet in area. A soundproof divider was installed in one large room of 1,500 square feet and in another of 2,000 square feet. Doors afford access from room to

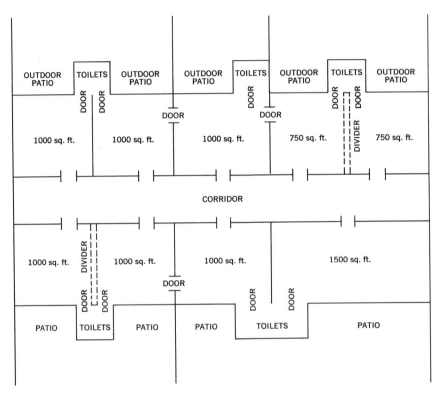

FIGURE 4.2 Flexible space arrangements in the new Englewood school unit.

room where access is not otherwise provided. Although still a rather conventional building design, the new facility expedited the plans of the teachers. The arrangement made it easy for groups of varying sizes to be brought together and for teachers to work in a variety of team arrangements.

The Englewood faculty discovered to its dismay that one change opens the door to a host of changes. New patterns in classroom organization suggest revisions in the curriculum. These, in turn, pose new teaching possibilities, and, before long, evaluation procedures must be revised, since information previously used for reports to parents is no longer adequate.

But the teachers in Englewood discovered and are still discovering the excitement and the satisfaction of making progress in enterprises that deeply concern them and the children they teach. We need more research to determine the relationship between such effort and faculty morale.

Patterns of Change

School improvement seems to move forward on an irregular, broken front. For several years, some phases of education attract vigorous attention, and improvement proceeds rapidly. Then a period of stabilization sets in, and activity spurts forward in another area not always clearly related to the first.

For nearly a decade after World War II, teachers concentrated on better understanding of children. Thousands of teachers across the nation took part in organized child-study programs. Thousands more engaged in informal study or enrolled in college classes in child development. No doubt the study led to deeper understanding of children, gentler treatment of them, and widespread changes in classroom practice. But the deeper understanding of children also produced frustration with what seemed to be inappropriate educational procedures.

For several years there has been a great deal of writing and even more talk about individual differences, marking systems, promotion policies, and reporting devices. Along with the writing and talking, there has been a good deal of tinkering with school procedures. But the old machinery remains much as it has been for decades.

Now we seem to be moving ahead again. Without any prearranged signal, schools scattered across the nation are seriously examining and changing, not just valves and buttons, but basic machinery. Hundreds of schools are studying the nongraded plan or trying somehow to break the lockstep of the graded school. Other schools from coast to coast are experimenting with team-teaching plans. These new developments in classroom organization significantly change the concept of a teacher-per-class-per-grade, a concept that has long dominated elementary education.

The nongraded plan should not be equated with the "social promotion" plan of previous decades. Social promotion was often little more than an abdication of responsibility for dealing with individual differences. This effort to escape the consequences of nonpromotion, however sincere the motives, failed to get at the heart of the dilemma of pupil progress and created as many problems as it solved.

The nongraded plan faces the realities of pupil individuality and encourages not a single standard of accomplishment for all but rigorous individual progress based on an analysis of each child's development and academic attainment.

Cooperative teaching plans attack the lock-step structure horizontally rather than vertically. They are not antithetical to the *concept* of the self-contained classroom. On the contrary, team-teaching experiments support the principles of unified learning basic to the teacher-per-class concept. At the same time, however, these newer approaches capitalize on the possibilities for improved teaching and learning that are created when more children and more teachers of varied interests and competencies take part in planning and teaching.

Cooperative teaching plans and the nongraded system supplement and complement one another. Together they present a new scheme of school organization. More varied opportunities for grouping pupils class by class are created when it is not necessary to preserve the conventions of the graded school. A greater variety of possibilities in grade-to-grade grouping is created when several classes and teachers work together to achieve shared educational purposes. With the lock-step broken, the creative mind is freed to explore the range of new possibilities for creating a stimulating setting for learning.

It is exciting to contemplate the school of tomorrow — the school that innovation and experimentation will produce in your neighborhood and mine. The concluding papers of this volume provide some sketches of what tomorrow's school may be like.

SELF-APPRAISAL IN NONGRADED SCHOOLS:
A SURVEY OF FINDINGS AND PERCEPTIONS

In 1960 we conducted a survey of practices in 89 communities in which there were reported to be about 550 nongraded schools. This paper presents the self-appraisal practices and the research findings reported by the 89 centers. A second paper discusses the procedures used in these communities to introduce nongrading, the specific program changes effected, and the plans these communities have for the future.

The data gathered in this study are not necessarily objective or fully representative of what is happening in schools labeled *nongraded*. Many answers to the survey questions tell only what the respondents perceive reality to be. Only one questionnaire was sent to each school system; consequently, the respondent was sometimes a member of the central ad-

SOURCE: Robert H. Anderson and John I. Goodlad, "Self-Appraisal in Nongraded Schools: A Survey of Findings and Perceptions," *Elementary School Journal 62* (February 1962), pp. 261–269. Copyright, 1962, by the University of Chicago. Reprinted by permission of the University of Chicago Press.

ministrative staff, sometimes an elementary-school principal. Not all respondents answered all questions. In the light of these circumstances, this cannot be a quantitative report. It is, rather, a commentary on the respondents' subjective assessments of the present strengths and weaknesses of the nongraded school.

Pupil Achievement

In the first group of questions the respondents were asked whether they gathered systematic data on pupil achievement and whether studies of achievement in nongraded classes included comparisons with control groups of graded classes (and if so, the nature and significance of differences that were found). As a check on the significance of differences in achievement, respondents were asked: Are you confident that the control group was actually different from the nongraded group with respect to the ways that the teachers used in dealing with the children?

Responses indicate that the overwhelming majority of schools depend on typical standardized tests to measure pupil learning. A few reported the use of tests that accompany reading series, and a few reported the use of devices such as reading progress cards, records of books read, logs for individual children, and samples of work, to estimate the rate and the adequacy of growth. Some responses indicated that nongraded classes had led to more testing and more diagnosis of test results.

Whenever control groups had been used, they were usually in graded schools in the same district. Some districts compared the rate and the nature of achievement gains with those made in previous years by graded classes, that is, before the adoption of nongrading. Several reported that data on control groups were gathered in neighboring districts. The majority, however, made no comparisons with control groups.

How much confidence did the respondents have that there actually were differences between the graded and the nongraded groups? To this question, most replied "no information." Several made interesting comments, however:

> Little doubt that we have had fewer discipline problems. By removing the fear of failure we have definitely improved the mental health of our pupils.
> The difference was not in the actual teaching, but in the way the children were dealt with: no pressure to achieve beyond their ability; no repeating of materials; an increase of teaching materials. [This community reported 25 per cent higher achievement in the nongraded schools.]

The enthusiasm for the newly developed philosophy and knowledge of new skills and techniques spread from teachers of the experimental

group to teachers of the control group. These, in turn, subconsciously re-
sorted to the use of the same teaching methods.

> I am very eager to compare our achievement with that of a really
> graded group. If you know of a school that is traditional in philos-
> ophy, that maintains strict grade standards, and is willing to compare
> results, I should like to contact that school.

The last comment illuminates one of the difficulties in conducting fruitful inquiry into the effect of nongrading on pupil growth. Nongrading as
a philosophy is probably congenial to the beliefs and the practices of most
teachers, even though for various reasons they remain surrounded by the
machinery of grade structure. It may be that a great many teachers attempt to individualize instruction and to soften the effects of grade organization in their work with children. This tendency makes it difficult to
compare nominally nongraded situations with nominally graded situations, since the environments could in effect be quite similar. As the fourth
respondent noted, we need data from classrooms that are literally graded
or literally nongraded. In the present study, we would like to assume that
the nominally nongraded schools have more characteristics of literal nongradedness than may be found in the control schools, but the extent to
which so-called nongraded schools truly represent the desired situation
remains open to question.

We are dealing for the most part with the perceptions of persons deeply
involved in, and enthusiastic about, the nongraded movement. Having
made these qualifications, let us turn to the achievement story as the respondents reported it.

Most of them acknowledged that their reports were incomplete, insufficient or tentative. Whenever a summary statement was made on differences between the graded and the nongraded classes, the statements indicated differences that favored the nongraded classes. Several studies
reported subscores that favored the control groups in a given area or for
a segment of the population, but each such study as a whole showed that
the nongraded classes had the advantage. Wherever statistical data permitted statements on the significance of the differences, a significant difference was rarely reported that was not in favor of the nongraded groups.

Pupil Adjustment

The second group of questions asked for objective and/or impression-
istic data on the social, emotional, and personal adjustment of children
in nongraded classes. The investigators were disappointed to learn that
little objective information had been gathered. Few schools had collected
scores on personality tests, for example. Whatever data were available,

however, definitely favored the nongraded groups. Eighteen respondents indicated that they had gathered no data of any kind on pupil adjustment. Twenty-seven respondents reported impressions on pupil adjustment; and, as in the question on achievement, the tenor of these comments was overwhelmingly positive.

Several respondents reported that in graded as well as in nongraded classes pupil adjustment is related to the caliber of the teachers. One respondent wrote:

> Subjective data suggest that children's attitudes towards school still stem more from response to teacher than to mechanical organization. We have always taken individual differences into account so there could be no gross change as from a traditional grade to some new kind of education.

Another respondent wrote:

> I don't know any good teachers who are using the lock-step type of instruction where everyone in the same room is expected to do the same things at the same time and at the same rate; therefore comparisons are hard to make.

Six respondents reported that slow children profited emotionally by the removal of the stigma of nonpromotion, and a dozen others reported this advantage indirectly. Several commented on the academic advantage to brighter children as well as to slower children. In the nongraded class, the brighter children were "no longer bored because of a lack of challenging work."

Many respondents reported a reduction in disciplinary problems. One community reported that there was less vandalism in the nongraded buildings. Another noted a reduction in absences and truancy. Several referred to the more responsible and more mature behavior of pupils in nongraded classes.

Although the data are by no means sufficient to justify definite claims about improved pupil adjustment, the reports of the spokesmen suggest that the teachers of nongraded pupils believe that their pupils are happier than they would be in graded classrooms.

Pupil Progress

In the third set of questions we tried to learn whether fast learners, who might have "skipped" a grade in earlier times, or slow learners, who might have lost a year through "failure," were progressing through nongraded schools at the rate of speed most desirable for them.

The schools were asked, "What number or per cent of children now take an 'extra' year or more to complete [the program], by comparison with your graded school experience?"

The replies indicate wide variance in practice. Unfortunately the responses are hard to interpret since virtually no respondents commented on the relative achievement of the children by the time they reached the next stage of their school career.

Typical of many comments was this one:

> Two per cent [require the extra year]. This is considerably less than when we retained children.

Another stated:

> Some children who appear to need an extra year when they are six years old, may, when they are seven, have shown that they can proceed at a faster rate. This kind of flexibility is almost impossible in a graded school.

Other statements on retention are also worth noting:

> Two per cent (retentions) in nongraded, 10 per cent in graded classes in this district; 6 per cent (retentions) in one school, 10 per cent in two others.
>
> In some neighborhoods, scarcely any children require four years in the primary; in other neighborhoods, 15 to 20 per cent may require four years.
>
> One to two per cent ungraded (retentions), 7 to 8 per cent graded. In low socio-economic neighborhoods, perhaps 20 per cent took a fourth year.
>
> More pupils now take an extra year to complete the primary unit . . . but there are practically no failures or retentions in the intermediate grades. Previously there were more retentions in Grade 4 than in any other grade. Now 16⅔ per cent compared with 33⅓ per cent under traditional setup.

It is evident that situations vary a great deal from community to community, that school people have varying feelings and beliefs about pupil progress, and that the nongraded philosophy is not yet evident in the practices of some presumably nongraded programs.

Some respondents expressed viewpoints that are inconsistent with the philosophy of the nongraded school:

> There has been no dramatic change, nor do we feel that there should be.
>
> Because of good grouping and excellent teaching practically all our pupils need only the customary three years.
>
> We have the feeling that each child is entitled to an equal number of years in the public school program. Except for a few cases, we do

not feel that a child should have to take more or less than the normal number of years in the program.

One question dealt with the extent to which more able children proceed rapidly. The most striking fact about these responses was that relatively few communities have encouraged acceleration that results in placing a child in a class of older children. Seven of the respondents indicated that the fast learners remained with their agemates but were given "enrichment," and five stated that fast learners were allowed to move into more advanced classwork. One respondent, for example, wrote:

> Relatively large portions of Primary Three children begin to work with fourth year materials during the third year of the program.

A question on the progress of "typical learners" yielded little information worthy of comment.

Classroom Atmosphere

Next we asked about the influence of nongraded organization on the atmosphere of the school. In short, we were interested in the implications of nongrading for the mental health of pupils and teachers. The question proved redundant, since most respondents had already provided information on classroom atmosphere in their responses to other questions.

Practically every comment of some fifteen respondents who attempted to answer this question was positive. One community reported:

> Teachers of lower ability groups not completely happy with program. Too much pressure by some parents for tutoring.

At other points in the questionnaire two respondents referred to difficulties encountered with some parents when they first realize that the child is going to need an extra year to complete the nongraded primary unit. However, seven respondents stated or implied that the parents' attitude toward an extra year is better in the nongraded school than in the graded school.

Impact on Teachers

The next question opened with this statement: "Adoption of nongraded organization presumably changes the ways in which teachers plan their work, operate their classroom, measure their effectiveness, and conceive their professional role. If any studies have been made of the way *your* program has affected *your* teachers in these respects, please report them here."

Perhaps this question is one that should have been asked of teachers rather than administrators. At any rate, several generalizations emerge from the opinions volunteered:

> There is greater positive emotional involvement in teaching on the part of teachers who participate in development of a nongraded plan.
>
> At first there is considerable apprehension and/or tension among some teachers, especially traditionally oriented teachers. This anxiety, most respondents seemed to feel, gives way to satisfaction within a short time. Teachers in nongraded classes engage in more planning and more cooperative study than they did in graded schools.
>
> Nongraded teachers appear to feel more relaxed about their work.

One comment, not necessarily typical, is worth noting:

> Perhaps the outstanding effect upon our teachers has been a growing realization of the need for close cooperation. This system lends itself well to team teaching and the teacher who cannot work well with her colleagues is definitely out of place.

Junior High School

The influence of the nongraded program on the junior high program was the next topic in the questionnaire.

Six respondents reported that the children are further along when they reach junior high school, that junior high school teachers note that children from nongraded classes are better behaved or that they pose fewer attendance problems. Two respondents indicated that their nongraded program extends to Grade 9. Eight respondents reported that the junior high school staff has in effect begun to use the nongraded approach, and four reported that the junior high teachers have shown a real interest in the new philosophy. One respondent felt that the nongraded school enjoys great respect among the secondary school teachers. Two reported that the advanced standing of pupils from nongraded classes was a source of annoyance or worry to the secondary school teachers.

On the whole, the influence appears to have been extremely positive, both in stimulating appropriate procedures in junior high school and in building a bridge between the two groups of teachers.

Impact on Curriculum Development

Since the adoption of nongraded classes, has there been any notable increase in the amount and the effectiveness of staff activity in fundamental curriculum revision?

By a ratio of about 8 to 1, the answer to this question was affirmative. Three of the five who answered "no" went on to explain that an active in-service program has always been characteristic of that community. Among the activities cited were: preparation of materials more suitable for slow and fast learners, for children of limited backgrounds, and for others; development of a new curriculum in the social studies; more individualized teaching in arithmetic and reading; decreased use of single-text adoptions; increased use of unit teaching; intensive effort to make enrichment experiences more appropriate; effort to organize subjects other than reading into "levels"; increased attention to grouping practices; and "deeper concentration on fundamentals."

Several reported that intensive in-service studies of curriculum and of child development had been conducted either before or concurrent with the introduction of the nongraded plan. One respondent indicated that the nongraded primary had caused the staff to look more critically at the kindergarten program, and two mentioned that intermediate teachers in graded classes had begun serious re-examination of their program in the light of the nongraded program in the primary grades in their schools. Several reported heightened concern for evaluation and a better approach to it.

The responses indicated that there is a qualitative as well as a quantitative difference in the nongraded schools, as far as curriculum effort is concerned. The initiative, the industry, and the enthusiasm of the teachers in the nongraded classes were noted in many responses.

One respondent put it this way: "The nongraded teachers seem to be more vulnerable to the newer things and do not resist change as much." Another noted that nongraded teachers in system-wide meetings are "confronted with many a raised eyebrow or sigh when other teachers become aware of the great flexibility . . . in our school."

One respondent summed up a feeling implied by many other reports:

> Once teachers are acquainted with the nongraded program they like it. I think the reason faculties and schools have been so slow to accept the plan is that they realize it is *not* the easy way to teach.

Parent Attitudes

Apparently nongraded programs have met with such a favorable reaction from parents that few schools have regarded it necessary to make formal studies of parent opinion. Six schools gathered questionnaire data, in two cases in connection with graduate theses. Returns indicated favorable feelings on the part of 83 per cent to 96 per cent of the parents. Most other communities have measured parent reaction through interviews (one reported a total of five hundred interviews without a single negative reaction); through study groups and PTA meetings; through comments on report cards and during parent-teacher conferences; and through comments volunteered to administrators and school board members.

The questionnaire probed for differences in the reactions of children who were academically talented, below average, or typical. The reaction of all three groups was very favorable. One community reported that parents whose children attended a nongraded primary school petitioned the board to remove grades in the next school (graded) to which the children are sent.

Comments about the parents of academically talented children generally included the word *enthusiastic*. One school, however, stated that its severest critic is a parent who feels that her son is academically talented. Another school reported that there is now less pressure from such parents for early entrance to kindergarten, since the nongraded program allows brighter children to learn at their own speed. Another respondent stated that "acceleration hysteria has been placated."

According to the questionnaires, the parents appreciated the reduction of unreasonable pressure on below-average children:

> The stigma of failure has been removed and (such) children have been happier and made more rapid progress.

While three schools reported that parents were dissatisfied when a fourth year is required, most other comments on the fourth-year problem indicated that parents were grateful for the "smooth situation" and "this kind of setting" for their child.

As might be expected, there was relatively little comment about unusual benefits for typical or average children. Responses to a question on the parental reports of pupil attitudes toward school, enthusiasm for the nongraded program, and general school morale were favorable with only one exception. These responses applied to children of all ability ranges.

Problems

In the last question, respondents were asked to describe the most serious problems the parents posed. Twenty-six respondents reported that the parents posed no problems; if there was a problem, it boiled down to cooperating with parents and keeping them informed, especially new parents.

Many respondents said that problems disappeared once parents understood the plan and its purposes. In communities where some schools are nongraded and others are not, or where only the primary section is nongraded, it is reported that "parents can't understand why the graded [classes] are allowed to continue as such." A few schools saw the persistence of grade-level vocabulary in the community (and among some teachers) as a problem. Two reported problems in transition to fourth grade or seventh grade. The following comments are of particular interest:

> [We must] convince those few who have children in the below average class that the program is the best for their child.
>
> [Some] parents are still more concerned with prestige than they are with educational advantages.
>
> [We must get] parents to take pressure off their children to "pass."
>
> One problem is the inability of some teachers to see the advantages of a nongraded program.
>
> One problem is parents who will not accept their child as a slow learner.
>
> The parent who knows he has a bright child who is achieving far above average wants recognition by a competitive marking system.
>
> Parents are not our problem. They are ahead of our teachers.

The parent of a child who requires an extra year said:

> I would still rather she should go on. I wouldn't want her to fail.
> Using the word *reclassified* doesn't seem to help.

These comments reveal something about the nature of the problems and their origins.

As we noted earlier, the schools now operating so-called nongraded programs engage in a variety of practices and hold to a variety of viewpoints that depart somewhat from a pure philosophy of nongrading. Yet on the whole a common spirit and ideal permeate their thinking, and they all appear to be carrying on their work with striking enthusiasm. The available data offer them much encouragement to believe that all parties concerned are in favor of what is happening.

Research and Evaluation

Inquiry into the progress and the merit of nongraded organization will be facilitated by an increase in descriptive reports and by careful attempts at self-appraisal.

Typically, the school systems that have nongraded programs have issued bulletins and handbooks which serve the dual purpose of informing parents and answering inquiries of educators.

Over the past two years the periodical literature has paid increasing attention to the nongraded school, and several professional associations or councils have conducted studies of nongrading. At least four doctoral studies and a greater number of master's theses or course papers on the subject are known to have been completed. Many colleges have sponsored courses or workshops on the nongraded school. There is also a growing tendency for guidance and mental-health people to engage in studies of nongrading.

One major difficulty of controlled research in this area is that clear-cut models of gradedness and nongradedness are not yet available. This problem is brought into sharp focus in a study by Robert F. Carbone [1]. Seeking to find differences between the two types of school organization, Carbone revealed in effect that the curriculum and practices of instruction in the nongraded schools in his study were imperfectly related to the theoretical ideal of nongraded practice. In other words, many teachers in the nominally nongraded schools were continuing to use "graded" practices and to pursue "graded" goals. Quite likely the reverse is true of many teachers in graded classes.

The research problem is further complicated by the limitations of traditional achievement tests, which are geared to the curriculum and the instructional practices of graded schools. It may well be that comparative studies using such instruments will show little advantage, perhaps even disadvantage as in the Carbone study, for the nongraded school. Hence, there is a great need for assessment procedures and instruments wholly compatible with the philosophy of nongraded schools.

REFERENCE

1. ROBERT F. CARBONE. "Achievement, Mental Health, and Instruction in Graded and Nongraded Elementary Schools." Unpublished Ph.D. dissertation (Department of Education, University of Chicago, 1961).

EDUCATIONAL PRACTICES IN NONGRADED SCHOOLS:
A SURVEY OF PERCEPTIONS

The first part of the 1960 survey, reported on previous pages, sought to determine what research and self-evaluation activities were underway in the schools. The second part of the survey sought information on reasons

SOURCE: John I. Goodlad and Robert H. Anderson, "Educational Practices in Nongraded Schools: A Survey of Perceptions," *Elementary School Journal* 63 (October 1962), pp. 33–44. Copyright, 1962, by the University of Chicago. Reprinted by permission of the University of Chicago Press.

for introducing a nongraded plan, on changes effected in any part of the school program as part of the process of bringing the nongraded plan into existence, on changes in program that followed introduction of the nongraded plan, on current modifications in school practices related to nongrading, and on long-term plans for the future. A separate question sought to inquire more deeply into practices of reporting to parents. The findings on these sections of the study are reported here.

The reader should be aware of the fact that what we are reporting here are largely the perceptions of supervisory and administrative school personnel. To what extent the practices reported to us actually prevail is another question. In view of this important fact, we seek to convey impressions and perceptions of possible trends. Data are quantified only when our intent is to suggest a trend.

Why Begin a Nongraded Plan?

In the first question in this section of the survey, we sought information on why schools introduced a nongraded plan. Forty-five per cent of the respondents used language revealing that improved attention to the individual and to individual differences was one result they hoped for. In fact, about 25 per cent of all respondents used the words "better provision for individual differences" or a similar phrase.

The second largest category of responses (about 35 per cent) could be interpreted as reactions against the lock-step of grading. Respondents spoke of the importance of eliminating grade barriers, of providing uninterrupted progress for pupils, and of eliminating retardation and nonpromotion, concomitants of the graded system. Some mentioned the need for greater flexibility in pupil placement and grouping.

The remaining responses were not readily classifiable except for a cluster of about 12 per cent that implied the possibility of effecting curriculum change through reorganization of the school. This cluster of responses cannot be summarized in a single sentence; however, the actual wording of the responses is suggestive. One respondent said, "We are concerned with enriching children's curricular experiences." Another said that teachers in the school moving into nongrading hoped to give more attention to measuring the growth of the individual pupil, in addition to or in place of rating children comparatively.

This first question was not designed to elicit, and did not elicit, responses on the effect of strong top-level leadership, the desire to keep up with other school districts, or a drive to get on a band wagon. Such factors do enter into educational decision-making, however, and may have influenced the decisions to initiate nongraded schools.

Introducing Nongrading

The second question inquired into changes made in the school program in order to bring a nongraded plan into existence. A nongraded structure cannot be plan-less; there must be some way of classifying pupils as they progress upward through the school. However, we suspect that some so-called nongraded schools are brought forth without a new plan of vertical organization. As a consequence, what emerges is really a graded plan under a new name.

Again, we found a substantial clustering of responses. About half of the replies indicated that an attempt was made to organize the skill areas of the curriculum into levels. Half of these efforts were in the field of reading, as one might expect, since many of the nongraded plans were primary (embracing the first three grades) and since reading accomplishment is recognized almost universally as of prime importance during these early years of schooling.

Frequently, respondents attached descriptive material showing the progression of levels. In the description sent by one school, twelve reading levels are defined for the first three years of schooling. A left-hand column defines the reading skills expected at each level. A right-hand column lists the appropriate reading material, most of it being the progression of textbooks in the reading series of a well-known publishing company. Another school system provided check lists to be used by teachers in determining whether the child had acquired certain skills in reading or certain concepts in arithmetic.

It was difficult to determine from the responses whether a genuine rethinking of curriculum scope and sequence had occurred or the main effort had been directed to stating more specifically what was to be learned at each step in the existing progression. Our evidence suggests that the latter predominated. The responses suggest, further, that the levels became a means for differentiating the rate of progress of a child while in a class and ultimately through the years of the unit itself. Frequently, too, the levels were used as a means of interclass grouping and, almost uniformly, as a basis for homogeneous grouping in reading within a single class.

The remaining responses defy generalization. Some schools attempted to define and use social maturity as a basis for upward progression. Several used a semester classification plan, simply moving children forward from semester to semester with no accompanying effort to speed up or slow down the total time spent in the nongraded unit. Some schools reported that teachers now had the choice of remaining with a group of children for more than one year, moving up with the group during two or more successive years. Two schools reported an effort to develop evaluation techniques that were related to the actual progression of the child rather than to his comparative position with other children. Some of the other replies appeared to be only remotely related to any effort to revise school structure.

Refinements in School Practices

The third and fourth questions were designed to find out what educational practices had been developed following implementation of nongraded structure and what further modifications were under way. Because the two sets of responses had so many duplications the composite results are reported here.

The responses cluster into general categories: grouping, curriculum, facilities and resources, evaluation, and reporting to parents. About 20 per cent of the respondents reported that textbooks had been redistributed to fit more nearly the needs of small groups of pupils. The fact that only four respondents reported an increase in supplementary books, materials, and resources arouses one's curiosity. One would have thought that any plan entered into in the hope of making "better provision for individual differences" would have resulted in a general clamor for supplementary materials.

On the subject of grouping, respondents reported the following: the use of reading levels as a basis for homogeneous grouping, the creation of a nongraded "open" room for orienting all new pupils before placement in a class group, the use of a wider range of criteria for considering pupil placement, the acceleration or deceleration of pupils at the upper and the lower ends of the achievement continuum.

Under "evaluation and reporting to parents," respondents told of increased emphasis on the preparation of cumulative records, restudy of test instruments, use of faculty study conferences on child development, renewed interest in how to communicate effectively with parents, more frequent evaluation of entire class groups, modification of report cards, and conferences among teachers on pupil placement.

Although only about 12 per cent of the respondents indicated that their school introduced nongrading to effect curriculum reorganization, more than 30 per cent responded either that curriculum reorganization was accompanying the existing nongraded plan or that nongrading had stimulated interest in and created a need for curriculum revision. The subjects most commonly mentioned as requiring restudy during the implementation stages were reading and arithmetic. The subjects most commonly mentioned for curriculum reorganization in later stages of nongrading were the social studies and sciences.

Reporting to Parents

Our previous experience with nongrading and our information about it suggested that techniques of reporting to parents soon become a central concern of any group of educators involved in nongraded structure. Consequently, we inserted a separate question on this item.

Nearly 50 per cent of the respondents replied that conferences with parents had been substituted for or added to the usual "report card" method of communicating with the home about children's progress. An additional 25 per cent indicated that nongrading had been accompanied by a modification of the existing report card. The balance reported either no change or minor modification in terminology.

Many respondents reported hesitancy in giving up the written report card. Some systems combined individual and group conferences with two written report cards each year. Others eliminated the report card except for a final written report in June.

Additional comments reported on the familiar problem of improving techniques for conferring with parents. Some teachers experienced discomfort in face-to-face reporting. Questions often raised by parents did not alleviate this uneasiness, especially if teachers were unable to present samples of pupils' work and other evidence of progress. Many respondents reported on the inadequacy of the written report card in communicating pupil progress. Others observed that conferences with parents had been as useful in explaining the philosophy of the nongraded plan as in indicating the progress of the individual child.

Plans for the Future

Responses to the question on plans for the future were general in character. The only clustering of responses referred to the need for improved understanding, among teachers and parents alike, of the rationale for the program. Respondents reported that teachers have difficulty in divesting themselves of the "graded" mantle and that parents sometimes ask to have children's progress translated into grade norms. In several school systems, in-service education programs are to be devoted to further exploration of the concept of nongrading itself. Other respondents reported plans for orienting new teachers to the scheme, for using supplementary materials for children at the upper and the lower ends of the ability continuum, for refining reporting practices, and for developing evaluation techniques to appraise a wider range of goals.

The need for materials geared to the range of pupil abilities and achievements was mentioned several times. This response suggests that there has been some pressure from teachers for better materials but that there is still dissatisfaction about what is available. The teachers' irritation with grade-level designations in textbook materials came to the surface.

The wording of some responses attests to the difficulty of eliminating graded connotations and expectations. One respondent wrote at length about the fact that teachers who had taught in the school at the third- or fifth-grade level before nongrading were still associated with these grades after the elimination of grade levels in practice. He pointed out that teachers should be prepared to teach children of varying ages and should move from group to group for their own good and for "destroying the concept of the graded teacher."

According to many of the concluding statements, movement toward and refinement of nongrading resulted in more and better attention to the individual. Respondents reported that teachers were finding it necessary to engage in detailed analysis of the individual to determine appropriate placement, to report specifically to parents, and to pass along adequate information to the next teacher. One principal summed up several observations with the following statement: "That the teacher be proficient in his ability to study and interpret the learner's behavior is inexorably demanded by the primary unit plan." Many respondents proposed that their school districts initiate in-service education programs to assist teachers in individual diagnosis, in collection and organization of data, and in techniques of reporting to parents.

In Conclusion

These perceptions of nongraded plans in operation have encouraging as well as discouraging elements. Depending on one's perspective, one could use the data for a biting indictment or a flowery indorsement of nongraded schools.

Responses to our survey suggest some misunderstanding about the nongraded concept itself. Rather frequently we found some reference to preconceived patterns of homogeneous grouping as central to nongrading. In much of our correspondence, educators involved in nongraded plans begin their letters somewhat as follows: "I am principal of a nongraded school. In our plan we group children from class to class according to their achievement in . . ." From here on, correspondents elaborate the grouping system or the plan of horizontal organization, failing to realize that nongrading is a scheme of vertical school organization. Vertical school organization provides a structure for classifying and moving children upward from entry into school to departure from school. The alternatives are grading and nongrading and such semi-ungraded arrangements as multigrading. Horizontal school organization provides a system for grouping learners and assigning them to available teachers. The choices are many, and they are usually based on analyses of children's characteristics, subject matter, or teachers' abilities and preparation. Every school has a pattern of vertical organization and a pattern of horizontal organization. The two dimensions should not be confused.

As a consequence of our studies and observations to date, we pose the hypothesis that a substantial proportion of the elementary schools that now claim to be nongraded have given little or no attention to the vertical aspects of school organization. Changes effected to date tend to be modifications more of horizontal than of vertical structure. Consequently, many so-called nongraded schools are nongraded in name only.

We are much encouraged by the concern the responses showed for individual differences and the individual child. But we are somewhat discouraged by two aspects of this concern. First, a large number of schools and school districts entered into nongrading to make better provisions for individual differences; however, they expressed little initial concern for curriculum reorganization.

We have consistently contended that school organization by itself does little or nothing to improve instructional practice. Elimination of grades merely creates an opportunity to provide curriculum and instruction adapted to the needs of the individual. A school or a school district ought not to develop a nongraded plan unless the staff is prepared to move on into major curriculum and instructional reorganization.

Our second reservation has to do with the levels plan of providing for individual differences in schools labeled nongraded. Too often, the levels are defined according to narrow, subject-matter expectations. Children are grouped horizontally according to their levels of accomplishment. This scheme does indeed provide for differentiated progress for individuals, but it does not necessarily take cognizance of the many unique traits emerging in the individual and the school's responsibility for developing these traits.

On the other side of the coin, admittedly, we need better descriptions of desirable progressions in the development of concepts, skills, and values if we are ever to move from comparative to more absolute estimates of pupil progress. In our judgment, levels, if used at all, should be part of the diagnostic proficiency of the teacher and should not be used as arbitrary hurdles comparable to the grade hurdles, which the levels presumably replace.

We are encouraged most by the frequent mention of actual curriculum revision or the expressed need for curriculum revision after the implementation of a nongraded plan. These responses, however, must be interpreted with care, because a nagging awareness of need for curriculum reform may have existed before the introduction of nongrading. Nonetheless, the data suggest otherwise, since the need for curriculum revision was reported more as a concomitant of nongrading than as an initial reason for it.

This finding supports our contention that nongrading is an unshackling concept. It forces attention to arbitrariness in the placement of content, to the need for a wide range of instructional materials, and to limitations in testing programs. A nongraded view of the school, free from the graded lock-step, appears to us to be compatible with a longitudinal view of the curriculum and the continuous progression of pupils.

We are well aware that attention to organizational problems alone sometimes serves as an escape mechanism for individuals who are unwilling or unable to examine fundamental issues of curriculum and instruction. But our experience suggests that search for an escape mechanism is almost always an accompaniment of any attempt at educational reform. Child-study programs, for example, often bog down in meandering discussions of arbitrary administrators, misunderstood teachers, and misunderstanding parents. Even direct attempts at curriculum reform frequently deteriorate into the production of dull handbooks that collect dust on teachers' shelves.

Take as a whole, the responses suggested few common directions for curriculum reform. This is not surprising, since educators have been unable to map out substantial areas of agreement on curriculum matters. Perhaps there are no patterns of curriculum and instruction that should accompany nongrading. At any rate, proponents of nongraded schools have been chary in spelling out specific instructional changes to go along with organizational reform.

We see nongrading as part of a much larger conception of school function and practice. This conception embraces a longitudinal view of the curriculum wherein concepts, skills, and values are identified and developed over several years of schooling. At any given moment, there are several classrooms — not just one or two — from which to select in placing a child for vertical progression through the school. Individual diagnosis serves to select the most promising classroom environment for each child. In the schools we envision, materials are distributed so as to provide a range of materials approximating the range of individual differences within a class group. Evaluation procedures are designed to determine the extent to which all school goals are being attained.

Organizational reform is but a beginning; it is not an end in itself. To move into a nongraded plan without simultaneously or subsequently giving attention to fundamental questions of school function, curriculum design, teaching, and evaluation is to court chaos or, at best, to create a school that is nongraded in name only.

CLASSROOM ORGANIZATION: REVIEW OF RESEARCH

Schoolmen have devoted much attention to classroom organization. The first purpose, presumably, has been to determine the conditions of grouping under which students learn most effectively. Other considerations have played dominant roles: ease of administration, economical use of teachers, teacher satisfaction, and so on. Vertically, from class to class, the focus has been upon determining organizational structure for moving students through the time sequence of an educational unit. Horizontally, the search has been for dividing content without losing communication from field to field. The result at present is something like a chopped salad; the school program and the students' academic life are cut into vertical grade units and horizontal subject units.

The movement toward defensible schemes of classroom organization has been complicated by an emerging body of lore concerning learners and their learning and by shifting perceptions of educational purposes. The wide range of differences among students of the same chronological age and the differences in understanding and achievement from subject to subject for a single student do not lend themselves to easy compression into the lock-step of grade levels. Since these ranges remain large regardless of class-to-class organization, the problems of grouping both within and among classrooms are in many ways similar. Research into the effects of experiments in classroom organization and the impact of that research on practice have been blocked by changing perceptions of educational function and desirable learning. It is difficult or impossible to interpret comparisons of two practices designed with differing intent. Furthermore,

SOURCE: John I. Goodlad, "Classroom Organization," *Encyclopedia of Educational Research* (ed. Chester W. Harris), pp. 221–226. Reprinted by permission of The Macmillan Company. Copyright 1960 by The American Educational Research Association.

a person who believes, for example, that elementary education is primarily a socializing process is not likely to adopt a new grouping procedure merely because it appears to produce somewhat higher arithmetic achievement.

There is a plethora of material reporting theory, practice, and some research in school organization over the past one hundred years. Most of the writing is argumentative; some is analytical; some describes experimental approaches; and the balance reports research. The effectiveness of experimental patterns has been determined largely by observations of administrative expediency, teacher satisfaction, acceptance of new plans within the teaching profession, and so on. Controlled research has concentrated on evaluating a limited range of objectives, such as the effect of general ability grouping on achievement in arithmetic. There are so many semicontrolled studies of this sort, especially before 1935, that it is impossible to select even a truly representative sample. Wherever possible, surveys of such studies are used in supporting the findings reported here.

Certain classroom practices — such as one-teacher-per-class group of 30 or so students, and graded structure in elementary and secondary education — tend to persist in modern education in spite of periodic efforts to dislodge them. Frequently, these efforts have been directed against admitted weaknesses in the time-honored practices and strongly supported by significant educational ideas of their time. But the innovations most often have lasted only for the tenure of their sponsors.

Vertical Organization

Our schools have not always been graded. Both the Dame schools of the seventeenth century and the "district" schools of the eighteenth century were without grade classifications. The Quincy Grammar School, although not the first graded-type organization, established a pattern that has persisted from its opening in 1848 to the present. By 1860, nearly all city schools were graded, and critical educators already were lamenting the swing from little system to almost all system. By 1870, graded classes, graded content, graded textbooks, and even graded teachers meshed together in a school mechanism that has undergone little redesigning to the present.

Nineteenth- and early twentieth-century attempts to break the lock-step of graded school organization sought to modify the arbitrariness of grade standards rather than to eliminate grades. The St. Louis Plan, first introduced in 1868, sought to reduce the rigidity of graded structure by reclassifying students at six-week intervals [1]. Both the Cambridge Plan, first introduced in 1893, and the Portland Plan, discontinued by 1915, permitted bright students to move more rapidly in a double-track system, completing a nine-year program in as few as seven years [2]. The Batavia, North Denver, and Santa Barbara Concentric Plans also recognized individual differences and sought to make special provisions for them within the limitations of graded structure [3]. Of more recent vintage, the Winnetka and Dalton Plans differentiated "academic" from nonacademic phases of the curriculum and then encouraged students to move through the academic work at their own rate. In one of the few controlled studies available, data revealed academic superiority for students in the Winnetka Plan on 23 of 30 comparisons with students in conventional programs [4].

These and other schemes are not always seen as attempts to break down vertical, graded structure. But they were designed to modify the effects of grading by helping students of varying abilities to move ahead unhampered by uniform grade expectations. They were a product of the creative thinking of their time and paved the way for the broadscale attack upon lock-step that characterizes the nongraded school.

The nongraded school, like the innovations described above, is designed to implement a theory of continuous student progress. The plan introduced at Western Springs, Illinois, in 1934 and since discontinued was the first, apparently, conforming to the modern conception of a nongraded system [5]. A plan begun in Milwaukee in 1942 appears to be the oldest of those now operating [6]. Most of 16 such centers surveyed in 1955 [7] and of 31 surveyed in 1957 [8] started between 1947 and 1950. Goodlad and Anderson [9], using an arbitrary definition of the nongraded school as one where the grade levels have been entirely removed from a minimum of two grade levels, concluded that there were several hundred nongraded schools operating in from 40 to 50 communities in the United States during the 1957–58 school year. Since then their number has expanded so rapidly that a reasonably accurate count would be difficult.

Nongrading is supported by some plausible-sounding claims and theories rather than by research. Two surveys of nongraded schools [8, 10] reported reduced tensions in students; increased teacher awareness of student individuality; and, from the increased involvement of the community in the change process, increased parental understanding of the school. Teachers in nongraded schools surveyed by Kennedy [11] reported freedom from fear of encroaching on "material reserved for the next grade" and, thus, freedom to move bright children forward with more stimulating tasks. In Milwaukee, 99 students in four nongraded schools were compared with 123 students in four graded schools. Test data in reading and personality adjustment, the two major areas reported, slightly favored the nongraded group, even though these students were a little younger and tested slightly lower in mental maturity [12]. In Appleton, Wisconsin, 10 fourth-grade groups were compared with three intermediate nongraded groups at the beginning of their fourth year in school. The median overall achievement grade placement scores were 4.57 for the graded groups in contrast to 4.833 for the three nongraded rooms [13].

Graded structure suggests a relatively common sequence of learning tasks, but lacks the virtue of facilitating continuous progress for learners of widely varying abilities. It is this lack, above others, that has motivated a century of attempts to modify the grade system. Subsequent experimentation with accompanying research must maintain perspective regarding the three central problems of learner variability, curricular commonality, and administrative expediency.

Horizontal Organization

At any given level in the vertical organization of classrooms, students must be grouped into horizontal instructional units. One central problem here is how curriculum content should be cut and classrooms organized around the divisions. The practice of separating classes according to subject fields is known as departmentalization. Platooning is a system of departmentalization or semidepartmentalization wherein students move from room to room for different types of activities.

Departmentalization is well established at secondary and higher educational levels. Some colleges have succeeded in breaking down departmental lines by establishing general studies in the humanities, social sciences, and physical and biological sciences. At the high school level, the most significant innovation of recent years is the core curriculum. Two or more subject areas, English and social studies in more than 90 per cent of the cases [14], are combined into a core of studies occupying a larger block of time in the schedule. It is difficult to determine the present status of the core movement, but surveys [14, 15] suggest that from 3.5 to 6.6 per cent of four-year senior high schools practised some form of core curriculum organization between 1952 and 1956 and that the number increased during the period. Research to date, insufficiently comprehensive and inadequately controlled, merely indicated that core, more than subject departments, does what core organization was set up to do in the first place [16].

With division of all children of a given grade into self-contained class groups of 25 to 40 students established as standard elementary-school procedure, much twentieth-century experimentation at this level has been with departmental-type plans. Surveys [1, 17, 18, 19, 20] conducted between 1910 and 1950 revealed shifting enthusiasm for departmentalization and platooning. Interest in departmentalization grew during the first two of these decades, even though the one-teacher-per-class plan became more widely used. The debate over respective virtues of departmentalized and self-contained classrooms grew intense during the third decade, with the advantages claimed for each being essentially the same [21]. In the fourth decade, 1940–49, more schools reported departmentalization on the way out than on the way in, although so-called special subjects such as music, art, and physical education increasingly were being taken care of in the big cities by persons other than the regular classroom teacher. Toward the end of the 1950–59 decade, departmentalization once more was picking up its advocates, with practice of it found most frequently in the upper elementary grades, particularly in the 8–4 pattern of vertical organization, and occasionally in the primary grades.

The research into the effects of departmentalization is inconclusive. Most of the problems and issues involved were highlighted by Rouse's study [22]. Rouse was able to identify differences in 14 factors pertaining to teaching, curriculum, and school operation, with advantages about equally distributed between the two types of organization. But the advantages of departmentalization were mostly rejected and the advantages of nondepartmentalization mostly approved by those then recognized as specialists in elementary education. In aspects of education where the research problems are complex and the findings inconclusive, practice is likely to reflect tradition and to respond to plausible viewpoints or administrative demands rather than to research evidence.

Ability Grouping

Perhaps the most controversial issue of classroom organization in recent years is whether or not students of like ability should be grouped together for instructional purposes. The debate has been accompanied by some experimentation and research seeking to promote and appraise a given viewpoint. Ability grouping is a consideration in determining both vertical and horizontal classroom organization. Even with a general pattern established, the teacher is faced with problems of individual differences within the classroom and the issue of whether or not to group on some ability criterion.

The terms *homogeneous grouping* and *ability grouping* frequently are confused. Homogeneous is the broader term. Ability grouping is only one of several devices for bringing students together on criteria of likeness or homogeneity. In ability grouping, an attempt is made to divide the students into classes or within a given class according to their ability to attain. Sometimes the criterion is general ability as revealed by an intelligence or readiness test. Sometimes ability is merely inferred from past general or specific accomplishments. More than 20 criteria, singly or in combination, have been used from time to time as bases for establishing classroom organization.

Conducting and interpreting research on the effects of ability grouping are complicated by the issue of whether or not ability grouping is socially desirable [23]. The arguments for and against tend to increase and decrease, respectively, as the focus of attention moves upward from elementary to higher education. A question accompanying this issue is whether or not student variability is materially reduced through ability grouping [24]. When a broad range of human characteristics is considered, the answer is "not much." As Williams points out, ". . . if we have sixty independent measurements, the chance that any individual will be in the median 50 per cent in all is about one in one quintillion" [25]. Research suggests the following generalizations concerning the extent to which ability grouping reduces variability in achievement: (a) Ability grouping only imperceptibly reduces student variability when a broad range of academic, intellectual, physical, and social traits is considered; (b) When students of a given grade level are divided into A and B classes or A, B, and C classes according to general ability, variability in school achievement is reduced about 7 and 17 per cent, respectively; (c) When this kind of grouping is accompanied by vertical regrouping so that bright and slow students advance on separate promotional tracks, attainment variability is reduced about 10 per cent more. One kind of frequently advocated ability grouping — segregating the bright and the slow from the average group on the basis of a general ability criterion such as IQ — falls far short of achieving the virtues claimed for it. For example, children with IQ above 120 and below 90 were removed from a fifth-grade class, but the range of reading ability in terms of grade norms among the remaining students still spread from 2.7 to 11.2 [9].

During the thirties, there was a great deal of research into the effects of ability grouping. Studies since that time have not added precision to the conclusions or clarification to the problems succinctly analyzed by Cornell [26] in 1936. Nor have these later studies in general taken cognizance of the research limitations pointed out by Cornell at that time. If they had done so, there would not be the repetition of studies wherein the conditions controlled for experimentation are inimicable to the underlying philosophy of the two plans compared. For example, when students in ability groups A, B, and C and in nondifferentiated groups are required to deal with the same topics at the same rate and with the same books, it becomes apparent that any potential advantages of ability groupings are likely to be nullified. Similarly the question of assigning cause arises when ability groups supported by appropriate curricular and instructional adaptations are shown to be superior to nondifferentiated groups for which similar adaptations have not been made. Studies reporting research of this kind are meaningless for comparative purposes, although they may be useful in revealing the educational procedures that should accompany organizational change.

The evidence, of limited value as indicated above, slightly favors ability grouping in regard to academic achievement, with dull children seeming to profit more than bright children in this regard. The advantage to bright children comes when they are encouraged to cover the usual program at a more rapid rate. In fact, the studies of ability grouping in subject areas such as English, geometry, history, Latin, and algebra contradict each other and results swing toward favoring ability grouping in promoting achievement only when, for example, content is enriched. An analysis of the many studies of ability grouping reported by Cornell [26] and by Petty [27] and of several more recent studies [28, 29, 30], suggests that curricular differentiation for the range of student variability represented in a given group is a more significant contributor to academic progress than is the basis for establishing classroom groups. Teachers tend to react more favorably to teaching groups in which the heterogeneity has been somewhat reduced, than to teaching randomly selected groups. This finding raises the serious question as to whether many teachers see in ability grouping a kind of Utopia in which undifferentiated teaching procedures and content will be applied to differentiated, "homogeneous" groups. The results would be far from Utopian for the students unfortunate enough to find themselves in such classrooms.

Class Size

One other question of classroom organization demands brief attention: Is there an optimum class size? Most of the studies before 1925 and a few since that time sought to relate class size to measurable student achievement. There is nothing in the evidence to suggest that large classes materially affected attainment in subject matter under teaching techniques considered typical at that time [31]. Subsequent studies of the relation of class size to student attention, discipline, self-reliance, attitudes, and work habits failed to establish a research basis for decisions on class size [31, 32]. At the college level, there has been some attempt to relate class size to the instructional activity. Large lecture groups are broken down into smaller groups for laboratory work or discussion. Elementary and secondary schools, however, tend to hold to classes of from 20 to 40 students for almost all activities. Unless reduced class size is seen as offering increased opportunity for certain essential learning activities, the economic drive for the largest possible ratio of students to teachers ultimately will prevail. Roff [33] points out that the number of initial interpersonal interactions in the classroom moves upward by 129 and 213 per cent, respectively, when class size changes from 20 to 30 and then to 35 students. (But this fact has little relevance if a teacher continues to lecture while class size moves downward from 35 to 30 and finally to 20 students.) Class size, like other problems of classroom organization, cannot be satisfactorily studied apart from the problems of curriculum and instruction tied up with it.

Current Status and Trends

In general, the classrooms of the United States are organized vertically by grades or years. At the elementary-school level, there is increasing interest in de-emphasizing grade demarcations by creating larger units in which two or more grade lines are merged or by removing grade lines entirely. At higher levels experimentation is more in the direction of acceleration, with gifted students traveling the established grade routes in shorter time. Horizontally, the classrooms of secondary and higher education are organized by subjects. Experimentation at the college level is toward general education sequences that break down departmental lines between related disciplines. At the secondary level, the core curriculum is the most significant departure from classrooms organized by subjects. Elementary-school proposals for reorganization invariably involve some breakdown of the self-contained classroom.

Student enrollments that outstrip teacher supply and the resulting larger classes, together with serious questioning of educational lock-step, pose thought-provoking questions for future classroom organization. Should classes be of equal size for all types of learning? For how long should young children remain with a single teacher in order to establish the secure base considered essential by specialists in child development and elementary education? Do large groups supervised by several adults provide more and better resources for learning without destroying other educational values? To what extent can and should electronic or mechanical devices, under certain conditions of classroom organization, relieve teachers to provide other kinds of assistance to learners? Should the complex organism that is modern education be turned toward the promotion of individualized learning wherein optimum class size is one student engaged in the pursuit of knowledge [34]? Gilchrist [35] and Trump [36] have reported some new ventures in exploring these and other questions

69750

Servire est vivare

LIBRARY

at the secondary-school level. Institutions such as Harvard University, George Peabody College for Teachers, and the University of Chicago have been cooperating with selected elementary and secondary schools in several experimental ventures designed to break the lock-step of both vertical and horizontal classroom organization.

On one hand, the continuing educational quest is for classroom patterns that preserve and enhance the significant differences among students in regard to general and specific ability, interest and motivation, energy, and creativity. On the other, the quest is for patterns that preserve unity in content and that utilize teaching resources effectively. This two-fold quest always will be tempered by considerations growing out of available funds, tradition, administrative expediency, and the building limitations resulting from each successive generation's inadequate appraisal of the future.

REFERENCES

1. HENRY J. OTTO. *Current Practices in the Organization of Elementary Schools.* Evanston, Ill.: Northwestern University, 1932.
2. C. S. HARTWELL. "The Grading and Promotion of Pupils," *Addresses and Proceedings.* National Education Association, 1910, p. 296.
3. FRED C. AYER. "The Present Status of Promotional Plans in City Schools," *American School Board Journal 46* (April 1923), pp. 37–39.
4. CARLETON W. WASHBURNE and LOUIS E. RATHS. "The High School Achievement of Children Trained under the Individual Technique," *Elementary School Journal 28* (1927), pp. 214–224.
5. LEONARD B. WHEAT. "The Flexible Progress Group System," *Elementary School Journal 38* (1937), pp. 175–183.
6. FLORENCE C. KELLY. "The Primary School in Milwaukee," *Childhood Education 24* (1948), pp. 236–238.
7. JOHN I. GOODLAD. "Ungrading the Elementary Grades," *NEA Journal 44* (1955), pp. 170–171.
8. KENT C. AUSTIN. *The Ungraded Primary Unit in Public Elementary Schools of the United States.* Doctor's thesis (University of Colorado, 1957).
9. JOHN I. GOODLAD and ROBERT H. ANDERSON. "1958 Progress Report: The Nongraded Elementary School," *NEA Journal 47* (1958), pp. 642–643.
10. JOHN I. GOODLAD. "More About the Ungraded Unit Plan," *NEA Journal 44* (1955), pp. 295–296.
11. DORA F. KENNEDY. *Does the Nongraded School Better Meet the Aims of Elementary Education?* Master's paper (University of Maryland, 1957).
12. *A Study of Primary School Organization and Regular Class Organization at Primary 6 and 3A in Eight Schools.* Milwaukee Public Schools, 1952.

13. *History and Development of Our Continuous Progress Plan.* Appleton Public Schools, 1957.
14. GRACE S. WRIGHT. *Core Curriculum Development.* U.S. Office of Education Bulletin 1952, No. 5. GPO, 1952, p. 104.
15. NELSON L. BOSSING. "Development of the Core Curriculum in the Senior High School," *School Review* (1956), pp. 224–226.
16. GRACE S. WRIGHT. *The Core Program; Abstracts of Unpublished Research: 1946–1955.* U.S. Office of Education Circular No. 485, 1956, p. 70.
17. MARY DUNN. *Trends in Institutional Organization in City Elementary Schools from 1920 to 1949.* Doctor's thesis (University of Pittsburgh, 1951).
18. HENRY J. OTTO. "Comparison of Selected Organization and Administrative Practice in 286 Public Elementary Schools and 46 Campus Demonstration Schools," *Journal of Educational Research 41* (1947), pp. 81–87.
19. THOMAS C. PRINCE. "Trends in Types of Elementary School Organization," *American School Board Journal 106* (June 1943), pp. 37–38.
20. JAMES H. VAN SICKLE. "Progress in City School Systems: XIII. Departmental Teaching in the Grades," *Annual Report of the Commissioner of Education, Bureau of Education, for Year Ended June 30, 1913.* GPO, 1913, pp. 139–141.
21. MARY DUNN. "Should There Be Any Set Type of Elementary School Organization?" *Elementary School Journal 53* (1952), pp. 199–206.
22. MARGARET R. ROUSE. *A Comparative Study of Departmentalization and Non-Departmentalization as Forms of Organization for the Elementary School Curriculum.* Doctor's thesis (University of Texas, 1945).
23. ALICE V. KELIHER. *A Critical Study of Homogeneous Grouping with a Critique of Measurement as the Basis for Classification.* (New York: Bureau of Publications, Teachers College, Columbia University), 1931.
24. MARVIN Y. BURR. *A Study of Homogeneous Grouping in Terms of Individual Variations and the Teaching Problem.* TC, 1931, p. 69.
25. ROGER J. WILLIAMS. "Individuality and Education," *Educational Leadership 15* (1957), p. 146.
26. ETHEL L. CORNELL. "Effects of Ability Grouping Determinable from Published Studies," *The Grouping of Pupils.* 35th Yearbook, Part I, N.S.S.E. (Bloomington, Illinois: Public School Publishing Co.), 1936, pp. 289–304.
27. MARY CLARE PETTY. *Intraclass Grouping in the Elementary School.* Doctor's thesis (University of Texas, 1952).
28. WALTER B. BARBE and TINA S. WATERHOUSE. "An Experimental Program in Reading," *Elementary English 33* (1956), pp. 102–104.
29. DARRELL HOLMES and LOIS HARVEY. "An Evaluation of Two Methods of Grouping," *Educational Research Bulletin 35* (1956), pp. 213–222.
30. KENNETH HOOVER. "An Experiment in Grouping Within the Classroom," *California Journal of Secondary Education 30* (1955), pp. 326–331.
31. JOHN I. GOODLAD. "Room to Live and Learn: Class Size and Room Space as Factors in the Learning-Teaching Process," *Childhood Education 30* (1954), pp. 355–361.

32. HENRY J. OTTO and others. *Class Size Factors in Elementary Schools.* University of Texas, 1953, p. 118.
33. ROSELLA ROFF. "Grouping and Individualizing in the Elementary Classroom," *Educational Leadership 40* (1957), pp. 171–175.
34. HERBERT A. THELEN. "Group Dynamics in Instruction: Principle of Least Group Size," *School Review 57* (1949), pp. 139–148.
35. ROBERT S. GILCHRIST. "Innovations in the High-School Curriculum," *The High School in a New Era* (Francis S. Chase and Harold A. Anderson [eds.]). University of Chicago Press, 1958.
36. J. LLOYD TRUMP. "Some Approaches to the Better Use of the Teaching Staff," *The High School in a New Era* (Francis S. Chase, and Harold A. Anderson [eds.]). University of Chicago Press, 1958.

PART III *Organizing the Curriculum*

How the curriculum of the school is organized sets limits and creates opportunities for teachers. A mere listing of topics encourages teachers to stress such topics or ones like them in their teaching — and to search for textbooks which deal with them. Emphasis in the institutional plan on fundamental concepts, principles, and generalizations turns teachers' attention to the value of such organizing elements over specific facts. Or so we like to believe. We have very little evidence.

Curriculum planning has been and is still a trial-and-error business, guided at best by precepts derived from experience. There are as yet no conceptual schemes or interconnected concepts comprising a science of curriculum. Consequently, research tends toward the "dust-bowl empiricism" variety and, as a consequence, is not yet cumulative.

Part III deals with problems of organizing the curriculum. The status of curriculum as a field of study and the need for conceptual systems to guide curriculum inquiry and practice comprise the substance of the two papers in Chapter 5. The first of these poses a scheme for classifying curriculum decisions based on levels of remoteness from the learner and uses it to examine curriculum research and curricular proposals during a three-year period. The second speculates on the possible structure and function of conceptual systems in curriculum and suggests some first steps toward their formulation.

One function proposed for such conceptual systems is the identification of promising data-sources for answering curricular problems and questions. Chapter 6 examines three data-sources commonly identified as useful: society, learners, and organized subject matter. Chapter 7 explores a cluster of key questions with which curriculum workers concern them-

125

selves and for which the data-sources discussed in Chapter 6 are presumed to have significance. A curriculum design for an educational institution or cluster of institutions is the end product, good or bad, of a series of decisions concerning the ends and means of education. The final paper of Chapter 7 — and of Part III — sets forth in broad strokes the design for science which emerged from the decision-making processes of curriculum workers in Montgomery County, Maryland. It was written by members of the curriculum office of that school system using theoretical concepts presented by the present author while serving as curriculum consultant.

The organization of the school and the organization of the curriculum influence each other. They merge comfortably or uncomfortably, depending on the values successfully built into them. The chapters of Parts II and III, taken as a whole, suggest compatibility among present-day insights into individual differences in students, school organization unbroken by arbitrary grade and class divisions, and longitudinal curriculum organization based on fundamental concepts, principles, and modes of inquiry.

5

Curriculum as a Field of Study

CURRICULUM: THE STATE OF THE FIELD

Scope of the Curriculum Field

Review of research on curriculum planning and development first necessitates agreement on what concepts, data, and processes are involved in an inquiry in the field of curriculum. Prevailing definitions of curriculum include the following [1]: (a) The curriculum is a design or plan of institutionalized education; (b) the curriculum consists of the actual learning opportunities provided at a given time and place; (c) the curriculum is an instrument for bringing about psychological changes in learners as a result of their activities in an educational institution. Though the second definition is more commonly stated as ". . . all the educational experiences that a learner has under the guidance of the school" [2], the term "learning opportunities" is substituted here for the term "educational experiences"; since an "experience" usually is defined as the result of an interactive process, such substitution is necessary if the distinction between definitions (b) and (c) is to be a real one.

Distinctions among these and other definitions of curriculum appear not to affect significantly the kinds of questions and problems dealt with in common by those who work in the field of curriculum. As Kearney and Cook [2] point out, even those who define curriculum as "something that

SOURCE: John I. Goodlad, "Curriculum: The State of the Field," *Review of Educational Research 30* (June 1960), pp. 185–198. Prepared with the assistance of Margaret P. Ammons. Reprinted with permission of the publisher.

happens to learners" devote their attention to problems involved in developing a curriculum plan or design.

This paper emphasizes curriculum as a field of inquiry and attempts a classification of problems and questions according to nearness to, or remoteness from, acts involved in the learning-teaching process. At the societal level are various analyses, pronouncements, and reports, conceived broadly, or concerned with some type of education — general, vocational, and professional; elementary, secondary, higher, or adult. At the institutional and instructional levels are proposals and programs pertaining to specific, identifiable institutions or groups of learners, and to the actual performance of teachers.

Succeeding pages draw primarily upon analytical and theoretical formulations, using selected research studies only to illustrate kinds of studies and data that can be pertinent. (What one chooses to call data depends upon the theory one constructs to explain phenomena.) Questions are raised in each section which may prove useful in the guidance of future research — questions about who should make what decisions, about appropriate sources of data for decision-making, and about how curriculum decisions are made. The materials selected were published during years immediately preceding the preparation of this paper.

The Societal Level and Curriculum Decision-Making

In all periods in history there have been practical and theoretical proposals for educational reform. It is virtually impossible either to identify the impact of long-standing philosophical formulations during any brief period, or to single out and predict the impact of fresh statements appearing during such a period. For example, how much and in what ways did John Dewey influence curriculum during the period under review? The John Dewey centennial was celebrated in 1959 with a rash of publications concerning the philosopher and his work [for example, 3, 4, 5]. Are curriculums anywhere being redesigned to correct what Snow [6] referred to as a long-standing and widening schism between two intellectual cultures, the literary-artistic and the scientific? He argued that, in today's world, standards of scientific literacy must be placed in importance side by side with standards of the traditional "literary" culture.

The years 1950–60 constitute a decade of unusual interest in, and debate over, education in the United States. Evaluations of U.S. education in the literature between 1956 and 1958 became more negative toward the end of this period [7], apparently as a result of the launching of the first Soviet satellite. Whyte [8] asserted that the school must become what Riesman [9] terms "counter-cyclical," throwing its weight against powerful socializing forces that shape "the organization man." With Commager [10], he maintained that the socialization of individuals is now being effected by other institutions and forces, and that the schools must place more emphasis on contributing significantly to the individual's intellectual development. Rickover [11] treated world affairs, economic resources, national crises, comparative education, philosophy, psychology, community organization, teacher qualifications and certification, and curriculum and instruction in formulating a bill of particulars for U. S. schools. Conant [12] endorsed the comprehensive high school that Rickover condemned.

It requires some stretching of both language and imagination to classify such material as curriculum research. The several authors do not hold positions in federal or state political structures concerned with, or directly controlling, public education, nor are they in positions involving responsibility for planning specific curriculums. Nonetheless, there is often a parallel between influential lay opinion of what curriculum ought to be and what happens within educational institutions. For example, within months after release of Conant's report, high schools in various parts of the country announced new graduation requirements closely coinciding with his recommendations. Rickover considered Dewey's influence so far from dead that he found it necessary to condemn him repeatedly; Derthick, justifying his 1961 budget request before the House Committee on Appropriations [13], was called upon to defend the U.S. educational system against the charges earlier delivered by Rickover before the same Committee. Rickover's appearance on NBC's "Meet the Press" brought the largest audience response in the 14-year history of the program, almost unanimously praising Rickover [13]. It would be interesting to know what curriculum changes, if any, have taken place in the schools of Park Forest, Illinois, which Whyte singled out as providing an example of what schools ought not do; and how much Stoddard [14] was influenced — even indirectly — by Snow's lecture in formulating part of the theory underlying certain curricular and organizational innovations in selected elementary schools involved in a project with New York University where Stoddard was dean; the resemblance in their theoretical base is striking.

Certainly, people with direct responsibility for education mold curriculums according to some conception of what education ought to be. In many countries — and particularly in the developing countries of Africa, Asia, and South America — political and educational leaders view education as essential to the advancement of whole peoples. In an awe-inspiring revolution of the human spirit, illiterate parents see schooling as essential to the future welfare of their offspring; educational effort is focused upon the establishment of primary schools and upon keeping pupils in them long enough to become functionally literate [15]. In the United States, with total literacy close to an established fact, but with national and individual survival thought to be heavily dependent upon science and technology, there is increasing emphasis upon science and mathematics [15].

The fact that curriculum decisions should, and inevitably do, reflect some human conception of what ought to be — frequently somebody's perception of someone else's conception of what ought to be — raises profound questions for curriculum theorists and researchers, answers to which have far-reaching implications for all citizens. Each question must be examined with a view to determining methods and sources of data appropriate to its solution. The question, for example, of who should determine the purposes and content of the educational program in the United States involves moral and legal issues, as Smith, Stanley, and Shores [16] so well point out. Questions of how to determine the best educational ends, of what they are, and of how to implement them, quickly acquire philosophical, political, strategic, and psychological considerations. Woodring [17] looked to the great philosopher (not necessarily the professional) to enunciate core values of the American people so clearly that the tasks of the school would become clear. He had little to say about procedures through which such values might be translated into educational programs. Lieberman [18], on the contrary, brushed aside philosophical issues and focused on the political machinery through which a powerful teaching profession might exert effective pressure in educational decision-making, presumably to achieve improved educational practices.

It is astonishing that curriculum research has dealt so sparingly with the questions of what is expected of educational institutions and how curriculum decisions are made. It is said over and over that the schools belong to "the people" and that "the people" determine the objectives of their schools. What do "the people" want? Downey [19], Seager [20], and Slagle [21] built a conceptual model of mutually exclusive unit-functions to define the tasks of elementary and secondary education. From this model, they derived an instrument for assaying the perceptions of educational objectives held by various sub-publics. They sampled 1286 past and present educators and 2544 noneducators in 15 communities — a residential suburb, an industrial center, and a rural center in each of five regions, the West, the Midwest, the East, the South, and Canada. Downey's study identified the three R's — "the skills for acquiring and communicating knowledge" — and cultivation of a "love for knowledge" to be the first and second priorities for both elementary and secondary education among all these sub-publics in all regions. Seager and Slagle found that these two priorities persisted when the educator group was separated from the noneducator group, and when occupation and age sub-publics were compared. Interesting variations from group to group and on the basis of differing levels of education were noted on items farther down the scale of priorities. Slagle found occupational classification to be more productive than income, age, or sex grouping in indicating differences of opinion regarding the task of the school.

To what extent do the people want what Commager, Conant, Dewey, Rickover, or some other "success figure" wants? Does the people's perception of what Conant and Rickover want coincide with what these men really want? Where and in what way should and do professional educators, subject specialists, foundations, and other groups enter into the decision-making process at the societal level?

To what extent and in what ways is the kind of education the people want actually implemented in curriculum decision-making? And, back to the question of authority and responsibility raised earlier, to what extent and in what ways *ought* the people's wants to be implemented?

Empirical research won't answer the "ought" questions. But, until "ought" questions are separated from "what" questions and cast into conceptual constructs from which explanatory hypotheses can be derived and tested, the kind of research needed to explain curricular phenomena and to guide the curriculum worker in his inevitable decisions of "how" and "when" will not be forthcoming.

Institutional-Instructional Levels and Curriculum Decision-Making

Curriculum decision-making at the institutional level pertains to a specific educational institution or group of institutions having identifiable students, teachers, patrons, service areas, and sanctioning bodies. There appears to be considerable agreement among curriculum theorists regarding the major tasks of curriculum planning and development encountered at this level [16, 22, 23]: determination of objectives; identification of the kinds and range of learning opportunities pertinent to these objectives; selection of designs or patterns through which these opportunities may be most effectively provided; and development of procedures for evaluating, changing, and improving the curriculum.

Educational proposals and decisions at the societal level become one of several sources of data to be considered in decision-making at the institutional level. As Lieberman [18] pointed out, however, it is naive to believe that local school boards actually control all the decisions — about the curriculums and about other matters — pertaining to their schools. Campbell [24] termed this belief "folklore," citing state and federal supreme court decisions to document his statement that the public schools have always operated within the framework established by the states and that federal influences have always been prevalent. He went on to observe: "Actually, current realities may be more in keeping with what our public policy for education ought to be than the prevailing fantasy is."

The question of who should make what decisions is as complex at the institutional as at the societal level. Hanna's [25] proposal for a national curriculum stirred much debate. Key questions regarding such a proposal are: "What curricular questions at what levels of generality and specificity can best be answered at the national level?" and "How are the answers to be used as data-sources for decisions appropriately left to the local level?" Conant [12] pointed to the uselessness of only one year of foreign language in high school; nonetheless, uninformed local decisions frequently condone such practice.

How institutional curriculum decisions are influenced and made is a provocative question for research. Certainly, the official pronouncements of boards of education or trustees responsible for specific institutions constitute inescapable sources of data for the professional. What views do board members hold? What views of what groups shape the decision-making processes of individual board members? Is there a relationship between values and/or educational viewpoints of certain groups and curricular practices at a given time in a given place? McPhee's [26] study of the relationship between individual values, educational viewpoint, and local school approval provided a basis for needed research. If the phrase "identifiable curriculum practice" is substituted for "local school approval," it becomes apparent that McPhee's model can throw light on the kinds of questions raised. Preliminary research into community power structure as it affects local school policy would give some needed indications of the most productive groups to sample.

In one sense, a rational set of goals for an educational institution would be those agreed upon by the sanctioning body (community), faithfully transmitted through the agency of that body (board) to the professional leader (superintendent), and accurately translated by the professional group (teachers) into specific educational objectives. The superintendent (or other top-level executive) is a cultural hybrid linking confused and confusing cultural expectations from without and professional decision-making processes within.* Hencley's [27] study, however, causes one seriously to question the rationality in the process at the vital point

---

* For clarification of this concept, the writer is indebted to Alicja Iwanska, "The Role of the Curriculum Maker in Cross-Cultural Perspective" (unpublished paper).

of this link. He examined congruence in perceptions and expectations held by school superintendents and their major reference groups with regard to the superintendent's role. The sample consisted of superintendents, members of the boards of education, and selected teachers, principals, and members of the PTA councils in 15 cities of Indiana, Illinois, and Wisconsin. Hencley found conflict between the superintendents' beliefs regarding their role and their perceptions of the expectations of these other reference groups regarding their role. Superintendents' perceptions of the beliefs of others and the actual beliefs of others also conflicted, but the actual beliefs of superintendents and of the several reference groups did not significantly differ. His data suggest that superintendents experience significant difficulty in assessing accurately the true expectations of others. The effectiveness of superintendents as interpreters of what various groups want for their schools must be questioned. Curriculum literature, emphasizing rational, intellectual processes of transmitting societal concerns into institutional curriculums, largely ignores certain operational facts of life.

The professional educator seeks to make formulations of educational objectives useful, whatever their derivations may be. Educational objectives, to be of maximum usefulness, should indicate both the kinds of behavior desired in the learner and the range of content or subject matter to be dealt with. There is a present trend toward emphasis on defining content to the neglect of other concerns. Such a trend, if not carried too far, might balance the trend, which has been developing slowly over the last 40 years, toward emphasis on the behavioral aspect of education [22, 23]. Interest in the behavioral considerations has found expression through a taxonomical analysis by a group of college examiners [28]. A study at the secondary-school level [29] supplemented an earlier study at the elementary-school level [30]; both emphasized learner behavior. All three studies are being used to guide test preparation and evaluation procedures.

Discussion of educational objectives up to this point has implied emphasis on teacher clarification of desired learner behavior. Such an emphasis could readily lead to the conclusion that appropriate teacher behavior is best derived from improved insight into learning and, subsequently, into how learning is best induced. Smith and others [31], while not denying the possibility of deriving a theory of teaching from a theory of learning, were not impressed by past progress toward this end. Teaching is one thing and learning quite another, they maintained. Smith and his research team, exploring the logic of teaching as exhibited in classroom discourse [32], broke such discourse into pedagogically significant units, which they then classified as logical operations. Their conclusion:

There are logical operations in teaching, some more prevalent than others, notably those of describing, designating, and explaining, in that order. Smith and his colleagues further noted a variation in frequency of these logical operations with a variation of subject matter.

As is so often the case with new and promising approaches, the surprising simplicity and straightforwardness of Smith's approach cause one to wonder why it was not exploited long ago. Smith would be first to admit that it is incomplete; his other writings make this point clear. Nonetheless, his findings have high-level potential significance as guides to the selection of procedures to assist teachers to perform according to the demands of certain kinds of teaching.

For several decades, teacher groups have engaged in formulating comprehensive sets of educational objectives. Nerbovig's [33], study revealed that elementary-school teachers, especially those with considerable teaching and curriculum-planning experience, use objectives to relate their planning, selection of learning opportunities, and evaluation of pupil progress to educational objectives. However, there appear to be no studies establishing an actual relationship between increased clarification of educational objectives and improved discrimination in the selection of classroom learning opportunities for students. In the realm of evaluation, Bloom and his associates [28] found little teacher appraisal of cognitive behavior above the level of mere possession of information, even when stated objectives called for more profound levels of cognition.

One of the reasons why a relationship between teachers' clarification of objectives and specific classroom practices has not been established may be that both aspects of curriculum planning have been global. Wood's [34] attempt to classify objectives for teacher education from an analysis of catalogs from 239 institutions of higher learning revealed part of the problem: For the most part, the statements of objectives were too general or broad to be classified by any taxonomical scheme. Provus [35] illuminated another part of the problem: Educators are likely to see only one type of behavior in an educational objective when, in reality, two or more may be involved. He investigated social problem-solving behavior, identifying two affective behaviors in what at first appears to be a strictly cognitive process. He did not identify any significant relationship between these affective behaviors and intelligence as measured by IQ. Failure to recognize the presence of these behaviors in an otherwise cognitive objective could well result in failure of teachers to provide instructionally for a significant part of the behavioral change sought. Further analysis of the structure of educational objectives is needed, together with analyses of the kinds of teaching and learning processes necessary to attainment of all parts of a single objective.

It is a popular belief in some educational circles that involvement of teachers in curriculum planning leads to increased satisfaction on the part of teachers and increased learning by students. McGuire [36], however, was unable to obtain evidence in support of the following proposition: The participation of teachers in cooperative programs of curriculum planning results, other things being equal, in significantly greater improvement in student achievement than that which occurs when the curriculum is planned either by administrative personnel alone or by teachers working individually. Sincock [37] formulated a model separating research (of an action type) from nonresearch methods, and consensus group processes from processes based on dependency on status leaders in curriculum planning. He was unable to establish a significant relationship between method or process used and satisfaction of teachers with curriculum study programs. Nonetheless, the teachers scored the consensus-research combination highest as their ideal model for curriculum study. Apparently, however, they were dissatisfied with the relative amounts of consensus-research experienced in the projects. Much remains to be learned about *what* should be planned by teachers in improving curriculum practices, and *how*.

School reorganization presumably demands curriculum reorganization. It is yet too early to determine whether the two-track plan devised by Stoddard [14], team-teaching projects, and widespread interest in nongrading will result in fundamental reordering of the curriculum. However, there is critical re-examination of content at all institutional levels, different approaches to curriculum organization and presentation in various fields, and earlier presentation of content formerly taught at higher grade levels. Such trends at the institutional level should be compared with proposals at the societal level reported above.

Rapid accumulation and reordering of knowledge render obsolete the old additive approach to curriculum planning. One alternative, long recognized by some theorists, proposes the selection of a few major principles, ideas, generalizations, or methods of inquiry and the organization of relevant content around them. The need for approaches of this sort is now urgent. Dooley's [38] dissertation, dealing with geographic concepts, and a series of dissertations in the social studies published by Stanford University [39, 40, 41, 42] offered methodological and substantial suggestions for organizing the various fields longitudinally. Until fields of knowledge are viewed and cataloged in this way, schools and school systems attempting to break down the lock-step of grade structure will not move far beyond the grade-level, topical placement of subject matter with which we are now plagued. There is no need, however, for the entire process of developing new approaches to be duplicated from the bottom up by each institution. This is the kind of undertaking best assumed by major research centers, which could then disseminate findings for appropriate consideration at the local level.

The college subject-matter specialist increasingly is becoming a self-styled expert in curriculum planning at lower levels of education. Ruml and Morrison [43], however, seriously questioned the ability of college personnel even to plan respectable curriculums at the college level, maintaining that college departments, in the main, are unable to rise above departmental self-interests to unbiased consideration of what constitutes first-rate general education. Ruml and Morrison recommended increased board study of curriculum questions and the establishment of faculty-trustee curriculum committees having powers transcending departmental authority. Goodlad [44] proposed a three-dimensional model for organizing and interrelating data relative to the subject, the learners, and learning processes at both institutional and instructional levels; such a model would provide a basis for balance in curriculum organization, thus avoiding the familiar swing of the pendulum from child-centered to subject-centered extremes.

Tjerandsen [45] observed an unfortunate tendency of curriculum recommendations in social-science general education to reduce complex or composite problems to only one, or a few, of the considerations involved. Such reduction, he claimed, ignores the fact that the problem of the curriculum necessarily involves method as well as subject matter, subject matter as well as aims, and some rational organization of these aspects of curriculum into a meaningful pattern. He developed a scheme involving these necessary components and used it to analyze 63 articles in the periodical literature dealing with general education and the social sciences. Among his findings were: (a) With but few exceptions, the papers omitted discussion of aims, or subject matter, or mode of operation, or two of these; (b) even though several kinds of conclusions about the curriculum were treated, they were not treated in terms of their interrelationships, and thus no structured form of the curriculum emerged; (c) in general, conclusions were offered without appeal to a sufficient range of grounds or sources of data to disclose adequately the reasons for arriving at them. Furthermore, only a few writers indicated their intentional restriction of treatment, suggesting a lack of awareness as to what an adequate treatment should include. It would appear that these social scientists, subject-matter specialists, strike out as curriculum experts.

Tjerandsen's study further supported the conclusion that curriculum is not yet widely established and recognized as a field of disciplined inquiry — with its unique problems, methods, and data-sources — even by educators planning for their own institutions.

In Conclusion

Curriculum study needs theoretical constructs from which hypotheses can be derived and empirically tested with a view to determining, for example, how curriculum content has been established. Out of a multitude of topics worthy of research, a few are proposed to suggest the richness of the potential harvest awaiting the eager researcher's whetted scythe:

1. Conceptual systems which identify the major questions to be answered in developing a curriculum must be rigorously formulated. The elements that tie these questions together in a system must be classified; subordinate questions must be identified and classified properly in relation to the major questions; sources of data to be used must be revealed in answering the questions posed by the system; and the relevance of data extracted from these sources must be suggested [46].

2. Theoretical constructs are needed from which research studies may be derived to demonstrate how values and expectations of individuals and groups find their ways through various channels of communication and political (conceived in the broadest sense) structures to influence curriculums.

3. Studies are needed to determine what types of subject matter (languages, for example) are best taught simultaneously, as contrasted with those best taught consecutively.

4. Studies are badly needed to show with rigor and precision how best to arrange material in a field for effective learning. This problem is of broader significance than the traditional problem of grade placement of content. The best solutions will not be forthcoming from analysis of subject matter alone. To lay out material according to some principles of increasing complexity derived from the subject is one thing; to provide sequences of learning opportunities according to insights derived for observing how students of varying abilities and past accomplishments best learn is quite another.

5. Taxonomical analyses of educational objectives must be extended into psychomotor and affective realms, and potential uses of resulting taxonomies must be more thoroughly exploited. In addition, structural analyses of objectives would help to reveal to teachers the range of specific behaviors with which they must cope in seeking to achieve any broad educational goal.

6. Global approaches to the establishment of relationships between curriculum-planning processes and improved instruction and learning must be replaced by research studies more precisely isolating and comparing process-product factors.

7. There is need for further research exploration of the teacher-pupil relationship (as revealed and expressed in the learning-teaching act) examined in the socio-psychological framework of reference groups and role conflict.

It is conceivable that the two-dimensional model developed by Getzels [47] and productively applied to the understanding of administrative behavior [48], supervisory processes [49], and instructional groups [50] could be applied equally productively to the understanding of certain curriculum decision-making processes. Curriculum theorizing to date is best described as abstract speculation; curriculum research as "dust-bowl" empiricism; and curriculum practice as rule-of-thumb guesswork (often a wet thumb, at that, held aloft to test the direction of the prevailing breeze). Perhaps increasing interest in curriculum as a field, and in curriculum problems generally, will lead to the development of conceptual schemes which separate logical from empirical questions and point to appropriate sources of data; theoretical constructs which lead to meaningful, cumulative empirical research; and curricular practices which stem from answering appropriate questions with tested data selected from pertinent sources.

REFERENCES

1. George A. Beauchamp. "Curriculum Organization and Development in Historical Perspective," *Review of Educational Research* 27 (June 1957), pp. 241–249.
2. Nolan C. Kearney and Walter W. Cook. "Curriculum," *Encyclopedia of Educational Research.* Third edition. (Chester W. Harris, ed.) New York: The Macmillan Company, 1960, pp. 358–365.
3. William W. Brickman (ed.) "The John Dewey Centennial," *School and Society* 37 (October 10, 1959), pp. 369–408.
4. Norman Cousins (ed.) "John Dewey Centennial: A Special Section," *Saturday Review* (November 21, 1959), pp. 1-62.
5. *School Review* 67 (Spring 1959), pp. 1–121.
6. Charles P. Snow. *The Two Cultures and the Scientific Revolution.* The Rede Lecture, 1959. Cambridge: Cambridge University Press, 1959.
7. David Ward Martin. *American Education as Seen in Periodical Literature, 1956–58.* Doctor's thesis. Columbus: Ohio State University, 1959. Abstract: *Dissertation Abstracts 20,* No. 6 (December 1959), pp. 2102–2103.
8. William H. Whyte. *The Organization Man.* New York: Simon and Schuster, 1956.
9. David Riesman. "Teachers as a Counter-Cyclical Influence," *School Review* 65 (March 1957), pp. 78–91.

10. HENRY STEELE COMMAGER. "A Historian Looks at the American High School," *The High School in a New Era.* (Francis S. Chase and Harold A. Anderson, eds.) Chicago: University of Chicago Press, 1958, pp. 3–19.

11. HYMAN G. RICKOVER. *Education and Freedom.* New York: E. P. Dutton and Co., 1959.

12. JAMES B. CONANT. *The American High School Today: A First Report to Interested Citizens.* New York: McGraw-Hill Book Co., 1959.

13. "The Commissioner Refutes the Admiral," *Phi Delta Kappan 41* (April 1960), pp. 299–302.

14. GEORGE D. STODDARD. "The Dual Progress Plan," *School and Society 86* (October 11, 1958), pp. 351–352.

15. United Nations Educational, Scientific and Cultural Organization. *World Survey of Education, II: Primary Education.* Paris: the Organization, 1958.

16. B. OTHANEL SMITH, WILLIAM O. STANLEY and J. HARLAN SHORES. *Fundamentals of Curriculum Development.* Rev. ed. New York: World Book Co., 1957.

17. PAUL WOODRING. *A Fourth of a Nation.* New York: McGraw-Hill Book Co., 1957.

18. MYRON LIEBERMAN. *The Future of Public Education.* Chicago: University of Chicago Press, 1960.

19. LAWRENCE W. DOWNEY. *The Task of the Public School as Perceived by Regional Sub-Publics.* Doctor's thesis. Chicago: University of Chicago, 1959.

20. ROGER C. SEAGER. *The Task of the Public School as Perceived by Proximity Sub-Publics.* Doctor's thesis. Chicago: University of Chicago, 1959.

21. ALLEN T. SLAGLE. *The Task of the Public School as Perceived by Occupation and Age Sub-Publics.* Doctor's thesis. Chicago: University of Chicago, 1959.

22. JOHN I. GOODLAD. "Current Curriculum Trends," *Materials for Reading.* (Helen M. Robinson, ed.) Chicago: University of Chicago, 1957, pp. 7–12.

23. RALPH W. TYLER. "The Curriculum – Then and Now," *Elementary School Journal 57* (April 1957), pp. 364–374.

24. ROALD F. CAMPBELL. "The Folklore of Local School Control," *School Review 67* (Spring 1959), pp. 1–16.

25. PAUL R. HANNA. "Design for a National Curriculum," *Nation's Schools 62* (September 1958), pp. 43–45.

26. RODERICK F. McPHEE. *The Relationship Between Individual Values, Educational Viewpoint, and Local School Approval.* Doctor's thesis. Chicago: University of Chicago, 1959.

27. STEPHEN P. HENCLEY. *A Typology of Conflict Between School Administrators and Their Reference Groups.* Doctor's thesis. Chicago: University of Chicago, 1960.

28. BENJAMIN S. BLOOM (ed.) *Taxonomy of Educational Objectives: The Classification of Educational Goals: Handbook I, the Cognitive Domain.* New York: Longmans, Green and Company, 1956.

29. WILLIAM M. FRENCH and others. *Behavioral Goals of General Education in High School.* New York: Russell Sage Foundation, 1947.

30. NOLAN C. KEARNEY. *Elementary School Objectives: A Report Prepared for the Mid-Century Committee on Outcomes in Elementary Education.* New York: Russell Sage Foundation, 1953.

31. B. OTHANEL SMITH and others. *A Study of the Logic of Teaching: A Report on the First Phase of a Five-Year Research Project.* Urbana: Bureau of Educational Research, University of Illinois, 1960. (Mimeo.)

32. MARY JANE M. ASCHNER. *The Analysis of Classroom Discourse: A Method and Its Uses.* Doctor's thesis. Urbana: University of Illinois, 1959. Abstract: *Dissertation Abstracts 20,* No. 1 (July 1959), pp. 221–222.

33. MARCELLA H. NERBOVIG. *Teachers' Perceptions of the Functions of Objectives.* Doctor's thesis. Madison: University of Wisconsin, 1956. 237 p. Abstract: *Dissertation Abstracts 16,* No. 12, 1956, pp. 2406–2407.

34. JEAN MARIE WOOD. *A Survey of Objectives for Teacher Education.* Washington, D.C.: Commission on Teacher Education, Association for Supervision and Curriculum Development, a department of the National Education Association, March 1960. (Mimeo.)

35. MALCOLM PROVUS. *Some Affective Modes of Behavior in Relation to Problem Solving Behavior in Social Studies.* Doctor's thesis. Chicago: University of Chicago, 1960.

36. GEORGE K. McGUIRE. *The Effect on Student Achievement of Teacher Participation in Curriculum Planning.* Doctor's thesis. Chicago: University of Chicago, 1959.

37. WILLIAM R. SINCOCK. *Teacher Reaction to Certain Practices in Curriculum Study Programs.* Doctor's thesis. Chicago: University of Chicago, 1957.

38. M. LOUISE HOLLAND DOOLEY. *A Compilation and Validation of Basic Geographic Concepts for Inclusion in School Curricula from Grades One to Twelve.* Doctor's thesis. Boston: Boston University, 1957. Abstract: *Dissertation Abstracts 17,* No. 10, 1957, pp. 2243–2244.

39. CLAY S. ANDREWS. *Social Science Generalizations for Use in the Social Studies Curriculum: Organizing and Governing.* Doctor's thesis. Stanford: Stanford University, 1957. Abstract: *Dissertation Abstracts 17,* No. 11, 1957, pp. 2464–2465.

40. HAROLD G. EMMERSON. *Social Science Generalizations for Use in the Social Studies Curriculum: Providing Recreation.* Doctor's thesis. Stanford: Stanford University, 1957. Abstract: *Dissertation Abstracts 17,* No. 11, 1957, p. 2534.

41. OWEN C. GEER. *Social Science Generalizations for Use in the Social Studies Curriculum: Protecting and Conserving Human and Natural Resources.* Doctor's thesis. Stanford: Stanford University, 1959. Abstract: *Dissertation Abstracts 19,* No. 11, 1959, pp. 2877–2878.

42. ALBERT D. PECK. *Social Science Generalizations for Use in the Social Studies Curriculum: Expressing and Satisfying Esthetic Needs and Impulses.* Doctor's thesis. Stanford: Stanford University, 1958. Abstract: *Dissertation Abstracts 19,* No. 2, 1958, pp. 254–255.

43. BEARDSLEY RUML and DONALD H. MORRISON. *Memo to a College Trustee.* New York: McGraw-Hill Book Co., 1954.
44. JOHN I. GOODLAD. "Three Dimensions for Organizing the Curriculum for Learning and Teaching," *Frontiers of Elementary Education III.* (Vincent J. Glennon, ed.) Syracuse: Syracuse University Press, 1956, pp. 11–22.
45. CARL TJERANDSEN. *The Adequacy of Current Treatments of General Education in the Social Sciences.* Doctor's thesis. Chicago: University of Chicago, 1958.
46. JOHN I. GOODLAD. "The School Scene in Review," *School Review* 66 (December 1958), pp. 391–401.
47. JACOB W. GETZELS. "A Psycho-Sociological Framework for the Study of Educational Administration," *Harvard Educational Review* 22 (Fall 1952), pp. 235–246.
48. DANIEL E. GRIFFITHS and LAURENCE IANNACCONE. "Administrative Theory, Relationships, and Preparation," *Review of Educational Research* 28 (October 1958), pp. 334–357.
49. GORDON MACKENZIE. "Expectations That Influence Leaders," *Leadership for Improving Instruction.* 1960 Yearbook of the Association for Supervision and Curriculum Development. Washington, D.C.: the Association, a department of the National Education Association, 1960. Ch. 3, pp. 67–87.
50. JACOB W. GETZELS and HERBERT A. THELEN. "The Classroom Group as a Unique Social System," *The Dynamics of Instructional Groups.* Fifty-Ninth Yearbook, Part II, National Society for the Study of Education. Chicago: University of Chicago Press, 1960. Ch. 4, pp. 53–82.

CONCEPTUAL SYSTEMS IN CURRICULUM [*]

Nowhere in education is there greater need for conceptual systems to guide theory-building, research, and planning than in the field of curriculum. By conceptual system, I mean a carefully engineered framework designed to identify and reveal relationships among complex, related, interacting phenomena; in effect, to reveal the whole where wholeness might not otherwise be thought to exist. Such a system consists of categories abstracted from the phenomena that the system is designed to describe and classify, categories which can be readily discussed and ma-

[*] I am grateful to Michael H. Millar for his helpful critique of my "Toward a Conceptual System for Curriculum Problems," *School Review*, LXVI (Winter, 1958), pp. 391–397, on which this paper is based.

SOURCE: Previously unpublished manuscript by the author.

nipulated at consistent, clearly identifiable levels of generality and which can be developed from different perspectives.

A conceptual system is more general than a theory, nurturing a variety of theories pertaining to parts of the system. Further, while giving rise to hypotheses (which are part and parcel of theories), it is neutral with respect to hypotheses. That is, a conceptual system suggests realms for fruitful hypothesizing but does not itself mandate a specific hypothesis. Such a system is, then, more than a theory in scope but less than a theory in precision and prediction.

Just as a conceptual system has structure, so does it perform functions. In curriculum, then, it facilitates the following: (1) the identification of problems and questions presumably having relevance to planning any instructional program; (2) the clarification of the types of inquiry likely to be productive in dealing with these problems and questions (*i.e.*, empirical-inductive or theoretical-deductive or some combination of the two); (3) the revelation of possible connections among these problems and questions; (4) the identification of promising data-sources for dealing with these problems and questions; and (5) the initiation of processes designed to reveal the relevance of these sources and of data extracted from them to the problems and questions classified by the system.

A conceptual system provides a bridge between general theory and specific practice. The worth of that bridge depends upon its ability to bear two-way traffic. If the theoretician cannot use the system to gain perspective and, subsequently, to formulate theories, build models, and conduct research, he turns his back to it. If the practitioner, even with great effort, cannot see in the theoretical models derived from the system at least blurred reflections of his daily concerns, he turns his back to them. In either case, the system is deprived of nourishing feedback, so essential to self-correction, and quickly perishes. The theoretician's inquiries remain narrow; the practitioner's endeavors remain in their deeply grooved channels.

Curriculum inquiry designed to give rather immediate and direct assistance to ongoing processes of curriculum has been a compelling preoccupation of American educators, especially since the second decade of this century. The work of Bobbitt [1], Bonser [2], Charters [3], Harap [4], Draper [5], and others readily comes to mind. The 1926 Yearbook (Part I) of the National Society for the Study of Education, *The Foundations and Techniques of Curriculum-Construction* [6], was produced by a committee of the period's leading educators: Bagley, Bobbitt, Bonser, Charters, Counts, Courtis, Horn, Judd, Kelly, Kilpatrick, Rugg (Chairman), and Works. Certainly, the existing problems have not been neglected by first-rate minds.

These men appear to have been interested primarily in analyzing the role of curricula in American life, posing steps for making important curricular and instructional decisions, and recommending specific curricular practices. All of them were much concerned with ends: the aims of education and the objectives of schooling. In recent years, literally dozens of theorist-writers have sought to develop a point of departure for dealing with curricular problems by extracting implications from characteristics of learners, subject matter, or all three.

These approaches, in general, depend upon a set of operational assumptions which, when followed through to their conclusions, produce specific recommendations for curriculum construction or reform. They are particularly useful in revealing where curriculum makers might arrive in their thinking and with their products when given beliefs or values are used in dealing with specific curriculum problems. These approaches are less useful in identifying categories dealt with in common by curriculum planners and in explaining what happens when alternative assumptions are applied. There has not been, therefore, a clustering of differing theoretical positions with respect to the same categories of curricular phenomena (that is, to the commonplaces of curriculum as a field of study) and the systematic testing of these theories through research. Consequently, the conditions for meaningful discourse and cumulative inquiry have not been present.

Nonetheless, curriculum speculation of the past has produced a formidable array of topics which now constitute the substance of some graduate courses labeled "curriculum" or "curriculum theory." Clearly, the curriculum specialist requires a vast background of knowledge if he is to push very deeply into them. Expressed as questions, a common list might read as follows:

1. In what ways does knowledge of learners, or of subject matter, or of society contribute to curriculum construction?

2. What is the potential contribution of an educational philosophy to curriculum construction?

3. What is the potential contribution of a psychology of learning to problems of curriculum construction?

4. How do differing patterns of curriculum organization affect processes of instruction?

5. To what decision-making processes in curriculum do studies in the behavioral sciences make a contribution?

6. Are there some guidelines for directing the absorption into the curriculum of new content in rapidly changing and expanding fields such as science and mathematics?

The practitioner can see at least some of his problems in such questions. Further, in contrast to the "ought" and "should" pronouncements so common to the curriculum field, they provide some basis for research. But what does the theoretician do with them? Do they provide perspective, visions of a larger whole? Ways of finding answers, of knowing when one has answers, and of using what one presumes to be answers are obscure.

The key explanation for this obscurity is that curricular phenomena — that is, commonplaces for purely curriculum discourse — are not identified. We know not what *curriculum* — in contrast to *a* curriculum — is, and choose not to name it.

Tyler [7] has moved above these questions to a more productive four:

1. What educational purposes should the school seek to attain?

2. What educational experiences can be provided that are likely to attain these purposes?

3. How can these educational experiences be effectively organized?

4. How can we determine whether these purposes are being attained?

This list appears to be more productive than the previous one for at least three reasons. First, it provides the practitioner with a rationale by means of which to examine his problems. Second, the questions presumably define *curriculum* and the answers to them provide *a* curriculum. Third, the actual phrasing of the questions suggests differences in their character, different procedures, therefore, for answering them, and some possible relationships among the questions. The "should" in the first question calls for an initial value position. The second question calls for a deduction from the first and suggests the possibility of comparing several means. The third is meaningless without answers to the first and second. The fourth is self-correcting within the limits set by the initial answer to the first and, when answered, could readily lead to a fresh round of answers to all four.

Most of the curricular questions raised from Bobbitt on down can justifiably be placed within Tyler's framework or legitimately translated into his terms. He has clarified and systematized what appear to be central questions running through the practical affairs of curriculum makers. It probably is fair to say that Tyler put the capstone on one epoch of curriculum inquiry and, in so doing, dramatized the need for another: to prepare the field of curriculum for theory-building through the construction of conceptual systems.

How shall we proceed toward the formulation of such conceptual systems? A conceptual system in curriculum concerns itself with general questions, questions which derive their viability from the fact that they persist in practice. Careful observation serves to identify what curriculum makers do. Strangely, although we have amply described curricula, we have little knowledge of what curriculum makers do. Perhaps, then, our first ill-formed constructs should serve only to describe, abstracting a common set of categories to make meaningful description, comparison, and generalization possible. Nothing in the work of curriculum makers dictates how a problem will be cast in the system, however; nor, for that matter, whether it will appear there at all. But again, the system must shadow practice to a degree or lose its usefulness.

From observation of curriculum planning and of curricula, we may find what *curriculum* is. Or, do we define it before we observe? Does our definition, however derived, influence our determination of fundamental categories and, if so, how? Is "objectives" a viable category or do we put ourselves in a straitjacket by thus suggesting a separation of ends and means? There may be no point even in speculating on such questions and, therefore, on the substance of our categories until the hard data from observation are before us.

To be useful, the categories of a conceptual system must be readily accessible to discussion and manipulation at consistent, clearly identifiable levels of generality and, to a reasonable degree, reflect practice. Curriculum workers almost invariably deal with the ends and means of education. These, therefore, are likely to be included in a substantive category of any conceptual system in curriculum. Preliminary observation of reality suggests, further, that curriculum planning occurs at several levels of remoteness from the learner and is carried on by a wide variety of persons. Although these levels overlap and responsibility for the substantive decisions of ends and means at each level is far from clear, construction of a three-level model can be defended: Instructional (with decisions primarily the responsibility of a teacher or team of teachers guiding a specific group of learners); institutional (with decisions primarily the responsibility of total faculty groups under the leadership of administrators); and societal (with decisions the responsibility of lay boards and legislators at local, state, and Federal levels of government). The societal level of decision-making might well be subdivided according to types of organizational entities. A conceptual system, then, that ignores these levels of decision-making in favor only of substantive categories is less than satisfactory.

Observation of reality reveals, also, that there is a dependent relationship between levels of curriculum decision-making although, again, the nature of this relationship is far from clear. Nonetheless, boards of education expect their decisions to be carried out, regardless of the bases on which these decisions are made. The superintendent of schools serves, then, both to facilitate expectations of the board (even though he usually contributes to determination of these expectations) and to interpret the meaning of societal decisions for institutional levels of decision-making. Similar *transactional* and *deductive* processes go on between institutional and instructional levels of curriculum planning. Presumably, a useful conceptual system in curriculum possesses categories that include such processes.

A conceptual system identifies data-sources to be consulted in seeking to answer problems and questions identified by the system and in conducting processes implied by that system. Ideally, one would expect curriculum workers to turn exclusively to the best knowledge available — that is, the data-source of funded knowledge — in making curriculum decisions. But observation of practice reveals otherwise. Board members and professional educators frequently employ popular beliefs, however archaic or anachronistic these may be in the light of specialized knowledge. Conventional wisdom rather than funded knowledge becomes the prime data-source. For some decisions, it is desirable to seek out what the body politic or subpublics of it believe to be true or to be good and desirable. For other decisions, it is desirable to seek out the viewpoints of specialists in given fields of knowledge. A conceptual system in curriculum should point to the data-source or sources likely to be most relevant to the kind of decision to be made.

Sketched in broad strokes, then, a conceptual system by means of which curriculum planning might be systematically studied would include at least the following:

1. An identification of levels of decision-making, specified according to remoteness from the learner. Three possible categories, moving successively away from the learner are instructional, institutional, and societal.

2. An elaboration of the substantive curriculum decisions and sub-decisions at each level.

3. A specification of the *type* of decision to be effected at each level and between levels of the system. This specification would include the processes involved in studying and effecting these decisions; hence, transactional decisions lend themselves nicely to empirical analysis, deductive decisions lend themselves to logical analysis, although such a neat separation oversimplifies.

4. An identification of appropriate data-sources to be consulted for each type of decision; *e.g.*, funded knowledge in contrast to conventional wisdom.

5. A clarification of authority and responsibility for decisions based on office and of authority and responsibility based on proximity of individuals or classes of individuals to appropriate data.

A conceptual system is not value-free. To accept curriculum practice as one beginning point is to express a value. But once having posed the problems and issues according to an initial set of values, a conceptual system should facilitate the application of alternative value positions to each commonplace of the system. Thus, over time, the consequences of approaching curriculum problems from different prespectives could be systematically studied.

As our conceptual systems are refined, we shall know more precisely where to turn for the purpose of resolving persistent curriculum issues. Some fields used as data-sources may prove unrewarding. We shall thus know that there is no point in coming back to them for knowledge they cannot yield. Other fields may prove potentially rewarding but too immature to provide the answers needed. We shall thus know not to abandon but to come back to them later. To search outside of education for answers to our educational problems is fruitless until we have first conceptualized these problems into systems that describe them, explain them, and point the way toward data needed in their solution.

REFERENCES

1. FRANKLIN BOBBITT. *The Curriculum*. Boston: Houghton Mifflin Company, 1918; *How to Make a Curriculum*. Boston: Houghton Mifflin Company, 1924.
2. FREDERICK GORDON BONSOR. *The Elementary School Curriculum*. New York: The Macmillan Company, 1920.
3. W. W. CHARTERS. *Curriculum Construction*. New York: The Macmillan Company, 1924.
4. HENRY HARAP. *The Technique of Curriculum Making*. New York: The Macmillan Company, 1928.
5. EDGAR M. DRAPER. *Principles and Techniques of Curriculum Making*. New York: D. Appleton-Century Company, 1936.
6. National Society for the Study of Education. *The Foundations and Techniques of Curriculum-Construction*. Twenty-Sixth Yearbook of the Society. Illinois: Public School Publishing Company, 1926.
7. RALPH W. TYLER. *Basic Principles of Curriculum and Instruction*. Chicago: University of Chicago Press, 1950.

▶6

Data-Sources for Curriculum
Decisions

SOCIETY: SOCIETAL PRESSURES AND
THE CURRICULUM

Much has been written about the need to examine society in determining what the schools should do. Much less has been said about the implications of societal conditions for what should be taught, how the content of instruction should be organized, and the educational climate conducive to learning. The intent here is to analyze several characteristics of present-day society that appear to have implications for education over a period of at least several decades. A long list of societal characteristics and their possible implications could be made. It is necessary, therefore, to be selective. The generalizations presented here are selected because they suggest implications that embrace a broad range of educational objectives, that can be stated rather specifically, and that demand far-reaching examination of existing curricula. Furthermore, the combined impact of these generalizations about society and their derivatives creates inestimable pressure upon humans to learn.

Some Societal Pressures to Learn

This last statement brings us to our first observation about the society in which we live. *Today's children and young people grow up in a society that expects them to learn and to go on learning.* A person of early middle age can remember when completion of high school was thought to provide

SOURCE: *Educational Forum,* XXIII (November 1958), pp. 73–80. Reprinted by permission of the publisher.

certain social and economic advantages. Today, many people regard the liberal arts graduate as having no unique advantages unless he completes specialized advanced training. A decade ago, the correspondence schools exhorted the value of a secondary education. Today, they cite impressive figures to support the claim that college graduates earn significantly more than high school graduates. Book clubs, record clubs, and other "dealers in culture" frankly appeal to education and the educated in building their mailing list and slanting their promotional activities. And now we appear to be entering the era of "education as national power." It would be difficult to believe that the goals and processes of education can go unaffected in such an atmosphere of pressure to learn.

Segments of society bring their particular concern for learning to bear upon the schools in unique ways. Many parents view the road up for their children to be an educational one. Schooling provides assurance that life for their children will be better than the life they themselves have known. Others view education as a part of one's birthright. The notion that "it" (often defined quantitatively) might not be forthcoming is simply unthinkable. Sometimes, they have difficulty in accepting a child's limited ability rather than teacher ineptness as a possible block to educational attainment. For still others, education is an assurance that, come what may economically, poverty will be at least genteel. Education thus promises participation in the true good that rises above the mere material.

These various, often-conflicting voices provide no clear-cut directives as to what our schools should do. The very disparateness and, on the whole, sincerity of the points of view expressed, however, suggest the need to examine them carefully in setting forth educational goals. Certainly, these differing expectations for education create pressures to be reckoned with in conducting the educational enterprise.

We live in a society that uses a complex variety of communication systems and places a premium on learning the communication systems of the groups to which one would belong. Although freedom to move rather freely from group to group is a prime ideal of the democratic society, there is a tendency for various groups to wall themselves off from other groups through the development of unique communication systems. Failure of an individual to learn the communication system (perhaps because the opportunity is kept from him) denies him group membership. Group members control the perpetuation of their group by controlling the educative process through which the communicative system is learned.

One example of a group communication system not readily available to all is that of certain old-line families. Very carefully guided internships are conducted by family adults or trusted long-time employees. This is a subtle kind of learning accomplished, probably, only by growing up in the family. A second type of group maintains its integrity in part by developing a mysterious code. This communication system is carefully controlled by those already admitted to the group. Obvious examples are the Masons and both social and professional fraternities and sororities. Such groups make a certain appeal to the desire to be set apart. Groups such as labor unions have a different sort of appeal and their correspondingly unique communication systems. The concept of "together we grow strong" is woven into the organizational fabric and ties the membership together. A new labor leader may express himself in novel ways and may stray to some extent from behavior patterns deemed desirable in the larger society. But he dare not deviate from the basic tenets of the movement nor fail to communicate its ideals in forthright fashion.

Most persons belong to several groups. Personal anxiety sometimes is caused by the necessity of learning several communication systems and of adjusting to their often conflicting demands. Intergroup tension arises from failure of one group to understand the communication system of another and thus to become suspicious of that group's intent. The danger to a democratic society arises not so much from the presence of such groups but from any lack of general opportunity to learn the communication system and thus to make intelligent judgments about a group's goals and the desirability of personal affiliation. This danger creates perplexing dilemmas and pressures for our schools.

Rapid advances in technology and communication have pushed formerly far-flung regions of the world into an elbow-to-elbow relationship that predates the development of any international language for clarifying this relationship. Very recently, the old and the new lived in separate worlds, each seeming right unto itself. Now, much of the world constitutes a monstrous anachronism with the old and the new standing glaringly side by side. Romantic notions of quaint differences among peoples fade, to be replaced by the grim knowledge that different people see the same things as different. Red becomes green and right bcomes wrong; one language appears not to be superior to another as a vehicle for conveying a common understanding. Diplomatic leaders despair on discovering that interpretations of their written and spoken words convey inadequate and distorted meanings to certain strategic audiences.

Studies in linguistics suggest that an awareness of language, and how language interrelates with the rest of culture, leads us away from the assumption that thought and ideas are universal and can be put into words by all languages in much the same way. Linguistic scientists tease us with the intriguing hypothesis that native speakers of different languages see the world in amazingly different ways *because of the different ways languages structure experience.* If this be fact rather than hypothesis, to think that we can bring about intercultural understanding through reading stories about the quaint customs of other peoples is to be naive. Perhaps, instead, we must come first to see the very way in which language structures one's perceptions of reality and thus come to see several different realities, one not better than another simply because it happens to be ours and not somebody else's. Some pressing problems for our language and social studies curricula lie before us.

The body of knowledge now available to man and the variety of techniques for discovering and exploring knowledge have long since surpassed the capacity of an individual to encompass them. Much of the knowledge possessed by man is disorganized or, at best, organized for self-containment. It has been organized for preservation rather than for dissemination and human integration. And much present organization is geared to the scholarly demands of uncovering new knowledge. Furthermore, the rate of communicating knowledge lags behind the pace of its uncovering.

Much of what one receives as knowledge is yesterday's knowledge, already outdated by new explorations and findings. We readily recall "facts" taught in bygone days and are startled to realize how much of what was dutifully learned is no longer fact. To what extent was the teaching of such facts in our schools a disservice? Obviously, there can be little understanding without facts. But, unfortunately, there can be facts without understanding. What is the school's role as as synthesizer of knowledge? As interpretive agent assisting the learner in the search for integrative principles around which new knowledge can be organized and thus supplant the old? The need for schools to find effective curricular means for dealing with knowledge is among the most demanding of pressures.

The rate of freeing man from his daily labors far surpasses the pace of freeing man to indulge fully in the rich and productive use of his leisure. Many of those persons gaining the greatest amount of leisure time lack the personal resources for using this time creatively. And so they turn to goods and gadgets that provide a few hours' diversion. The luxuries of yesterday became the necessities of today. It has been facetiously observed that the mass drive for such goods may well force men back into a longer work-week in order to be able to purchase the gadgets required for their leisure!

Today's adult frequently grew up equating education with earning a living rather than with enjoying life. Furthermore, he may well have been reared in a home where work was a virtue and leisure a sin. The role of the father and husband was to provide for his family and in so doing he established himself as worthy in his own eyes and in the eyes of others. Work took on a religious significance with all the accompanying spiritual connotations. Little wonder, then, that increased leisure for some brings with it an uneasy sense of guilt. Resulting anxiety prevents the individual from mobilizing his energy creatively and valuable time is frittered away aimlessly. Bored and frustrated, he may plunge into a second job, joining the ranks of the "moonlighters." Perhaps the resulting physical fatigue is better for him in the long run than the emotional draining that might well occur otherwise. But in neither case is he refreshed and invigorated. He perishes without dying, never knowing what might have been.

There are obvious implications for adult education in the above. But with all the progress that has been made in this field during the past decade, only the barest surface scratching, in comparison to what will someday be, has occurred. It is conceivable that the ranks of the adult educators, within the forseeable future, will outnumber the combined teaching force of all other levels and types of education. There are clear implications, too, for the creative behaviors that goals for all educational institutions must embrace. In the course of the exciting journey toward the attainment of such goals, human beings everywhere may come to have at least some understanding of the power of education "to set the human spirit free."

Some Implications for the Curriculum

In examining the curricular implications of the foregoing, let us temporarily pass by the first observation. Today's pressure on young people to learn is a pervasive one; in fact, such pressure represents the combined impact of all the others. And this impact profoundly influences the classroom climate for learning and teaching.

Let us turn, then, to the generalization about groups and intergroup communication. According to linguistic scientists, physiologically normal persons learn the complex systems through which human communication goes on by about five and one-half years of age. Before entering the first grade, then, a normal youngster acquires language, kinesis, vocalizations, and so forth. He has learned something of the power of language and with facility uses his voice to express surprise, terror, joy, and anger. The range and depth of these important learnings, unaided by formal schooling, is impressive.

We tend to assume, however, that since the child can't read when he comes to school he must be taught his "language." But we really confuse language and writing. In part because of this confusion we place a high premium on writing and the reading of writing. Surely we aren't assuming that no communication can go on before the child learns to read and write. Obviously, a great deal of communication takes place among six-year-olds who cannot read and took place for years among these children before their arrival at school. Furthermore, each little subgroup has been busily learning a special "language." The "blue stocking" child learns the communication system for her set whether or not she learns to read and write. Similarly, the electrician's son learns the language of the labor group whether or not he learns to read and write. Frequently, we can scarcely identify the various communication systems let alone understand and teach them.

Most of us believe that the opportunity for all to learn to read and write is the greatest culturally unifying force in a democracy and it may well be. But a formidable one, too, is the opportunity to learn through the public schools the subtle communication systems of the various groups and classes that make up our society. Should not, then, the goal implied parallel the reading and writing goals held high for elementary education? Can such a goal be adequately achieved so long as formidable segments of our population, whether by choice or circumstances, never participate in the necessary intergroup communication? And in this period when ability grouping is being rediscovered we must examine the extent to which this practice, proved advantageous in the achievement of certain education goals, may be equally disadvantageous in the attainment of others. Significant progress toward the goal of intergroup understanding (certainly demanding the learning of group communication systems) may require a scheme of classroom organization wherein learner heterogeneity is deliberately planned. In this way, the schools would provide opportunity for individuals to learn the unique communication systems of many groups as well as to read and write.

In the first part of this paper it was suggested that the elbow-to-elbow relationship of people around the world today carries significant implications for our language and social studies curricula. The social studies program is vitally concerned with problems of human living and relationships among people. Where and when one lives in large measure determine the character of the problems of living one must face and one's relations with others. These problems, their environmental genesis and their disposition in the hands of men, became the catch-hold point in social studies instruction. But, too often, our social studies programs are a far cry from such procedures. Their learning circumscribed by a textbook, students move ploddingly forward with placenames, products, and land features stripped of the human struggles with which they might readily identify. Little wonder that children express great interest in topics that belong in the social studies, but boredom and dissatisfaction with the social studies program itself.

It becomes evident that the content of social studies curricula, especially in the lower grades, requires overhauling. Is there any good reason, in these times, why pupils of eight and nine years of age should not study the customs of other peoples? It has been argued that students cannot meaningfully study other times and places until their time-space concepts are well-developed. But the aspects of culture young children might study most meaningfully do not demand such understanding. It could be argued, too, that our schools already give much attention to the study of other peoples. They do, but the emphasis is historical and geographical, with much of the latter being of the casual "tourist" variety. A much greater infusion of anthropological and sociological content is called for. Such material is of immediate interest to children and youth. It would be necessary, of course, to organize it so that the developmental levels of the students would be respected in regard to both content and reading level.

If the experience be the sole determinant of one's reality perceptions, then the study of different cultures through the approach indicated above may well be adequate. But if thought and ideas depend, too, on the nature and structure of the language vehicle, then something more is called for. Studying a culture without paying attention to the language portion of that culture, if language contributes to the structuring of experience, would result in a serious gap in seeking to understand a people. The beginning point, most probably, is in the study of the structure of our own language and linguistic scientists have indicated both content and method for such study. Unfortunately, their recommendations are only slowly finding their way into the secondary-school curriculum and scarcely at all into the elementary school. Specifically, these recommendations suggest greater emphasis in the lower grades upon the differential aspects of language; that is, the elements that give a language its internal structure and unique characteristics, quite apart from the inferential or referential aspects to which we normally pay much attention. For example, *hat* is different from *hot* because of the internal characteristics of the words as well as because of the different meanings we attach to them. At higher levels of schooling, where the teaching of formal grammar is introduced, this recommendation would call for the substitution of grammar arising out of differential language considerations for the referential grammar that has predominated traditionally.

While such analysis of our language has significance in its own right, we are not likely to move forward from such studies to greater understanding of other cultures. An understanding of differing reality perceptions among various peoples may well be enhanced, however, if study of the structure of our own language is accompanied by a study of the structure of another. This may well prove to be the strongest argument for inclusion of a second language in the elementary and secondary curriculums.

Our next generalization about the society in which we live refers to the staggering amount of knowledge now available to man, much of it disorganized or, at best organized for preservation rather than instruction. The amount of specific information that can be digested in, say, twelve years of schooling bears a relationship to that available for learning comparable to the relationship between a handful of straw and heaped tons of it in twenty scattered silos. To think, then, that we can meaningfully prescribe *the* content for elementary and secondary education is to be unrealistic. It should be possible, however, to select appropriate, representative content for revealing the methodology and organizing principles of given fields of knowedge.

A significant task for educators is the identification of curricular organizing elements drawn from both the methodology of inquiry and the results of inquiry in the various fields. Thus, from mathematics both processes of deductive thinking and concepts of number, quantity, and relationship are derived. In history, we see an historical method wherein human decisions are reconstructed and certain generalizations about time-place determinants emerge. The selection of organizing centers — catch-hold places for teaching and learning — in the curriculum is then guided by the clarity of the relationship between the proposed centers and the methodology or the particular concepts, skills, and values deemed worthy of long-term educational development. Naturally, the content introduced in the process must have value in itself, but the maturity and concerns of the learners can now be considered realistically in choosing one classroom activity over another.

Through the curriculum building process suggested here, relatively stable guidelines for instruction are determined. It is conceivable that they would facilitate some nationwide agreement in curriculum planning. And yet, teachers and learners would still be free to decide locally upon the specific catch-hold points to use in day-to-day learning. The deadly weight of "having to cover" prescribed content that already may be out of date is removed without belittling the value of content carefully selected to reveal methodology and first principles.

The inability of millions of people to engage productively in the creative use of their leisure time readily poses two major educational implications. We already have ample evidence to suggest that most adults, with only a little well-timed guidance, could learn to plumb the depths of their own experience with considerable insight and to express these insights in a variety of creative ways. The increase in leisure time and in our knowledge of the unfortunate mental health concomitants of using this time poorly suggests the present urgency of tapping the folk arts of the American people. Increasingly, our communities must have centers to which our people may come and where, with the skillful guidance of qualified teachers, they will explore various artistic media. It is often said that America is in a period of adolescent culture. With the advent of general adult participation in the arts, we will have entered into an era of cultural maturity.

An obvious corollary paralleling the inference for adult education is that today's young people must have ample opportunity to participate in the arts, programs for which are not yet well-established in elementary, secondary, and higher education. There is an alarming tendency for boards of education, when under budgetary pressures, to eliminate any existing special resources for art and music in the elementary school. These subjects are sadly underrated electives in secondary education. And only a handful of colleges give to art and music anything like the attention paid to athletics. In fact, these two departments frequently (and illogically) are among the most undernourished of the liberal arts constellation. Throughout the hierarchy of organized education, there is appallingly little planned provision for challenging human creativity and channeling its expression through the arts.

Toward Creative Learning

This last observation turns us back full-cycle to where this paper began: Today's children and young people grow up in a society that expects them to learn and go on learning. Societal pressures to learn exert their ultimate impact upon the human organism. If this impact creates undue anxiety, the human organism will not, cannot, learn up to the full potentiality for learning it possesses. Energy subsequently consumed in coping with this anxiety is lost in meeting the challenges imposed by a demanding society.

Optimum human achievement appears to be the product of blending intelligence, motivation, energy, and creativity. Educational institutions can create the climate wherein optimum blending of these human characteristics may occur. First, they can endeavor to screen out those societal pressures that create unrealistic, damaging expectations for learning. Among the most vicious of these is the expectation that all individuals can achieve a given standard equally well, especially when this expectation is accompanied by the connotation that there is something disgraceful or sinful about failing to achieve such a standard. Second, educational institutions can place emphasis upon appropriate ends of learning. Ends that encourage processes of intellectual inquiry are appropriate; ends that place the search for teacher approval above the search for truth are not. Third, educational institutions can seek for order in the curriculum;

order of such nature that the timing and pacing of individual learning can be meaningfully guided. Anxiety is as likely to grow out of the tasks of education as to be carried into them and can be prevented only by careful planning. Fourth, educational institutions can seek to keep open-ended the basic human drive that is creative expression. For, most assuredly, without creativity the human spirit shall perish.

LEARNERS: THE LEARNER AS A DATA-SOURCE

Three fundamental questions to be dealt with in planning to promote any learning are: *Can* it be induced? *Should* it be induced? *How* is it best induced? Answering these questions calls for analysis of and speculation about the species *homo sapiens,* the systems through which the species cluster and communicate, and the human personalities representing consistent and variable expression of the species. The learner, then, as representative of a class of creatures, as members of various groupings, and as unique individual, is a data-source to be examined and consulted in making educational decisions.

The above might be reduced to the simplest of platitudes: We must take the learner into account in teaching and planning for teaching. The platitude covers up the complexity of the problems involved, however. The learner, obviously, is not the only data-source to which one turns in making curricular decisions. Awareness of this fact, when coupled with an inadequate conception of the total context of educational decision-making, leads us to scream, "You've forgotten the children!" when someone attempts to analyze the place of subject matter, and "You've forgotten the subject matter!" when someone seeks to analyze the place of the learner. Thus, a sterile debate arises out of our inability to see two quite different parts as essential to a larger whole as well as unique within themselves.

A much more complex problem in considering the place of the learner in the total school program arises out of seeking to determine the application of *specific* knowledge about learners to the decisions for which data about learners are appropriate, while remembering that knowledge about subject matter also is appropriate to aspects of the same decisions. Now

SOURCE: *Educational Leadership,* XIX (October 1961), pp. 11–14. Copyright © 1961, by the Association for Supervision and Curriculum Development. Reprinted by permission of the publisher.

we find ourselves not simply in the midst of a sterile debate over the importance of learners as contrasted with the importance of subject matter but in a chaotic no man's land where curricular and instructional decisions often are made in response to political pressure, the drift of the tide, or personal whim and bias.

In seeking to make complex decisions rationally, one identifies the category of knowledge or experience within which appropriate data, if available at all, might be found. This category is the data-source. Thus, the behavioral sciences constitute a broad data-source bringing together knowledge, principles and theories pertaining to human reproduction, individual differences, patterns of learning, and so on.

In the realm of educational decisions, however, the data-sources and the lines separating them are dimly defined. The data presumed to lie within them are transitory or, at best, timidly endorsed. Educators must base their decisions upon the evidence of experience and the analysis of that experience, until such time as the necessary theory and scientific studies are available.*

Basic Questions

In the early conduct of practical arts which have now become applied sciences, the absence of a theoretical base from which to predict the consequence of choice probably was not unduly frustrating to the artisan. The scope of his operations was relatively limited; the range of alternatives appeared finite and manageable. Today's educator, however, embraces, in one sense, the whole of human experience. The array of decisions to be made appears endless; the alternatives infinite. At the same time, the educator is aware of what appear to be relatively sophisticated inquiries into human behavior. Surely, somehow and somewhere, these inquiries pertain to him and his work! Blindly, he may reach out for them, unaware that the findings are themselves significant for a developing fabric of knowledge but often inappropriate to the task for which he seeks help. Little wonder that he often turns away from knowledge that seems to serve him ill . . . and hardly fair to call him anti-intellectual for so doing! Why *not* bite the hand that fails to feed you?

Education, as a field of inquiry, is now able to offer at least simple formulations to assist the practitioner in sorting out the general kinds of questions with which he must deal, the broad categories of knowledge pertinent to such questions, and scatterings of data within these cate-

---

* For an analysis of different classes of evidence applied to educational decisions, see: James B. Conant, *Trial and Error in the Improvement of Education*. Washington, D.C.: Association for Supervision and Curriculum Development, NEA, 1961.

gories. Let me illustrate by turning to the three questions of planning with which I began — can you? should you? how best to? — and apply these to just two problems of planning the school program. The problems are in the realm of nursery school education and education of the gifted.

Inquiry into the nature of the young human being suggests a natural pacing in what appear to be certain essential learnings. One set of such learnings involves establishing at least a self-preserving relationship with adults. The general category of the behavioral sciences appears to be an appropriate data-source within which to hunt for data about what young children do and, therefore, might be taught to do well.* We examine the data and conclude that two-year-old children evidence little discomfort in relating themselves both to their parents and to a variety of other adults — baby-sitters, uncles, neighbors. In other words, they *can* do it; this behavior appears to be educable.

It follows, then, that we might be able to direct this kind of childhood behavior in a variety of directions. Why not create nursery schools in order to educate the two-year-old in social directions we choose to call desirable? But *should* we? Now we have a decision that is quite different from the preceding one, calling also for data from the behavioral sciences but perhaps from other realms within this general category. On examining pertinent evidence, we discover that young children are preoccupied with the task of relating themselves to their parents. We discover, further, that youngsters who seem still to be struggling unduly with this task at the age of six or seven often appear to be handicapped in seeking to devote themselves profitably to tasks, such as learning to read, posed by the school.

We now turn back to re-examine our proposed creation of nursery schools and ask ourselves whether these young children *should* be separated from their parents at this early age in order to struggle with a variety of adult relationships when the parental relationship is of such fundamental importance. Perhaps, we conclude, admission to nursery schools should be delayed until the necessary parent-child relationships are established.

My third question of *how* best to conduct the nursery school program now evaporates. If the child's task of relating himself effectively to his parents is so important that it must not be interfered with through the interposition of nursery school teachers, then we refute the previous justification for such schools and, consequently, eliminate the question of

---

* The illustration is to be considered hypothetical in that my purpose is to illustrate the *kind* of inquiries that might provide rational approaches to educational decisions and thus to avoid the fruitless either/or debates which now consume so much of our valuable energy.

how best to conduct them. (Again, I remind you that the specifics of the illustrations are hypothetical, even though some specialists in child psychology seriously question the wisdom of nursery schools for two-year-olds, except where there are no parents.)

There are, of course, alternative answers to the three questions, arising out of the application of different values than those guiding me. Nonetheless, the rational procedures that would be applied in getting to other answers would be comparable. Some people might say that childhood struggles toward satisfactory parent relationships are debilitating, often resulting in unsatisfactory compromise and, in fact, inadequate self-realization. The answer, therefore, is to remove the child from the parents at birth, placing him with a dozen other infants in a nursery-school situation. Then, however, if these children simply placed the teacher in the parent role and competed with one another in seeking a parent-child relationship, we might have additional evidence to question the desirability of this alternative line of reasoning and so strengthen the first.

Let us turn to the second example. It has been amply proven that gifted high school students are capable of grasping advanced mathematical concepts. It becomes clear that the answer to the "can" question is "yes." Since they can, we tend to assume that the answer to the "school" question likewise is yes. But the *should* question is a different order of question than the *can* question; the answer to the former cannot be deduced from the answer to the latter, present practices to the contrary.

Examination of *how* best to promote rapid advancement of the gifted through advanced courses reveals some of the limitations of attempting to deduce answers to *should* questions from answers to *can* questions. Recently, an exponent of automated teaching observed that, with improved programing of teaching machines, some high school students of algebra will be able to cover in a few weeks what formerly took years. "What will the poor teachers do then?" he inquired. In posing this question, he may have revealed present-day rigidity (often sterility!) in thinking about what schools are for.

Some recent studies of adolescent values reveal infinitesimal changes over the four years of high school. Does this mean that adolescent values cannot be changed? Or does it mean that inadequate emphasis is given to value formation as end and to appropriate techniques of value change as means? Or are there other alternatives?

Let us assume the second, hypothetically, as the most plausible assumption: Inadequate attention is given to value development in today's high school. We conclude that more time and new measures are needed for producing deliberate change in affective behavior among high school students. But we observe that high school students, using machines, are now able to learn in a half-hour of daily self-instruction twice as much algebra as they did a few years ago. The state then places a programed machine in every home and the home takes over responsibility for education in algebra. The high school now uses this time for education in human values and valuing. (Or is abolished if the *only* function of the secondary school is to teach algebra.)

It becomes clear that evidence to the effect that adolescents *can* learn advanced algebra at amazing rates of speed does not necessarily lead to the conclusion that high schools *should* teach algebra. On deciding that high schools should not teach algebra, according to the line of reasoning outlined, the question of *how* best to teach algebra in high school now evaporates, although the question of how best to teach adolescents algebra at home remains.*

My total analysis reveals, I think, that consideration of learners in planning the school program is not merely desirable; it is inescapable. The analysis reveals also, I believe, that a more systematic identification and treatment of the questions inherent in program planning, together with identification of valid data-sources and data appropriate to each specific question would eliminate the empty subject/child dichotomy. Such analyses might even reveal that current defensive attitudes toward subject-matter organization and programed learning on the part of some members of our profession are misplaced. Perhaps, instead, we should be viewing with keen anticipation the prospects of automated learnings, removing entirely from the realm of human interaction — and thus from schools as we now know them — many subjects now constituting a subject-centered curriculum. And, then, individual pupil interests, needs and purposes might well become the catch-hold points for developing through our schools ideal men and ideal societies of the sort speculated upon in man's best dreams.

* Again the reader is reminded of my purpose in seeking to separate several of the different *kinds* of educational decisions to be made. It should not be assumed that the field of algebra has no place in seeking to achieve a broad set of educational goals. Nor should it be assumed that whenever teaching machines are employed the teacher must be a supervisor of these machines or that the machine is to be used only if it can be encompassed within the span of control of the classroom teacher as conventionally perceived.

ORGANIZED SUBJECT-MATTER: THE CHANGING
CURRICULUM OF AMERICA'S SCHOOLS

Today's educators have a formidable task in seeking to select what to teach, especially in cumulative fields such as the natural and behavioral sciences. If this accumulation is plotted on a time line, beginning with the birth of Christ, it is estimated that the first doubling of knowledge occurred in 1750, the second in 1900, the third in 1950, and the fourth in 1960.

Whether or not these are only rough approximations, they have impressed upon educators an inescapable fact, well stated by Professor Schwab of the University of Chicago: It is no longer merely difficult to select and package for instruction the most important bits and pieces of knowledge; it is impossible! The search is on for something more lasting than "the bits and pieces" emerging as residue from the advance of knowledge, something more permanent around which to organize learning.

Some of the guiding questions are old ones. What is worth knowing? What knowledge prepares for the acquisition of new knowledge? What kind of education is most likely to help individuals become self-propelling during a lifetime of learning?

Clearly, a massive reformulation of what is to be taught and learned in the schools of the United States is under way. Talk of the "new" mathematics, the "new" physics, and the "new" biology is now commonplace. Various scholarly groups and individuals, handsomely supported by the National Science Foundation — and, to a lesser degree, by private philanthropic foundations — have developed new course outlines and instructional materials for mathematics, physics, chemistry, biology, anthropology, economics, geography, English, and foreign languages. New textbooks are in wide use, both in this country and abroad. Tens of thousands of teachers and students in elementary and secondary schools have participated in the preparation and trial use of these materials. Many of these teachers and thousands more have attended institutes on the new content and how to teach it.

The beginnings of the current curriculum reform movement are commonly identified with the successful launching of the first Russian satel-

SOURCE: *Saturday Review* (November 16, 1963), pp. 65–67, 87, 88. Reprinted by permission of the publisher.

lite in the fall of 1957. This spectacular event set off blasts of charges and countercharges regarding the effectiveness of our schools and stimulated curriculum revision, notably in mathematics and the physical sciences. But the roots of change go back further, to the years immediately following World War II. The recruitment of young men for the armed services had revealed shocking inadequacies in the high school science and mathematics programs of high school graduates. The problem was partly the limited quantity of work in these fields, partly the quality of what had been taken. The high school curriculum too often reflected knowledge of another era, not the scientific advances of the twentieth century. Recognizing their responsibility for this unhappy state of affairs, scholars in a few fields began to participate actively in what has now become a major curriculum reform movement.

Sometimes an individual took the initiative, sometimes a learned society (the American Mathematical Society, for example), prompted by a few articulate members. In either case, the subsequent course of events was surprisingly similar from project to project. First, a group of scholars came together to review the need for pre-collegiate curriculum change in their field. Then, in subsequent summers, scholars and teachers invited from the schools planned course content and wrote materials. These materials were tried out in cooperating schools during the regular school year and revised in the light of this experience. Meanwhile, in summer and year-long institutes, teachers were educated in the new content and methodology. Throughout, participants have been agreed, apparently, that new materials are central to basic curriculum change.

The current curriculum reform movement is now too far advanced to warrant the adjective "new." In some fields, notably mathematics, the first wave is about to be followed by a second. The "new" new mathematics is in the offing.

There is grave danger, however, in assuming that curriculum change has swept through all of our 85,000 public elementary and 24,000 public secondary schools during this past decade of reform. Tens of thousands of schools have been scarcely touched, or touched not at all, especially in areas of very sparse or very dense populations. Tens of thousands of teachers have had little opportunity to come to grips with what advances in knowledge and change in subject fields mean for them. Tens of thousands hold emergency certificates or teach subjects other than those in which they were prepared. In elementary schools, teachers with any appreciable backgrounds in science and mathematics constitute a species that is almost as rare as the American buffalo.

Suburban schools have fared well by comparison, with extensive participation in curriculum projects, ability to attract qualified teachers, and resources for providing in-service education. The gap between the haves and have-nots persists and, in some ways, is accentuated.

Curriculum planning is a political process, just as it is an ideological process of determining ends and means for education. Proposals must find their way successfully through the political structure into educational institutions or slip into obscurity. Almost without exception, these projects have had their genesis outside of the formal political structure, having been conceived primarily by scholars in colleges and universities who were joined by teachers from elementary and secondary schools.

Projects have been generously supported from funds that are predominantly federal in origin, testifying to the fact that the education of its youth is a primary interest of the nation. But the relationship among local, state and Federal governments in the support and conduct of school affairs is a sensitive one that has materially affected the ways by which the various curriculum projects have entered the bloodstream of American education. Conditions of the grants have cautioned recipients against promoting their wares in any way; project directors have been limited to descriptive information, articles and, on request, speeches. But their efforts are in vain unless the benefits find their way to local schools and school systems. It is not surprising, therefore, that products, largely in the form of textbooks, often have been turned over to commercial publishers who have their own effective means of reaching state and local school authorities. These products now come into the schools through the expenditure of state and local funds. This whole fascinating series of events warrants further study.

The curriculum reform movement has been sharply focused on single subjects planned, generally, from the top down. This focus and the "national" character of the projects have attracted first-rate scholars into pre-collegiate curriculum planning. But these characteristics also have attracted scholars from fields not normally included in pre-collegiate schooling, who sense, apparently, a fresh opportunity to include their particular roads to the good life in the curriculum of elementary or secondary schools.

This competition among fields places severe burdens upon instructional time. Just how all of the subjects will share this time remains to be seen. Demands will exceed time, even if the school day, week, and year should be lengthened. Some subjects will have to be combined or left out — there is not room for twenty academic disciplines in the kindergarten. Arguments for the root nature and basic value of a discipline notwithstanding, problems of what subjects shall prevail are resolved largely in the political realm at Federal, state, and local levels of educational responsibility, with national concerns largely determining the priorities today. Consequently, the humanities and social sciences will gain increasing favor with any appreciable reduction in world tension.

The strengths and weaknesses of the several projects stem in part from the nature of American education, with its characteristics strengths and weaknesses. For example, there is no single set of aims for America's schools; there are many. Therefore, each curriculum project is free to formulate objectives for its own particular segment of the curriculum. Some have; some have not. Rarely are objectives defined with such precision that one would know exactly what to evaluate in determining the success of a given project. It might be argued that those undertaking the various curriculum activities have no responsibility for the formulation of objectives; that local school districts set their own and gear materials to them. Each project is responsible only for setting forth what to teach in a given subject. But can ends and means be thus separated in any aspect of curriculum planning?

Although objectives are vague or not stated, documents describing the several projects express an almost uniform point of view. The current curriculum reform movement is seeking more in the student than the mere possession of information, however updated that information may be. The student is to sense *intuitively* the *structure* of a field. By "structure" is meant the concepts, principles, and methods that constitute the discipline. "Intuitive" refers to glimpses of abstraction that go beyond immediate practical experience. Sometimes the stated goal is for the student to think like the physicist or the historian.

Goals of this kind have a certain mystical quality. What does a student do when he senses the structure of a field intuitively or thinks like a physicist? How does a teacher decide that the student has acquired these commendable traits? And how are they best developed? Some project directors are deeply preoccupied with such questions. Others have brushed them aside, either because adequate answers appear to be hard to come by or because they believe that their programs already answer such questions reasonably well.

Most of the projects have sought to bring the student into the structure of the subject by identifying a few key concepts (number, quantity, energy, time, space, supply, and demand) which are to be developed persistently and with increasing depth over several years of schooling. The curriculum is thus organized into units, each unit progressing in difficulty and both reviewing and extending one or more concepts introduced earlier in the student's experience. Very often, the subject-matter is similar to that of conventional programs. But the treatment called for is different. For example, the textbook for grade 9 in the program produced by the School Mathematics Study Group concentrates on algebra, as is common in conventional curricula. Emphasis, however, is on the behavior of numbers rather than the solving of algebraic equations.

Some of the new programs depart radically from conventional content. Suppes and his associates, in their Experimental Project in the Teaching of Elementary School Mathematics at Stanford University, are developing their instructional materials around the concept of set. A set is simply any collection or family of objects. The putting together of sets of physical objects is a more concrete operation than the addition of numbers. According to Suppes, operations on sets — rather than the more abstract and difficult operations on numbers — permit the child to understand the way a number is related to a set of objects and lays the groundwork for the abstractions constituting mathematical thought. This is quite different from the arithmetic most of us learned in the primary grades!

Those involved in the various curriculum projects may have started out to reform the *content* of their fields, but few stopped there. In many instances, content has been pushed down or expectations for the year increased. There sometimes is provision for gifted high school students to go as much as two years into work normally reserved for college. Throughout, as noted earlier, emphasis is upon unifying concepts, principles, and methods of inquiry, with each successive topic designed to develop a central theme or element. Usually, subject matter is very carefully arranged — "programed" in the jargon of the trade — in a step-by-step sequence. Often, self-instructional programed workbooks accompany the familiar textbook. By means of these workbooks, students are able to work independently and at their own speed part of the time.

Perhaps the most comprehensive instructional package is that produced by the Physical Science Study Committee for a year-long course in high school physics. The first tool of learning is a new textbook, carefully developed by a team of outstanding physicists working in collaboration with high school teachers. Other tools include laboratory experiments and bits of simplified apparatus, a set of films, achievement tests designed to test the application of knowledge and techniques to new problems, a library of paperbound books on special and related topics, and a teacher's guide. Neither laboratory activities nor films are supplementary or for enrichment. Films demonstrate experiments that go beyond the confines of high school laboratories or otherwise provide a perspective not attainable in the classroom. Textbooks, films, laboratory experiments, and class discussions are planned to fit into a consistent, unified whole. With such tools so conveniently available, teachers' talk and chalk are extended as never before.

With grade placement of content determined, and with textbooks, teachers' guides, and supplementary materials published, some project directors see their work as nearing completion. Fearful that the relentless quest for knowledge in their own fields will pass them by, they are anxious to get back to research and teaching, usually maintained only with tag ends of energy during project years. Others, however, have become inescapably caught up in those fascinating learning and pedagogical problems that have alternately intrigued and frustrated psychologists and educationists. Patrick Suppes, for example, of the Stanford Institute for Mathematical Studies in the Social Sciences, as much a psychologist as a mathematician, wants to know what mathematics young children can learn, what they learn with ease and what with difficulty, and why. His materials on sets and numbers for the primary grades are little more than by-products of his central activity.

David Page, now of Educational Services Incorporated in Watertown, Massachusetts, is not enamored with the search for precise grade placement of subject matter. He seeks, instead, what he calls an "intermediate invention" of great power: power to stimulate an almost infinite number of mathematical operations, power to incorporate most of the basic mathematical concepts and principles, power to absorb and challenge children of vastly differing abilities. In one of his intermediate inventions, "maneuvers on lattices," children explore general rules, laws, and proofs for numbers through a simple table of numbers and a system of arrows variously pointing up, down, to left, to right, and diagonally. With the teacher's sweep of an eraser and scratch of the chalk, a new set of stimuli is on the board before the class. The limits of exploration and invention defy grade barriers. There is something here for children of all ages.

Although there are gross similarities in approach among the several dozen curricular projects now under way, probing reveals marked differences. Mathematics, with an array of projects embracing both elementary and secondary education, again provides an excellent illustration. Is mathematical insight enhanced by the verbalization of concepts? The organization of some projects reveals the careful coordination of mathematical operations and their verbal counterparts.

Beberman and his associates of the University of Illinois Committee on School Mathematics maintain that the early, often glib and incorrect, verbalization of mathematical concepts inhibits or distorts insight. They believe that precise verbalization is necessary for purposes of communication and proof, but this verbalization should come *only after* the individual has become thoroughly familiar with the generalization and has had adequate opportunity to test and refine it. "Precise communication is a characteristic of a good textbook and a good teacher; correct *action* is a characteristic of a good learner."

Mayor and his associates of the University of Maryland Mathematics

Project seek a close and supporting relationship between the verbal and the operational components of mathematics. Both the sequence of mathematical operations and the appropriate vocabulary for them should be planned side by side and pedagogy designed to promote the simultaneous attainment of both.

Page, in the University of Illinois Arithmetic Project, is impatient with "the hindering verbiage (minuend, dividend, partial product, and the rest)" of conventional arithmetic. He seeks what he calls "new frameworks for mathematical ideas" through which children are challenged to explore mathematics — to develop, invent, and extend. Page avoids technical languages in his teaching, encouraging children to invent their own, which, he says, often is better. They will come to the use of precise language soon enough, he thinks, when situations demand appropriate communication.

One of the shortcomings of the current curriculum reform movement, running almost uniformly through the projects, is the poverty of data regarding their effectiveness. There are, indeed, gratifying testimonials from teachers and students who have been involved. But are students learning fundamental concepts better than they did in conventional programs? If so, does insight into these concepts provide increased power in dealing with unfamiliar problems? Are all students able to proceed satisfactorily and with satisfaction to themselves in the new mathematics, physics, chemistry, and biology, if allowed adequate time? If so, does this place a solid high school curriculum in these subjects within the reach of all?

Most of the testing to date has compared students in new curricula with students in the old, using test items based on the latter. This is hardly fair to the new ventures. Nonetheless, students in the new curricula have shown up about as well as their counterparts on these conventional achievement tests, except where vocabulary or other specific memory items were called for. In those few instances where students in new curricula have been compared with students in the old using items thought to be more appropriate to the former, students in the old have performed rather poorly.

The scarcity of evaluative data has been defended on the ground that an overwhelming job of curriculum reform had to be accomplished quickly. Time and resources have not yet permitted broad-scale appraisal. The argument has merit. Nonetheless, one must still regret the disproportionate attention to evaluation in projects that sometimes have gobbled up as much as a million dollars a year, not collectively but individually. By and large, the several projects have been conducted apart from the regular teaching and degree-granting structure of universities. Consequently, there have not been the theses and dissertations that might have been stimulated otherwise.

Prospects for the future look somewhat brighter. Several projects have built long-term evaluation into their fiscal and personnel policies. Some have contracted with private testing agencies for the preparation of instruments appropriate to project goals. These provisions, in turn, should force the more precise definition of each project's goals.

The most significant question for the future is whether the current curriculum reform movement, long overdue, has built-in mechanisms to guarantee continuing self-renewal. Are present accomplishments to be enshrined within the covers of textbooks, there to remain (with periodic minor revisions) until some crisis precipitates another massive reform? The answer probably depends on whether or not highly competent, dedicated educators can either reproduce their own kind or attract successors of like competence and reputation into the enterprise. This, in turn, depends on the continuing intellectual challenge of that enterprise.

First-rate curriculum development demands the coordination of a vast array of resources: subject matter specialists, experienced teachers, educationists with a broad understanding of the schools, psychologists, programers, film makers, publishers, and skilled managers to get the most out of this talent. Experience has shown that scholars will participate for a few days during the year and for several weeks during the summer. But pre-collegiate curriculum building is not their primary interest. Nor is textbook writing a rewarded activity in universities. Some psychologists are interested in the learning problems involved, but the contribution demanded of them usually is of an applied rather than a basic research nature. Most of the problems are of central concern to educationists but their interests usually cut across subject lines. They know only too well the difficulties of putting together all the separate subjects so that a reasonable and realistic curriculum emerges. Further, they are more than a little skeptical about establishing pre-collegiate curriculum building as an ongoing university enterprise in view of their own long-term frustrating efforts to have such activity recognized as important by the academic community. If the current effort is to continue with vigor, it must either become established within the research and development framework of universities or be taken over by new institutions capable of reaching both the resources needed and the schools.

Whether the controlling agencies be universities or other nonprofit institutions, they must exert influence on the education of teachers. Today's teachers came up through the programs which they are now being asked to replace. The college curricula from which they graduated are in need of wholesale reform. To expect these teachers to depart radically from what they know best is expecting a great deal. Many are making the change — and experiencing a sense of adventure in doing so. But the big change in pre-collegiate schooling will come about in twenty years when today's children in changing schools are teachers — provided the present momentum of reform is maintained.

It is fair to say that the current curriculum reform movement has not yet developed effective means for influencing content and pedagogy in those colleges and universities preparing tomorrow's teachers, school leaders, and teachers of teachers. Until it does, it will not provide for continuing self-renewal.

▶7

Curriculum Decisions

INSTITUTIONAL: TOWARD IMPROVED CURRICULUM ORGANIZATION

A curriculum consists of all those learnings intended for a student or group of students. Since curriculum, as defined here, is something *intended* for students, there must be a plan specifying and justifying what they are to do and, hopefully, learn. The problems of setting forth such a plan are essentially problems of determining desirable ends for learning and of designing effective means for attaining these ends. The curriculum plan presumably aids the student in organizing separate entities into a small group of related experiences that can be kept readily in mind.

Decisions of Curriculum Organization

Educational Objectives ▪ Educational objectives (ends) should provide the first clues for determining the learnings (means) to be arranged in the curriculum. Unfortunately, school systems commonly lack a comprehensive and reasonably consistent set of objectives to guide them in making other curriculum decisions [1]. More often than not, schools possess a rather vague statement of philosophy and of goals for each subject taught. The so-called philosophy rarely is sufficiently rigorous to serve as a criterion in determining what should or should not go on in the schools,

SOURCE: *Planning and Organizing for Teaching* (Washington: National Education Association, 1963), pp. 25–50. Project on the Instructional Program for the Public Schools. Reprinted by permission of the publisher.

and the goals for subjects already in the curriculum certainly do not help in trying to determine whether other subjects should be taught.

This problem of aims goes back, in part, to the long-standing debate in American society over the purpose of our schools, a debate that is now characteristic of many societies in which, until recently, the function of schooling was scarcely questioned. Back of this debate, in turn, is the search for values to guide all phases of human activity. Since the nature of the good life in the good society is likely to remain elusive and illusory, the function of the schools is unlikely to remain static or to be satisfyingly clear.

But it is essential that societies establish and maintain processes whereby the aims of education are formulated and continuously reformulated. Such processes demand the systematic evaluation of national and worldwide trends and problems, appraisal of individual freedoms and restrictions upon them, and documentation of significant advances in knowledge. From these studies emerge implications for education.

School boards, which seldom assume adequately their responsibility of determining aims for the schools under their jurisdiction, lack the resources for conducting such studies. *We need to establish several independent regional curriculum study centers staffed with specialists in the relevant fields of inquiry for the purpose of conducting the necessary studies and disseminating their findings.* The results of their work could be of inestimable value to school boards.

Lacking the more comprehensive societal data which the proposed centers could provide, one way for boards to proceed is to poll the citizens as to their expectations for schools. Admittedly, the results of a poll reflect, at best, only wants and perceptions rather than funded knowledge. But a comprehensive expression of public sentiment provides school boards with a useful picture of lay expectations for education and a yardstick for placing vociferous criticisms of the schools in proper perspective. From such an expression, school boards have a basis for setting forth general statments of direction referred to here as *aims*.

When the expectations of many groups and individuals differ and these differences are not resolved, educational decisions are unlikely to be satisfactory to many people, regardless of how much these decisions reflect appropriate data. When the expectations of many groups coincide and educational decisions reflect this agreement but not appropriate data, these decisions are likely to be satisfactory to many people but, nonetheless, to be inadequate. But when the expectations of many groups affected by education coincide and educational decisions reflect this agreement *and* the best data available, these decisions are likely to be both sound and productive of general satisfaction.

When school boards, using competent help, set forth comprehensive sets of educational aims reflecting both funded knowledge and a considerable degree of consensus among the citizenry, school people will have directives to go by in determining objectives for learning. Objectives are statements of educational intent expressed so specifically as to establish criteria for selecting and organizing what is to be taught. A valid set of these objectives is a set that adequately reflects societal aims for schools.

A good educational objective defines both the behavior sought in the learner and areas of human experience through which this behavior is to be developed. An analysis of educational objectives [2] has revealed extensive educational commitment in our schools to the development of three types of human behavior: cognitive, psychomotor, and affective. This is a very arbitrary classification; any comprehensive human act probably involves all three types of behavior. Nonetheless, this taxonomy provides a useful tool both for determining what must go into the curriculum and for evaluating the results of teaching. Any comprehensive pattern of curriculum organization must identify the concepts (cognitive realm), skills (psychomotor realm), and values or attitudes (affective realm) to be used as guides in the selection of specific learnings.

Scope and Sequence ▪ With objectives specified, three kinds of decisions remain in organizing a school's curriculum. First, there are the decisions of arranging learnings in some kind of sequence so that one learning builds upon another. In making these decisions, one deals with the curriculum vertically or longitudinally. Second, there are the decisions of arranging learnings side by side so that they buttress each other. In making these decisions of *scope,* one views the curriculum horizontally. Third, there are the decisions of selecting the actual focal points for learning through which the school's objectives are to be attained.

Nowhere in the educational literature is there a term that conveys satisfactorily what is intended in these focal points. The words *activities* and *learning experiences* are used most frequently but are somewhat misleading. Under the circumstances, there is virtue in using the technical term *organizing centers.* Although somewhat awkward, the term does permit the inclusion of such widely divergent focal points for learning as units of work, cultural epochs, historical events, a poem, a film on soil erosion, and a trip to the zoo. The *organizing center* for teaching and learning may be as specific as a book on trees or as general as press censorship in the twentieth century. *Organizing centers determine the essential character of the curriculum.*

The problem of sequence in the curriculum is that of determining what continuing emphases are to be used in the effort to relate each subsequent learning to what has gone before and what is to follow. Bloom identifies these continuing emphases as "integrative threads" and defines them as "any idea, problem, method, or device by which two or more separate learning experiences are related" [3]. Tyler defines these threads as "organizing elements" and identifies them as concepts, skills, or values around which specific learnings are to be woven [4].

The problem of scope is that of determining how many of these integrative threads or *organizing elements* are to be developed simultaneously in a segment of the curriculum or in the curriculum as a whole. For example, should the social studies curriculum deal only with organizing elements from history, or should elements from sociology, anthropology, geography, economics, and political science be selected and combined? To a very large degree, the extent to which elements from a variety of fields are planned together determines the extent to which teachers, in turn, are likely to attempt to interrelate these elements in their teaching.

The curriculum plan should specify the organizing elements — the fundamental concepts, generalizations, and modes of inquiry to be developed throughout the school — and set forth illustrative organizing centers by means of which these elements might be developed. The teacher should have great freedom, however, in finally selecting organizing centers — the topics, problems, and units of work appropriate to the maturity of the class and relevant to the organizing elements of the school's curriculum. In this way, intended curricular sequences are clarified. Hopefully, sequence in students' learning is enhanced.

Balance in the Curriculum

Much recent and current controversy over the curriculum centers on the question of what kind and how much attention to give learners and subject matter, respectively. The prospect of stressing one to the exclusion of the other appears scarcely worthy of consideration. Nonetheless, the interested observer has little difficulty finding school practices emphasizing one component to the impoverishment of the other.

For the past decade, the stress has been away from learner-centered and toward subject-centered curriculum reform. One rarely hears terms such as *children's needs* and *developmental tasks,* so common in the late forties and early fifties. These have been replaced by subject matter concepts and structure. Already, however, there are evidences of some reversals in the current trend. Increasingly, the subject matter specialists involved in precollegiate curriculum reform are turning to psychologists and child development specialists for help in pacing learning so that it will not be accompanied by undue stress and fatigue.

The evidence from a rash of trial-and-error experiments with the early teaching of physics, chemistry, logic, and other subjects to very young children suggests that these youngsters are perfectly capable of learning fundamental concepts in these fields if properly taught. These concepts, in turn, when thoroughly understood, appear to lead to the appropriate interpretation and retention of new items of evidence. As yet, we lack the research evidence necessary for drawing conclusions about *when* students *can* master various learnings most effectively. The factor of economy — in both time and money — always must enter heavily into educational decisions. Consequently, it may be wasteful to introduce certain fundamental concepts in the physical sciences to five-year-olds when these same concepts could be developed several times more quickly with several times less effort a few year's later. Because of a few scattered studies into the delayed teaching of arithmetic and spelling conducted many decades ago, a few schools experimented with delaying the formal teaching of these subjects until the upper years of the elementary school. The evidence as to whether children graduating from such programs were comparable to youngsters graduating from regular elementary school programs in their later achievement is inconclusive or missing. Long-term longitudinal studies of this kind are badly needed. But we are not likely to have very soon the evidence needed in seeking most economical and effective placement of various school learnings.

A related issue is even less amenable to research. This involves questions pertaining to the kinds of learnings in which students *ought* to engage. Every institutional commitment to devote time to a given learning raises the possibility of detracting from some other kind of learning. From concluding that five- and six-year-olds *can* learn certain fundamental concepts of physics, chemistry, and logic, it is an easy step to conclude that these young children *should* learn these things. But such a conclusion does not necessarily follow. We have other bodies of evidence — some of it emerging from psychoanalytic inquiry, for example — suggesting that children have central, human preoccupations, the character of these shifting from developmental period to developmental period. The child struggling with the establishment of some kind of satisfactory relationship with his parents at the age of three or four also will be struggling with the refinement of certain reading skills later. The development of an impaired parental relationship may interfere with these attempts to read. We do not know.

The evidence on all of these matters at present is inconclusive. But the number of documented case studies of youngsters who fail to read and to write and spell passably well because of a variety of complex personal problems should be sufficient to restrain any zealots for educational reform who envision a long daily bout with the academic fundamentals as the good life for five-year-olds. At the same time, however, the evidence of successful downward extension without apparent damage to the psyches of children should be sufficient for those who would condemn such practices. Perhaps, for the present, to be fully conscious of the fact that answers to the question of whether or not children *can* master certain fundamental learnings do not completely answer the question of whether or not they *should* cope with them is sufficient vaccination against excess. Regrettably, concern for the illogic of deducing answers to "should" questions directly from answers to "can" questions is conspicuously absent from much current curriculum change.

To bring a field of study up to date for inclusion in the curriculum is one thing, in itself of great importance. But to actually include it in the curriculum is quite another. The new material cannot simply be slipped into a slot as one might replace a window pane or hang a door. The importance of one field must be judged against the importance of many others, some of them already in the curriculum, some not. The sequence of content in a field must be determined not only on the basis of presumed sequence of difficulty, but also on the basis of the readiness of individuals — uniquely different individuals — to learn it. Further, one must raise the question of whether these individuals, clearly capable of learning the material, might better learn something else.

Learners in Curriculum Organization ▪ Recent high points of concern for the learner in curriculum planning occurred during the thirties and forties. Efforts to translate such concern into a specific pattern of curriculum organization produced vehement and sometimes vitriolic condemnation of "life-adjustment education," the core curriculum, and proposals to organize learnings around "persistent life situations" or "developmental tasks." These patterns, often incorrectly grouped as one and the same, varied in their concern for both the learner and the realities of his society.

Recent criticisms of the schools, such as the following, imply that neglect of the fundamentals of knowledge is a result of "misplaced, sentimental overemphasis on the individual": Schools emphasize athletics too much; students are not taught the real discipline of systematic learning; success in school is measured by athletic and social activities, not by learning achievement; schools have watered-down courses; there are no intellectual standards for receiving diplomas in the high schools; anti-intellectualism is prevalent in schools; schools have degenerated into a system for coddling and entertaining the mediocre; students are allowed to choose their subjects too early; automatic promotion, automatic graduation, and report cards on which rarely is heard a discouraging word have become the rule, and children are not inspired to do their best; and teachers cannot teach as they should because they are too busy collecting milk money, attending assemblies, advising clubs, and so forth [5].

These criticisms are misleading because one can always find instances to support such generalizations, depending on where he goes and the color of glasses he chooses to wear in making his observations. Similarly, one can find sufficient examples to give rise to a different type of criticism: School curriculums are based upon a narrow conception of intellectuality; students are promoted or retained in the grades on the basis of a narrow conception of standards which is unjust to both the gifted and the slow; learning proceeds in an environment that inhibits creative individual processes of inquiry; and so on. Nonetheless, considerable educational writing of the past 30 years implied the maturation of the human self to be merely a process of unfolding in which the school was to have little more than an observing and congratulatory role. The quality of the developing self depends not only on a process of *unfolding* but also on the quality of cultivating the opportunities for *interacting and interrelating made available to the individual.* In contrast to the empty concept of unfolding is the pregnant concept of all living things having "an urge to grow and develop and to become" in keeping with their nature.

Whereas recommendations for curricular reform in the thirties and forties urged greater attention to the social and emotional needs of the learner, most current proposals emphasize the intellectual component of human individuality. Specific suggestions take two forms. Many specialists in physics, mathematics, history, literature, and languages see having knowledge as basic to functioning intelligently. This group, certainly concerned with the individual human being, proposes curricular reform that is in line with that proposed by persons who stress preservation of the cultural tradition. All of these views are lumped together in the section on subject matter which follows. Another group of specialists, however, made up primarily of psychologists and educators, is preoccupied with knowing. They stress problem solving, critical thinking, creativity, and even intuition in the individual.

Recent research into inquiry and creativity suggests that a narrow concept of school expectancy does not foster the divergent thinking so valued by this last group of specialists. Bruner, for example, fears that schools too often emphasize explicit formulations and the ability of students to reproduce verbal or numerical formulas, to the neglect of what he terms "intuitive" understanding. He sees intuition as implying "the act of grasping the meaning, significance, or structure of a problem or situation without explicit reliance on the analytic apparatus of one's craft" [6]. Bruner speculates that a process that is intuitive must call for learning general heuristic rules if it is to be taught at all. A heuristic procedure is a nonrigorous method of achieving solution to problems and is akin to the calculated or educated guess which Bruner doubts is cultivated in school. He urges the fostering of self-confidence and courage in the student, a willingness to make honest mistakes in the effort to solve problems. Then Bruner comes around to the inevitable need for balance between developing a trait of personality and knowledge of a subject. "It is no particular credit to the educator to help build the first without building the second. The objective of education is not the production of self-confident fools" [7].

Bruner's caution reminds us that there are two distinctly different kinds of curriculum planning processes that are indistinguishably intermingled in any school's curriculum but which must be sharply differentiated for both theoretical and practical aspects of planning. As stated earlier, these are as follows: first, the problem of identifying the kinds of elements around which specific learnings are to be organized; and second, the selection of specific organizing centers for learning upon which as much as possible of the learner's entire being is to be focused. The first of these is the subject of analysis in seeking to determine whether considerations extracted from learners or from subject matter are to constitute the primary basis of the curriculum plan. The second is involved in seeking to identify the specific content, learning processes, kinds of materials, and so on to be involved in the learner's inquiry. Although the first of these two kinds of problems is the one under consideration here, the second inevitably slips into the picture simply because of the intimate relationship between the two in any actual curriculum.

With respect to the first of these problems, literature on curriculum planning suggests that a curriculum organized around learners is psychological and a curriculum organized around subject matter is logical. Logical presumably "refers to an order among statements, an order which enables one to ground a given statement on more general premises and to draw further conclusions from it" [8]. By contrast, psychological is presumed to be some ordering of a learner's experience *resulting from* exposure to learning opportunities. Part of the difficulty in curriculum planning and discourse grows out of a failure to recognize the importance of distinguishing between the two processes. Ignoring the simple distinction between logical as a way of preordering and psychological as a way of describing what happens within the learner, curriculum planners have attempted to distinguish between two different kinds of preordering, one logical and the other psychological. Thus, presumably, there is a psychological curriculum organized around considerations growing out of understanding the learner and a logical curriculum growing out of understanding about subject matter. This is an illogical series of deductions basic to the much-discussed but unreal dichotomy between learners and subject matter in curriculum planning and teaching.

A scheme of curriculum organization can be logical or illogical, but it cannot be logical or *psychological*. What happens to the learner as a result of the plan of curriculum organization can be psychologically good or psychologically bad. Presumably, we seek a logical scheme of curriculum to produce outcomes in the learner that are psychologically good and, at worst, only rarely psychologically bad.

Patterns of curriculum organization differ in the bases selected for seeking a logical ordering and in the extent to which the plan, when finally put together, actually is logical. Consequently, when curriculum planners seek to use concepts of learner need, developmental tasks, or personality characteristics as a primary basis for organizing the school curriculum, the plan produced is in no way psychological even though the learner was the primary object in view throughout. The result simply is to some degree logical or illogical depending upon the degree of success obtained in using information about the learner as a basis for relating proposed learning opportunities one to another.

In spite of the millions of words written or spoken about child-centered curriculums, no detailed plan of curriculum organization based upon a consistent theory of child development ever has been worked out. Many people have sketched features of such a plan or have described in great detail the kinds of developmental processes desired in the learner. The kinds of learning processes desired in the learner do not define a curriculum plan of organization, however; they describe the desired outcome of such a plan. Perhaps Dewey [9], more than anyone else in modern times, provided us with a logical basis of planning the curriculum so that learners will start with the data of primary experience and progressively reorganize them. Interestingly, one of the important psychological outcomes sought from this particular logical scheme of curriculum organization is a perception of order among phenomena. To seek to perceive order among phenomena is to get involved with subject matter.

Subject Matter in Curriculum Organization ▪ Many people who see this perception of order as a desired end for schooling propose subject matter as the primary basis around which to organize learning opportunities. If number is a constituent element of mathematics, then number becomes a primary organizing element in curriculum planning. Similarly, if historians employ a method or methods by which to reconstruct the history of human experience, then a given historical method becomes a basis for ordering a series of activities through which such a method is to be learned.

Concern for knowledge and for knowing, presumably imbedded in the subject matter disciplines, is clearly evident in many statements of educational objectives: to develop an appreciation of the role of science in improving man's quality of living; to develop an understanding of and appreciation for scientific method; to develop skill in applying the methods of science to the practical problems of everyday living; to understand and appreciate order in the life cycle of all living things. Two different kinds of human motivation for schooling are expressed. First, ways of thinking have a *practical* utility in the immediate problems of living. Second, knowledge and ways of knowing may not have any immediate practical utility to the individual but are worth preserving because they are our cultural heritage. They are the means by which man remembers for a longer time than through the life span of a man or a woman and are thus the basis upon which a culture grows and continuously enriches itself.

During the past several decades, schools tended toward a practically oriented subject matter component of the curriculum. Textbooks sought to justify material that might not appear practical by listing human activities in which the specific learnings might have a clearly visible use. For example, square root is useful in building a set of wooden steps and aspects of trigonometry are applicable to the reading of maps.

Increasingly, however, curricular materials emerging from the new projects in mathematics, biology, chemistry, physics, geography, anthropology, and other fields are emphasizing ultimate rather than immediate practicality. Concepts become increasingly useful in the affairs of men if seen as part of a whole syntactical structure or discipline. The greater practicality of a curriculum organized to emphasize the structure of a field is argued by Schwab in this way: "Its vast superiority lies in the fact that it enables us to *anticipate* practical problems, not merely to wait until they are upon us. It provides for our future as well as our present. For scientific knowledge is knowledge ready and available of the stuff, the things, the doings, the undergoings, of which we inevitably must forge all our know-hows. Hence, theoretical or disciplined knowledge is practical knowledge virtual: a massive potential of capacities to do, to make, to alter, and to modify. . . ." [10]

In all probability, however, schools will move toward curriculums in which the immediately practical and the ultimately practical are kept reasonably in balance. This is in part because of societal expectations. Lay persons must perceive the utility of the subject matter if they are going to support it in the curriculum. But it is also because of pedagogical justification. The student is given a chance to provide tangible proof of his mastery of the nature of the discipline in dealing competently with problems of immediate practicality.

"The disciplines are practical only virtually and it is beyond all bounds of possibility that we can, in the schools alone, teach the disciplines and impart the semi-disciplines by which the lay public can extract unaided what it needs from the disciplines for present needs. Hence, there should be, not only mathematics as set theory, but mathematics as simple arithmetic calculation, as simple factoring of equations, as information about the more useful properties of curves and angles. There should not only be physics as a construction of elegant theories of atomic structure and as the derivation of theorems and equations from fundamental conservation laws and basic constants but also physics as the behavior of levers and dynamos, vacuum tubes and atomic energy plants. In biology, there is not only the almost-elegance of genetics and evolution, but also some simple consequences of our misbehavior with respect to natural resources; some facts and simple ideas about medicines, digestive tracts, sewage disposal, fluorine and water supplies, diet and cleanliness" [11].

The issue of immediate versus ultimate practicality in the organization of a subject carries over somewhat into the question of which subjects should be taught. This is an organizational problem if it can be shown that some subjects are basic to others and, therefore, should be taught before others.

Man has developed may different systems by which he classifies knowledge and the processes of knowing. For convenience and simplicity, let us identify here only four very familiar classifications of subject matter: the humanities, the social sciences, the biological sciences, and the physical sciences including mathematics. Various claims have been made for the prior significance of one or the other of these divisions and of the subject matter classifications encompassed by them. One classic organization is that erected by Comte in which physicals are the ultimate units of matter; chemicals, as next in line, are organizations of these physicals; biologicals are then organizations of chemicals, and so on. This kind of thinking is embraced in modern proposals for the hard-core subjects and often blocks the inclusion of newer disciplines or newer branches of old disciplines into the college curriculum. Delay in getting disciplines into the college curriculum delays their entry into the curriculum of elementary and secondary education. Consequently, the absence of sociology, anthropology, and psychology from the high school curriculum is apparent.

Perhaps, over the centuries, the subject matters that prevail in the curriculum are those that have been tested and retested as having root nature. But the status of a subject matter in the curriculum at a given moment in time depends heavily upon the circumstances currently believed to be most threatening to the preservation of the culture. The present emphasis on mathematics and science is due not so much to any root nature of these sciences but more to their pre-eminence in the present struggle for human survival. Should we survive the years immediately ahead, fraught as they are with the danger of human annihilation, predominant societal interest may shift to a different body of subject matter, perhaps the humanities.

The problem of establishing a rank order of subjects according to basic root nature is profoundly difficult. But the problem of establishing order at any given moment in history places subjects in competition with each other, not according to their root nature but according to their perceived contribution to the resolution of highly critical human problems. Once again, the basis of decision making shifts from the substantive to the political realm. We have no highly viable evidence as to the prior virtue of one field of inquiry over another. Sometimes we like to believe that subjects that take for study the very nature of man are themselves more virtuous than others in promoting man's humanity to man. Regrettably, a conniving priest, a thieving poet, a self-deceiving artist, and an intemperate theologian stand as occasional examples to teach us otherwise.

Still another question of organizing the curriculum around subject matter is that of placing various learnings in the sequence of topics. The approach differs according to the prevailing view of subject matter. Traditionally in arithmetic, for example, various manipulations have been arranged through the grades: adding, subtracting, multiplying, and dividing whole numbers and fractions; estimating interest; measuring rectangles, circles, and triangles. In spite of the arbitrary way in which these maneuvers are allotted to the years, months, and even weeks of schooling, there is little in their character to dictate such ordering. Consequently, there is nothing sacred about what is placed in the tenth grade; tradition rather than tested validity determines its placement.

In the structural approach to subject matter, the learner is introduced to small doses of the disciplined component at a relatively early age. Learners engage, too, in the kind of inquiry presumed to be central to the methodology of the field itself. The disciplined components increase in complexity as the learners move upward into junior and senior high school.

It has been pointed out earlier, however, that very few subject-matter specialists are able to avoid coming to grips with considerations of human development when they approach these tasks of curriculum planning. Similarly, the most child-centered curriculum worker has grave difficulties getting around the demonstrated usefulness of principles drawn from subject matter disciplines in dealing with vital life problems. To pose curriculums based solely on analyses of subject matter or solely upon observations of human development is not to pose curriculums at all. In the first instance one ends up merely with an elaboration of subject matter; in the second, with a description of the maturation processes of the learner. Neither is a curriculum as defined in this volume. It is difficult to conceive of even a theoretical mathematician, preoccupied with the elegant structure of his discipline, who would not concede the significance of data about young learners in planning a mathematical curriculum for them.

It has been said that "good teachers circumvent any shortcomings in curriculum planning" in order to teach well. But teachers should not find it necessary to expend their energies in circumventing the inadequacies of school plans for instruction. Somewhere between no planning at all and planning to the point of usurping teachers' instructional freedom lies the school plan embracing appropriate concern for learners and subject matter.

Patterns of Curriculum Organization

Good curriculum plans contain illustrative *organizing centers* at all levels and in all areas of instruction. The organizing center defines the substance of learning: the book, event, problem, epoch, experiment, or field trip selected to achieve one or more educational objectives with specific groups of learners. A basic criterion for selecting and arranging organizing centers is the *organizing element* that provides curricular continuity and sequence.

The organizing element is the thread running through a series of organizing centers, holding them together like beads on a string. The element can be a concept such as energy, selected from physics, developed through an organizing center on magnets in the primary years and an organizing center on the solar system at higher levels of schooling. It can be a generalization such as "problems of human living are a product of where and when one lives." Or the organizing element can be a mode of inquiry such as historical method.

The organizing element runs vertically through the curriculum, guiding the upward progression of students. Organizing centers are tied on to organizing elements, specifying what is to be taught to whom, listing instructional materials, and even suggesting ways of proceeding.

The organizing center may be narrow in scope: for example, when it is selected to develop only a single organizing element such as the concept of number in mathematics. Or, the scope might be somewhat broader, the organizing center being designed to develop three or four mathematical concepts simultaneously. However, so long as the center is selected to develop elements drawn from a single field, a single-subject pattern of curriculum organization emerges. Students study physics or chemistry but not general science; history or geography but not social studies.

On the other hand, the scope of the organizing center may be very broad. For example, when the teacher selects a study of the Aztecs and seeks to develop simultaneously such diverse organizing elements as historical method, art form, historical concepts of time, and geographical concepts of space, a broad-fields or core pattern of curriculum organization emerges. Students study general science but not physics or chemistry as separate subjects; social studies but not history or geography as separate entities.

Core and broad-fields patterns of curricular organization, popular in the thirties and forties, are in decline today. Current curriculum reform stresses the separate-subject pattern of organization. But what is being replaced is not all bad, nor is the new all good. As a consequence, the pendulum of change will soon swing back toward at least some features of core and broad-fields patterns of curriculum organization.

These patterns, cutting across subject divisions, favor the selection of broad organizing centers that accommodate many levels of student accomplishment and a variety of student interests. Sometimes, however, a subject supposedly taken care of in the organizing center is neglected. For example, students can compute costs of materials in a social studies unit without learning much mathematics. It is not surprising that the mathematicians (and the historians and geographers) rebelled and insisted that their subject be treated separately. But there is not room in the precollegiate curriculum for all the disciplines, treated separately, and so some must be combined or left out. At least one curriculum study is now exploring ways of combining mathematics and science in the elementary school. Further work of this kind, across the full spectrum of elementary and secondary school subjects, is likely to follow.

One of the difficulties encountered in seeking to differentiate one pattern of curriculum organization from another is that a school's curriculum plan must be described. This calls for "putting something on paper." Subject matter and paper are highly compatible, and so efforts to describe a broad-fields or core curriculum often end up simply as elaborations of content. To put on a two-dimensional page a three-dimensional process involving the creative synthesis of learners, subject matter, and the kinds of learning intended (cognitive, for example) is a task that tries the imagination. At the point that ideas must be translated onto the page, a kind of rigor mortis sets in. The dynamic interchanges envisioned collapse into a dull listing of topics for study.

One approach to circumventing this problem is the elaboration of resource units, a particular type of organizing center. In the core curriculum, the resource unit begins with a persistent social problem determined through the joint planning of students and teacher. Not just any problem suffices. The problem must be one which is of interest to students of the age group. Further, it must be a problem of vital significance to society. Third, it must permit extensive use of source materials and the organization of data. Fourth, the problem must hold promise for leading the group to a subsequent problem for study.

Of the many criticisms directed at the social problems type of organization, two have predominated. First, critics see too much freedom of student choice in the plan, with the resulting danger that student involvement in planning will lead to the selection of trivial problems that do not add up to a sequential pattern. However, there is nothing in the theory itself to say that this development is a natural result. In fact, proponents of the core curriculum see the danger and offer criteria to protect against it.

The second major criticism, perhaps more pertinent, is that the *disciplined* as contrasted with the *practical* component of subject matter is neglected. Maintaining syntactical or substantive relationships in a variety of subject fields brought together in a social problem is no easy teaching task. It is fair to say that core-type curriculums in practice emphasize the problem selected for study rather than the organizing elements around which these units are to be arranged. Consequently, teachers and students alike, in their enthusiasm for the topic, may very well lose sight of the need to develop some fields of inquiry in a systematic fashion.

Another type of resource unit, increasing in popularity, is one organized around problems growing directly out of components of the discipline. Thus resource units can be developed using a series of problem situations in which aspects of the substantive concept of energy recur. Exponents of this approach are enthusiastic over the ease with which even very young children of normal intelligence grasp abstract relationships among phenomena when the situations within which these phenomena are introduced are sufficiently simple, concrete, and appealing to the children.

This approach begins with subject matter and looks outward to see how the subject matter can be made vital and interesting to children. Consequently, the organizing elements for determining continuity and sequence are drawn from the substance and syntax of the field itself. Because of this fact, critics of such an approach maintain that only lip service is given to the progressive development of learners. They maintain that the learner is considered only to the degree that the organizing centers can be made appealing and attractive. Thus, motivation always is extrinsic. There is a fear that determination of what children *should* learn is deduced only from what children *can* learn. Consequently, these critics claim, there is the tendency to ignore the developmental cycles of child and adolescent development within which satisfactory adjustment to parents, peers, members of the opposite sex, and ultimately to one's self are of vital importance.

Again, there is a need for balance. During the 1930's, 1940's, and into the 1950's, some educators overemphasized the importance of so-called psychological readiness. There were fears that too early exposure to hard subjects, long periods of uninterrupted work, and pressure of subject matter were conducive to poor mental health and warped personalities. There is little evidence to substantiate such claims. There is even less evidence to support the present grade-level designation of required learnings involving so much addition and subtraction in the second grade, so much multiplication and division in the third, and so much long division in the fourth. Clearly, there is a need for extensive research not only into the best time for introducing a variety of learnings — neither too early nor too late — but also into the circumstances surrounding the learning processes which are most conducive to the sound psychological development of the individual.

It will be noted from the above analysis of resource units that a supposed strength of the learner-centered unit is a supposed weakness of the subject-centered unit and vice versa. Consequently, in any elaboration of units based on some theory of child development, it is of vital importance that organizing elements from *subject matter* be clearly identified or the disciplines may be ignored because of preoccupation with sequences of human development. Conversely, in resource units organized around some concept of subject matter structure, it is essential that keen attention be devoted to elaborating crucial developmental stages in the life of the learner and describing how these may be affected by the proposed subject matter teachings.

The kind of behavioral outcome intended is a key factor in determining the kinds of activities to be built into the organizing center for learning. If the intent is to develop attitudes toward people of other lands, of other races, and of other religious groups and yet all of the learning is directed to a textbook-oriented, cognitive analysis of differences, the desired attitudes may never develop. In many kinds of cognitive learnings, an actual background of experience with the phenomena studied is a desirable prerequisite. In the development of motor skills, an analysis of the present development of the child is crucial. In the development of value and attitudes, concrete examples that serve as models have their place. The degree to which any one of these considerations is emphasized depends in large measure upon the outcome intended. An analysis of proposed organizing centers for learning in books, courses of study, and teacher handbooks suggests that extraordinarily little attention has been given in the past to identification of the precise outcome desired and to the description of learner activities compatible with the attainment of such outcomes.

Conclusions and Implications

Previous pages suggest many needed improvements in curriculum organization. School boards need to assume responsibility for formulating comprehensive sets of educational aims. From these, in turn, the professional staff must formulate precise objectives for the guidance of instruction and evaluation. A school's curriculum plan must emphasize fundamental concepts, skills, and values, leaving the teacher relatively free to select specific activities appropriate to the development of individual children.

An analysis of current curriculum practices reveals that, at best, only a handful of school districts is dealing with these tasks in anything approaching adequacy, even though much curriculum reform is under way. Few school districts possess any over-all scheme by means of which the several tasks are placed in perspective and on some timetable of attack. Few states possess adequate policies regarding the respective roles of state and local school districts in curriculum building. In fact, most curriculum bulletins developed by state departments of education contain a hodge-podge of specifications, ranging from lists of values and aims to elaboration of techniques for teaching specific subjects.

Local school districts still use committees of teachers for the development of curriculum guides, although this practice has declined in recent years, especially at the secondary school level. Their work often is cyclical in nature. The teachers take many of their cues for what should be taught from existing textbooks, and textbook publishers, in turn, use these curriculum guides in determining what should go into the texts. Little wonder that the curriculums of America's schools need revision!

The updating of curriculum content and materials is now following a new route. Committees of specialists and teachers in mathematics, physics, biology, chemistry, and more recently, social sciences and humanities, supported by substantial foundation grants, are developing and testing revised content, teaching procedures, and instructional materials. Their products are then produced and distributed by commercial publishers.

To date, one important element in this process appears to be missin'

The responsibility of determining aims, objectives, subjects to be taught, relationships among subjects, and so on, rests (as it should) with state and local school authorities. They, in turn, are heavily dependent upon political forces and subject to the exhortations of textbook publishers. As pointed out earlier, the respective responsibilities of state and local education agencies are not at all clear. *These agencies need, then, the advice of bodies divorced from both political and commercial affiliations. These might very well be the regional curriculum study centers recommended on the opening pages of this chapter.*

These centers might be located in the eastern, western, central, and southern sections of the country. They would require, in addition to a central staff of persons knowledgeable about the theory and practice of curriculum planning, access to competent specialists in the behavioral sciences and in each of the academic disciplines. Because of this fact and the need for these centers to be independent in their inquiry, they should be located in major universities possessing rich graduate resources.

At the outset, each center should select an area of curricular emphasis and plan to cooperate with other centers. One center might select as its initial emphasis the collection and dissemination, at regular intervals, of data providing a status picture of curriculum and instruction in the public schools. A second might emphasize experimentation in curriculum sequences, seeking to determine appropriate timing and pacing for introducing learnings and regulating the progress of learners of varying abilities. A third, perhaps located near Washington, D.C., might study patterns of curriculum decision-making at local, state, and national levels. A fourth might develop techniques for appraising instructional materials and release the results of its analyses for professional groups involved in the selection of learning resources.

These should not be degree-granting centers, although many members of the staffs should be members of university departments in which courses and seminars for degrees are offered. The involvement of professors in these centers would enrich their teaching. The centers most certainly should provide a wide range of refresher clinics and mid-career institutes for teachers, supervisors, curriculum directors, and administrators. Any school system seeking to bring its staff members up to date in their respective fields would have the opportunity of sending able personnel to these centers. In this way, of course, school districts would participate in the financial costs of maintaining the centers. In return, they would receive both consultant help from a considerable field staff and the upgrading of their own personnel.

Such centers would provide unique opportunity for the cooperative participation and mutual profit of Federal, state, and local governmental agencies. With access to center status studies, the U.S. Department of Health, Education, and Welfare would be able to determine at any given moment the need for educational personnal deemed in too short supply for national welfare. The U.S. Office of Education could then make available to all centers funds for the selection and mid-career training of educational specialists. The work of a center emphasizing experimentation with curricular sequences for learners of varied abilities would provide state departments of education with evidence for guiding them in providing funds for the teaching of various subject fields. Instead of authorizing expenditures for any schools desiring instruction in a foreign language, the state might choose to provide funds for the center to experiment with several cooperating schools. Local school boards, confused and perplexed over community pressure to use certain instructional materials, could draw upon expert analyses carried on in a setting of impartiality.

The establishment of university centers for inquiry, experimentation, and research in curriculum planning could alleviate much of the lag and professional confusion over curriculum problems and issues. At present, substantive and political considerations are almost hopelessly interwoven. Political realities, part of the process of human action and compromise, become confused with philosophical, biological, psychological, and sociological knowledge and understanding. The data of political feasibility and strategy become indistinguishable from the data of human desirability and confused to the point of panic over desirable ends and means for our schools.

REFERENCES

1. MARGARET P. AMMONS. *Educational Objectives: The Relation Between the Process Used in Their Development and Their Quality*. Doctor's thesis. Chicago: University of Chicago, 1961.
2. BENJAMIN S. BLOOM ed. *Taxonomy of Educational Objectives*. New York: Longmans, Green and Company, 1956.
3. BENJAMIN S. BLOOM. "Ideas, Problems, and Methods of Inquiry," *The Integration of Educational Experiences*. Fifty-Seventh Yearbook, Part III, National Society for the Study of Education. Chicago: University of Chicago Press, 1958, pp. 84–85.
4. RALPH W. TYLER. *Basic Principles of Curriculum and Instruction*. Chicago: University of Chicago Press, 1950.
5. These criticisms are culled from a list of 25 gathered from an examination of newspapers, magazines, and books. See C. E. MERRILL. *Professional Reactions to Criticisms of the Schools*. New York: Council for Administrative Leadership, December 1959, p. 2.

6. JEROME S. BRUNER. *The Process of Education.* Massachusetts: Harvard University Press, 1960, p. 55.
7. *Ibid.,* p. 65.
8. JAMES E. McCLELLAN. "The Logical and the Psychological: An Untenable Dualism?" *Language and Concepts in Education.* (Edited by B. Othanel Smith and Robert H. Ennis.) Chicago: Rand, McNally and Company, 1961, p. 147.
9. See especially: JOHN DEWEY. *Democracy and Education.* New York: The Macmillan Company, 1916.
10. JOSEPH J. SCHWAB. *Education and the Structure of the Disciplines.* Paper prepared for the Project on the Instructional Program of the Public Schools, National Education Association. Washington, D.C.: the Project, September 1961. (Duplicated)
11. *Ibid.,* p. 46.

INSTRUCTIONAL: THE TEACHER SELECTS, PLANS, ORGANIZES

The right decision at the right moment is the essence of good teaching. Right decisions are those that time learning perfectly for the individual student. A series of such decisions moves the student forward at an optimum pace. Obviously, such timing and pacing are no more accidental than is a perfect catch by the professional outfielder. They are the result of careful planning and organizing on the part of the teacher.

The teacher must have a reasonably clear picture of what the learner will know or do when he has accomplished certain learning. Otherwise, how can the teacher know if anything worthwhile is resulting from the teaching-learning effort? He must see to it that what the student seeks to know builds readily on what he already knows. He must decide when to begin an activity and when to bring it to a close; when to use a student interest and when to pass it by; when to insist on exactness and when to sacrifice exactness to feeling. All these things and more the teacher must take into account in timing and pacing students' learning.

Some components of the learning-teaching act are quite predictable. The teacher can select the book to read, the problem to study or the skill to master. He can anticipate who will grasp new ideas quickly and who

SOURCE: *Learning and the Teacher* (Washington: The Association, 1959), pp. 39–60. Copyright © 1959, by the Association for Supervision and Curriculum Development. Reprinted by permission of the publisher.

will grapple with them in a cumbersome fashion. The experienced teacher can even predict the kinds of difficulties the class will encounter and who in the group will express greatest frustration. These things are the environmental conditions in teaching; they exist. They can be consciously encompassed within the teacher's "span of control," if the teacher chooses to do so. Or, these factors can be ignored, left to operate quite by chance.

But the learning-teaching act is profoundly affected by powerful forces that cannot initially be brought within an operational span of control. Teachers and learners alike are "carriers" of pressures, prejudices, optimism, pessimism and other attitudes which may aid or retard learning. The teacher plans carefully by bringing into synthesis those conditions that are known to him. And then, variable winds loaded with radioactive materials blow in upon the scene contaminating all that they touch. The best-laid plans are distorted or obliterated. Nonetheless, to the extent that the teacher carefully accounts for all that is relatively stable, to that extent variables are likely only to modify rather than destroy what has been planned.

The job of the teacher is to set up a series of catch-hold points — organizing centers for learning — that will initiate certain desired reactions on the part of students. It is impossible (and undesirable even if it were possible) to prescribe the series of such organizing centers to be set up for any group. It is possible only to analyze what is involved in the planning-organizing process. Consequently, this paper proceeds through the following phases:

1. An analysis of the factors (environmental conditions) that the professional teacher should take into account in planning the learning-teaching act.

2. An analysis of certain variables that must be screened out or used constructively if initial plans are to be successfully modified in action.

3. A presentation of criteria to be applied in actually setting up the stimuli from which learners are to derive their educational experiences.

An Episode in Planning

The following episode involving a teacher and a supervisor illustrates, in part, key points in the preceding introduction. The left-hand column records the discussion just as it proceeded. The right-hand column provides a running analysis to reveal: (a) some of the factors that can and should be encompassed within the teacher's span of control; (b) some of the variables that intrude and that can impede or aid learning and teaching; and (c) some of the considerations that should enter into the selection of situations in which students are to learn.

EPISODE · ANALYSIS

Scene 1

Teacher: I wish you would help me with social studies; it's the poorest time of the day. I don't know what the trouble is.

Supervisor: Well, why don't we begin there.

T.: Well, as you know, the social studies framework lists "The Community" for the second grade.

Specific content to be taught determined in advance of the actual situation.

S.: And are you doing "The Community"?

T.: Oh, I'm doing "The Community" all right. I began with the Police Department; next we did the Post Office; now we're up to the dairy and the grocery store.

The process of learning being promoted seems to imply a rather static concept of learning: we "cover" things; we "did" the Post Office.

S.: Have the children responded?

T.: I can't seem to get them interested or to hold their interest. In years before, I felt that I was successful but not with this group. They just don't seem interested in anything.

Recognition on the part of the teacher that she must have interest and attention from the group if the children are to derive any learning. Absence of interest and attention in this group is noted by the teacher.

S.: Have you tried other things?

T.: It wouldn't do any good; all they want to do is look out of the window at the steam shovel. We're having a new addition, you know.

The teacher displays a certain personal futility. She notes the intrusion of a factor not planned for that currently is working as a deterrent to the learning she visualizes for the group.

S.: Maybe we could build a unit around that.

T.: Oh, I wouldn't know enough. I don't know a thing about machinery, and besides I'd feel guilty.

The teacher reveals an insight into herself as an informed person. She expresses insecurity over the prospect of proceeding with learning activities not indicated in the course of studies.

EPISODE	ANALYSIS
S.: About what?	
T.: About not doing the dairy and the grocery store — they're in the course of studies, you know.	Teacher reveals a narrow view of the curriculum as topics to be taught because they're included in the course of studies.
S.: As "musts"?	
T.: Yes; or maybe . . . Well, I don't know for sure.	
S.: What have you done in social studies?	
T.: Well, when we studied the Police Department, I told them about the work of the police.	
S.: Did they see a policeman?	Supervisor points to the necessity of direct experience in concept formation.
T.: Oh no, we aren't incorporated, you know. We have a deputy sheriff here when we need him.	
S.: And the Post Office?	
T.: That wasn't successful either. I didn't take them to our Post Office. It's so little and uninteresting. If we could have gone to the downtown city Post Office it would have been different. I just had them read the Post Office books instead. But they weren't interested and the books seemed too difficult.	Sterile viewpoint regarding the learning process is demonstrated again.
S.: Suppose we think about the steam shovel for a minute. How long has the crew been working?	Supervisor introduces the possibility of turning a negative influence into a positive one.
T.: Only a few days, but it seems like an age. The children could give you a blow by blow account. They know it by heart.	
S.: Why don't we ask the foreman if he will talk with us a little about the possibilities of giving	

the children some real information regarding the work?

Scene 2 (Teacher and Supervisor
have returned from excavation.)

Teacher: I never would have realized there was so much to be
considered. How can I make the
most of it? I know I will have to
plan, of course, but what always
bothers me is what to have them
do later. There are steam shovel
stories, I know.

Supervisor: Why not have them
write their own story?

T.: The words will be so difficult — motor, excavation, time
schedule, night crew. Maybe we
could substitute some easier ones.

S.: Let's try using the real ones.
You know, we often talk about the
value of vivid real life experiences
in accelerating children's reading
and speaking.

T.: And using the hard words?

S.: Maybe we'll test that, too;
which are hard, which are easy?
What makes words "hard," any-
way? The smallest words — the,
and — often seem the hardest for
children because they have nothing to hang onto them.

T.: What about the steam shovel
stories?

S.: We can always use them
later.

T.: What about arithmetic?
We're doing two-column addition.

The teacher begins to think about
a range of factors that must be
taken into account in planning a
different kind of setting for learning. The need for initiating plans,
for following through, and the
need for materials are brought
into her thinking.

The supervisor injects the idea of
using one initiating point for fulfilling several educational ends.

Again, the supervisor introduces
a view of learning that is compatible with research and theory of
recent decades.

The supervisor challenges some
conventional notions about sequence based on apparent complexity.

The teacher shows an awareness
of the need for having learnings in
one area relate to learnings in another.

S.: How are you getting along?

T.: Oh, it's the same old story. The fast ones can do it; the slow ones are struggling.

S.: Maybe this steam shovel business will give us an opportunity to put the children's keen interest to work on arithmetic, too.

T.: Like the reading groups?

S.: Why not?

T.: I think I'm beginning to see. Some children could keep daily records while others could add up the hours in the week. This would help all of us; the parents are a little anxious about the children's success in addition.

The teacher reveals the familiar difficulty of dealing effectively with individual differences in many areas.

Again the supervisor demonstrates the consistent application of a modern view of learning based on evidence.

The teacher begins to relate a number of considerations that must be taken into account in planning. She begins to visualize what the children would be doing. This is quite a step from viewing learnings as topics to be "covered."

This conference between supervisor and teacher brings to our attention virtually all of the factors that must be accounted for in planning the learning-teaching act: the content of instruction, the learners themselves, the processes through which effective learning proceeds, and the materials to be used. Reading between the lines, two other factors are seen as significant in teacher planning. The teacher possesses a sense of direction, a view of where he is going with a particular group of learners. In addition, the teacher has a view of himself as a teacher and a person: what he can and cannot do, what he knows and doesn't know, and so forth. Taken together these factors constitute the teacher's span of control.

The conference reveals further that what insight one possesses in each of these categories makes a significant difference to his planning. This teacher's view of direction focused attention on what was to be covered and, as a result, the curriculum was equated with a course of studies. For her the prospect of moving away from prescribed content created guilt feelings of such proportions as to inhibit this teacher in seeking to function as a creative human being. As a result, her insight into the importance of interest and attention was relegated to an academic status. She intellectualized her awareness but did not put it to work.

The episode reveals, too, the influence of factors not initially brought within one's span of control. For example, the steam shovel moved unexpectedly to adjacent ground and noisily announced itself as a threat to both planned activities and the teacher's sanity. To the teacher it was just a nuisance, a disruptive influence. To the supervisor it was an opportunity to make learning real and meaningful. Some such intrusions are, indeed, a very real threat (as, for example, administrative instructions to follow the course of studies) and the teacher must do everything in his power to keep them from contaminating the learning process. But others are pennies from heaven to be used as premium payments on the learning capital.

In the conversation, the supervisor implies certain conditions that characterize the desirable catch-hold point for learning. For example, she points out the significance of finding a stimulus that fulfills several educational objectives simultaneously. The teacher, too, recognizes that very little learning results unless the organizing center challenges learners at several different attainment levels.

The balance of this paper develops and illustrates the central concepts about planning and organizing that have been introduced so far. Of the six factors already identified as significant in the teacher's span of control, only three are used in developing this concept further: learners, learning processes, and content.

The Teacher's Span of Control

Classroom climate is dependent upon the interoperation of factors which can be modified. Each teacher must develop a framework for organizing and interpreting data pertinent to the guidance of learning processes. The range of factors that might constitute such a framework already has been indicated. The extent to which these factors are brought into the teacher's decision-making constitutes his span of control. Facts, principles and theories regarding the factors included and the composition of a teacher's span of control may not be in close agreement. The teacher may encompass and draw from little more than tradition. But the opportunity to be more scientific is ever present. Happily, then, one's span of control can become more precise and useful through dedicated personal effort.

The teacher's span of control should be comprehensive enough to include all the major factors which are pertinent to teaching. At the same time, however, it must be limited enough so that the entire group of factors may be considered in decision-making. The categories must be able to absorb relevant data. And the categories must be flexible so that outdated facts and principles can be eliminated and new findings included.

With a sound span of control, the teacher is in considerable command of the *science* of teaching and ready to engage in the *art* of teaching.

Learners in the Teacher's Span of Control ▪ Courses in educational psychology, child development or adolescent psychology are standard in pre-service teacher education programs. At the in-service level, thousands of teachers across the land have participated in various kinds of child study programs. The teaching profession obviously believes that it is important for teachers to understand the learners they teach. But perhaps this is only "soft" pedagogy, a concern motivated by ends other than rigorous learning. Does inclusion of the learner in the teacher's span of control really make any difference to the student's learning? Or, must the teacher's effort to understand learners be written off as humanitarian or "the thing to do"?

There is some evidence to suggest that teacher knowledge of human development in general, and of a specific group in particular affects the teaching-learning process. Ginther [1], in a comprehensive survey of one large child study program, found that the classroom performance of teachers who had participated for three or more years could be differentiated positively from that of teachers who had not participated at all. His study points to the importance of gaining general insight into human development and the characteristics of successive age groups. Sturgis [2] explored the relationship between teachers' knowledge of the groups they taught and the achievement of these classes. College physics teachers were each given detailed information about one class section and practically no information about parallel class sections. The findings suggest that college students achieve more when their instructors have a great deal of information about them as individuals.

Studies such as these support theories attesting to the importance of rapport between students and their teachers. Energies used in coping with teacher-student conflict are not available to the teacher for teaching or to the student for learning. The effort, then, to plan and organize the classroom around what we know about human beings in general and about these individuals in particular is not peripheral. It is central to the function of schooling and the task of the teacher. Knowledge of learners, then, must be included in the teacher's span of control.

Learning Processes in the Teacher's Span of Control ▪ More than 25 years ago, when the writer began his teaching, he believed that adequacy of learning is the product of general ability, as revealed by intelligence quotient, and of motivation for the tasks to be accomplished. From this beginning, he went on to equate motivation with time and drill. And so, several spring afternoons each week when the days were lengthening and young adolescents' thoughts were wandering even more than usual, a dozen weary seventh graders and an even wearier young teacher gave extra time to the intricacies of common fractions. The results were far from encouraging. The class drilled on the three types of manipulations involved in the range of percentage problems. But, when ultimately a simple problem was posed, the youngsters invariably asked, "Which type do I use?"

Studies by Haggard [3] and others reveal the need for a more comprehensive learning formula than the one once used by the writer. Certainly intelligence and motivation are essential to high level learning, other things being equal. But intelligence must be functional in that it can be put constructively to work. And motivation can be of such order that the student activity is reduced to inertia. The individual must have energy for learning over and above the energy needed for coping with personal daily needs, otherwise he cannot approach problems creatively, in a way that results in learning increments. Learning, then, is a product of intelligence, motivation, energy, and creativity. This is the kind of learning formula that teachers must encompass within their span of control and put to work in planning and organizing the learning-teaching process.

Content in the Teacher's Span of Control ▪ Teachers at all levels of education are predominantly content-centered: They depend heavily on what is to be taught to carry the burden of instruction. This remains true in spite of the concern expressed in recent decades for learners and learning. But one can become a student of learners and of learning without significantly enhancing his ability to teach. Teachers have found that psychological principles must be translated into implications before they are useful. Similarly, one can become a student of history, chemistry or the fine arts without giving enough thought to the relation of his field to teaching.

Content is organized into subjects to preserve knowledge and to expedite the accretion of new knowledge. To serve education, content must be organized for instructional purposes. The most significant organization for teaching is that which exists at a given moment in a teacher's mind. The teacher must be both a student of content organized for preservation and an organizer of content for instruction.

Certain aspects of English teaching provide a useful illustration of the teacher's role in synthesizing content for instruction. For years our elementary and secondary schools taught what the linguistic scientist calls "referential" grammar. For example, a noun is defined as the name of a person, place or thing and thus refers to something outside of language structure itself. The linguistic scientist insists that "differential" grammar should be taught. That is, a noun should be differentiated from other parts of speech according to the function it performs within the sentence itself. The student then learns the structure of his language rather than a series of definitions which carry him away from how our language is put together. The English teacher whose concept of grammar is of the old-fashioned variety denies his students the view of content they should have. Such a teacher includes content within his span of control but it is misleading content that language specialists do not approve.

Considerations of content do not alone determine planning and teaching. But knowledge has its own integrity, an integrity that must be respected in the face of other considerations in the learning-teaching act. The elementary school teacher who, for example, concentrates entirely on only the social-usage aspects of arithmetic ignores the fact that mathematics is built upon a deductive system. After years of exposure to such arithmetic, the student remains unaware of mathematics as an organized field of human inquiry. Similarly, unless the social studies teacher is familiar with historical method, the class may move romantically from era to era and locale to locale without coming to grips with the rigorous method of the historian. A too limited or an erroneous view of content in the teacher's span of control deprives all but the self-directing student of an education.

Synthesizing the Components of the Learning-Teaching Act ▪ In planning for teaching, the skilled teacher visualizes a synthesis of the student, something to be learned, and a process through which student and something to be learned are to be united. As previously suggested, the kind of synthesis depends on the teacher's internalized conception of where he hopes to go with a given group of learners and certain insights into his own ability to carry the group forward. It is conditioned, too, by the materials, facilities, time and space at the teacher's disposal. In effect, the teacher poses certain organizing centers for learning — catch-hold places — for moving forward educationally. In large measure, the adequacy of these centers is dependent upon the adequacy of the organizing framework — span of control — developed by the teacher.

The needs, interests and wants of students are inadequate as the *sole* basis for organizing the instructional program, however important such considerations may be as a beginning point. Similarly, subject matter must never be *both* the point to begin and the point to terminate learning. But learners and subject matter, together with the processes through which behavioral changes occur, constitute the solid matter of the learning-teaching act [4]. These factors are largely controllable in that the teacher knows they will always be present and that a body of lore about each is available. New insights constantly emerge but at least the teacher can develop a framework for encompassing and dealing with additions and changes. In many ways, the information in these categories provides the basis for a science of teaching. Insight into them is requisite to planning and, ultimately, to setting up effective centers for learning.

Variables in Planning and Organizing

The creative teacher is an artist who synthesizes the components of the learning-teaching act under conditions that cannot always be predicted. Influences that shift like the weather upset the planning of even the most mature and experienced teachers. These influences find their way into the classroom through teachers and students who become "carriers" of attitudes which affect learning. The teacher serves both as a screen in keeping some influences out of the classroom and as a guide in dealing effectively with others. His success in dealing constructively with influences that could be disrupting stems in large measure from his control of the more stable factors that can be anticipated in planning. Following are a few samples of the variables that cannot be neatly planned for, but which can become positive influences when the teacher is aware of them.

Conflicting Goal Perceptions ▪ To get launched on his first teaching experience in an eight-grade one-room school, the writer was given three courses of study: a pink one for the primary grades, a blue one for the intermediate grades, and a yellow one for the two junior high grades in the class. Each of these formidable documents contained an impressive list of educational objectives challenging teacher and class to work toward all the virtues ever expounded by human beings. The writer taught 56 periods a day in pursuit of these goals: According to his primitive arithmetic, seven subjects for each of eight grades gave a total of 56 lessons. But not much constructive learning occurred. After six weeks of frustration for teacher and students alike, both became vaguely aware that something was wrong. Teacher and students now held a goal in common — the identification and solution of a discomforting problem. And for the first time, paper goals were in some danger of accomplishment!

Teachers have drives and these do not always coincide with high-sounding statements of educational objectives. Students, too, have drives and these often conflict both with the paper statements and the drives of their teachers. These personal drives of teachers and students are dynamic in contrast to the static nature of paper goals. They channel human energy in their expression, energy that is thus diverted from the attainment of less compelling goals.

Attainment of program objectives is unlikely when teacher goals and student goals are at cross-purposes. Teachers must plan, then, to let students have a meaningful part in the planning so that teacher goals, student goals and paper goals come to the surface where conflicts may be examined. Little children can help decide what they will do next and how they should behave when the teacher leaves the room for a few minutes. Older children can plan their day and evaluate its effectiveness. By the time students are in the intermediate and upper elementary grades they should be planning both their weekly schedule and units of several weeks' duration. Students who leave the elementary school without such skills are walking indictments of their teachers. They learn these skills by having many opportunities to practice them.

The creative teacher sets goals. But he anticipates the emergence of goals that cannot be planned for in advance. When unproductive goals appear to block productivity, he provides the opportunity for these new goals to be expressed and, hopefully, to be dissipated. When unanticipated goals appear to be productive, he strives for group acceptance of these in order that all members of the group may move toward common purposes.

Inadequate Perceptions of the Curriculum ▪ The courses of studies prepared for and by teachers are intended only as guides to planning and teaching. But, often, teachers come to view the suggested content as sacred. As the teacher said to the supervisor about the dairy and the grocery store, "They're in the course of study, you know."

Teachers are urged to use the interests of learners and the problems of the community as organizing centers for learning. But can one pay simultaneous homage to both the topics outlined in the course of studies and children's interests or community problems? The supervisor suggested that the steam shovel be studied, but what would happen to the Post Office and the Police Department? The dilemma of the teacher and the apparent conflict here often create tensions not conducive to learning. The dilemma and the tensions can be relieved in part by distinguishing between constants and variables in the curriculum.

In planning, the teacher must search for guides to the selection of what is to be taught. The concepts, skills and values in well-defined statements of goals provide criteria for selecting learner interests and community problems around which instruction can be organized. The teacher then asks regarding such emerging interests and problem, "Will they contribute to the building of this concept or that skill?" If no unique interests and problems emerge, he may then decide to proceed with the topic in the course of studies. Vision of the concepts, skills and values to be developed provides stability and degrees of freedom in teaching. The framework thus established gives the teacher security in departing from the course of studies in the selection of topics for study. These concepts, skills and values are the relatively constant curricular threads; topics in the course of studies, learner interests and community problems are the multi-colored beads from which specific learning stimuli may be selected.

Prevailing Perceptions of Coverage ▪ Teachers are guided in varying degrees by prevailing expectations for what shall be "covered" in given periods of time. General expectations are derived from the graded lock-step of American elementary and secondary education: long division in the fourth grade, fractions in the fifth and sixth, percentage in the seventh and eighth, and so on. Specific expectations often are set by departmental chairmen, principals or supervisors. But perhaps the most formidable concept of coverage is that imposed by the teacher upon himself and subsequently upon his class: up to here by Thanksgiving, to this page by Christmas, half the year's work by the end of January, and so on.

Arbitrary, content-dominated prescriptions can and do block the teacher from using dynamic principles of learning. Students should indeed pursue a pace that challenges the slowest and the quickest. But this means differing rates of progress for differing capacities, as Chapter Four points out. A pace determined in advance for all on the basis of content-to-be-covered is a destructive pace, ill-suited to the differences present in every group of learners.

The teacher, of course, needs an awareness of what constitutes adequate progress for "average" students of a given age. Such an awareness helps in seeking to quicken the pace for the fast and to retard it for the slow. But such an awareness is something to be brought within the teacher's span of control and not into the classroom. The teachers must "screen out" the inappropriate pressure of arbitrary coverage and set a pace appropriate to classroom realities.

Prevailing Perceptions of Standards ▪ Throughout America is heard a cry for higher standards in our schools. It would not be difficult to show that many students are neither using certain capacities nor developing others to their full potential. Any conscientious teacher dealing each day with 35 (or 150) widely differing individuals will readily confess that seeking to challenge all of them is probably the most frustrating aspect of his work. But the threat of imposing an arbitrary higher standard upon all is unlikely to produce higher levels of performance by all.

In some communities in the South, educators have been told that they should seek to raise the standards of Negro students in order to prepare them for easier integration with white students. The word has been passed along to teachers — often with devastating classroom results. Raised standards do not equate with increasing the pressure to learn. The learning that results often is of a sterile, rote sort. The writer visited the classrooms of some dedicated Negro teachers who reacted conscientiously to this kind of call to elevate standards. In many classrooms, they had completely eliminated the use of direct experience so essential to concept formation. Field trips, for example, were too time-consuming, they said. "We must get on with our teaching." The kind of discussion in which values are clarified had been all but eliminated. Teaching and learning were predominantly textbook-centered, with teachers asking factual questions and the students responding parrotlike. The educational clock was turning steadily backward. In learning, the shortest distance between two points is not necessarily a straight line.

The only concept of standards that has any validity to educators is that of providing quality learning experiences for all. This is what schools are for. The application of arbitrary achievement standards demands neither schools nor teachers. It requires merely test-makers and examiners who will call our young people together periodically to measure what has been memorized.

Quality learning experiences cannot be of "high standard" based upon an arbitrary norm for all. But they should be of high standard in regard to certain internal characteristics. These internal characteristics are discussed in some detail in the next section of the chapter. Above all, quality learning involves a dedication to learning of the sort discussed in Chapter Eight. Such dedication is not too much to ask of all enrolled in our schools.

When teachers pay attention to the expanding body of lore that underlies professional behavior and encompass it firmly within their span of control, they discover that achievement standards go up. The faculty of the Englewood (Florida) Elementary School engaged each year in concentrated study of a curricular area. In 1955–56, science was selected for study [5]. The group, in regular weekly meetings, never referred to higher standards as such. But it talked much of curricular organization, the scientific abilities to be developed in all, the basic concepts appropriate to elementary school science, and the kinds of instructional activities appropriate to certain age groups. In the achievement tests given just as these discussions were getting under way, the fourth grade scored 3.4 years when, according to national norms, the average score should have been 4.8 years. Twenty-four months later, the group was tested again. The score now was 7.1, a gain of 44 months and an average achievement of 0.4 years above the specified national norm [6]. What appeared many times to be the long, slow way around — improvement in the quality of learning for all — actually proved to be the shortest distance to "higher standards" of accomplishment.

Surely all teachers receive a warm glow of satisfaction from the accomplishments — all kinds of accomplishments — of their students. They will be denied these satisfactions if they allow inappropriate pressures to seduce them into planning shortcuts to learning that violate what they know about the nature of learning. As attractive as such seduction may appear to be, it can lead, nonetheless, only to disillusionment.

Certain Perceptions of the Learning Process ▪ Almost everyone who has had a little learning thinks that he knows something about learning. To the average layman, learning appears to be the simplest of accomplishments, even though his own learning may have involved considerable travail. You simply take a child of a certain age and expose him at a reasonable pace to what is to be learned and — presto, he learns! If he does not learn right off, prod a little. Perhaps even a mild threat or loss of some privilege will do the trick. Teaching becomes a process of keeping the seat of a child's pants to a chair and his eyes to the page. Lack of learning is largely a result of "poor discipline" on the part of the teacher and perversity or downright laziness on the part of the child. Little wonder, then, that teachers and psychologists have had such a difficult time in convincing the public that the notion of emotional blocks to learning is anything more than pedagogical gobbledygook thought up to confuse the gullible taxpayer.

The limited concept of learning suggested above, particularly if held by authority figures such as parents, can be devastating in its effects upon students' learning. As pointed out earlier, it is becoming increasingly apparent that energy and creativity in addition to intelligence and motivation are essential to learning. A highly motivated and highly intelligent person can be a highly anxious person. A highly anxious person may be tense, rigid and noncreative. Energy that might be used in learning gets swallowed up in coping with anxiety. Adults whose view of learning is limited impose the very demands that dissipate student energy, stultify creativity and inhibit learning.

The teacher's grasp of learning processes may be quite adequate but his planning must still provide for the management of anxiety that is carried into the classroom by the students themselves. He cannot effectively screen out anxiety arising beyond the classroom. But he can seek to provide an environment wherein inappropriate stresses can be analyzed and their fraudulent nature exposed. Above all, he can seek to provide the timing and pacing that keep nonproductive anxiety arising from classroom tasks down to a minimum.

The Teacher Selects Centers for Learning

In planning, the teacher views alternatives for classroom action. He projects his vision to the point where his students actually catch hold of a problem, idea, theory or principle and move it somewhere in time and space. Such a catch-hold point is referred to in subsequent pages as an "organizing center" for learning. Something as concrete as a book may become an organizing center for learning. But a book is a book and nothing more until it is made to serve human motives. When it is made to serve teaching motives, it is an organizing center for learning.

Organizing centers are productive or nonproductive to the extent that they satisfy certain specific criteria. These criteria are derived from the various factors comprising an adequate teaching span of control. The characteristics of the good organizing center enumerated below, then, are guiding principles derived from the wide variety of data discussed earlier and are applicable to the highly specific task of selecting classroom alternatives for learning.

The good organizing center for learning encourages student practice of the behavior sought. If students are to develop problem solving skills, they must practice problem solving. But if they are to solve mathematical problems, they must practice solving this particular type of problem; problems of minority groups will not do. If cognition is seen only as the possession of information, it is unlikely that the teacher will plan for problem solving of any kind. It now becomes crystal clear that the behavior sought must be visualized at the planning level. Such visualizing demands the advance testing of a variety of possible organizing centers to be sure that they have almost literally built into them ample opportunity for student activity involving the behavior sought.

The good organizing center for learning is economical in that it contributes to the simultaneous attainment of several educational objectives. For example, a Viennese painting, *circa* 1925, may well serve to demonstrate effective use of color, to stimulate discussion of the political uncertainties of the time, and to encourage several sessions of creative writing. A potential catch-hold point must be critically examined, however, for negative as well as positive possibilities. A poorly selected problem in arithmetic may provide opportunity for quantitative thinking but also may leave the impression that a mortgage may be secured at 3 per cent interest. Time is ever in insufficient quantities. Much time can be saved by planning to make double and even triple use of it.

The good organizing center for learning encompasses ability floors and ceilings of the group. This criterion involves attention to the nature of content as well as to the nature of differences in the learners. Some kinds of content, such as mathematics and science, require the development of rigorous concepts. Solving mathematical problems demands high-level insight into concepts of quantity. Learning to read involves acquiring skill in word attack. There are very definite limits to the range in concept or skill development that can be challenged by a single organizing center for learning. When these limits are narrower than the range in group abilities *in the particular skill or concept sought,* the teacher must plan to make the two more comparable by dividing the class into smaller groups. The development of certain social skills, on the other hand, demands the interaction of individuals varying widely in interests, abilities and backgrounds. The best organizing center for such learning may be one that plans for inclusion of the entire class. Either the organizing center deemed desirable must challenge the entire class or, then, the class must be divided so that the center is used for only the most appropriate group.

The good organizing center for learning builds on what has gone before and prepares for what is to come. Continuity and sequence are old concepts in planning. Interpreted positively, they mean simply that learning is more effective when an important idea or skill is repeated, each time at greater depth or increased refinement. Earlier, the concept of organizing elements was introduced. An organizing element is a curricular thread — a concept, skill or value to be developed and deepened. An organizing center is like a bead on that thread; and an important concept is built up bead by bead. The teacher must ask in planning: To what does this particular catch-hold point contribute? Does it emerge logically from what has gone before? Does it prepare for deeper learning? Positive answers to such questions suggest that the proposed learning is timed well in the sequence of things.

The good organizing center for learning buttresses and supports learnings in other fields. Other variables being equal, it is desirable to plan to study the literature, art and music of nineteenth-century England at the time of studying political and economic developments of that period. Many elementary school teachers plan art, music and literature activities in part around the seasons of the year. In the elementary school, where a single teacher guides all or most of a student's learning, such juxtaposition is quite readily attainable. But careful dovetailing of several teachers' efforts is essential at higher educational levels. Otherwise, learning can readily be disintegrative rather than integrative. Instead of buttressing each other, several fields may contradict the learning-teaching effort.

The good organizing center for learning has educational significance in its own right. It was indicated earlier that few topics for study are sacred;

that most are interchangeable. But this does not mean that any organizing center appearing to satisfy a passing whim of the teacher or student is acceptable. Whatever consumes the valuable time of teacher and students must in and of itself be worthy of their attention. It takes time to study the use of line and color in graphic art. Why not use good paintings for the development of these insights? Iambic pentameter can be understood only through the analysis of appropriate lines of verse. Why not use good poetry in developing this understanding? Good paintings and good poetry need not be beyond the understanding of even very young children. In fact, again and again we are astonished to find how badly we tend to underestimate the readiness of children for many kinds of learning. This is especially true in the more creative and aesthetic fields where children's perceptions have not yet been contaminated by the plethora of sorry examples around them. Let us be sure in planning that the stimulus for desired learnings is itself worthy of storing on the ever-expanding shelves of human recollection.

The good organizing center for learning is comprehensive in that it permits inclusion of several ideas and several catch-hold points for differing student interests. An organizing center of limited complexity is soon exhausted of its appeal and must be replaced by another. The energies of a single teacher cannot keep up with the voracious consumption of a group of young learners, even when the students are brought into the planning and selecting processes. But a truly comprehensive center invites exploration at several points and poses a variety of student appeals. Once under the surface of the center, the student is only beginning to see the possibilities. For this reason, a broad social problem, a political issue or a unit on some phase of human life is virtually selfpropelling and carries student interest from day to day.

The good organizing center for learning ties together students, ideas and materials in some meaningful fashion. In planning, the teacher perhaps sets forth several questions relating to censorship: Why was a certain movie censored? Why has a local committee undertaken the task of screening certain magazines from the drug-store counters? He sees these questions simply as means for focusing student attention. Then he plans possible next steps. How can questions such as these be used to guide discussion into large issues? What issues would be most appropriate to the backgrounds of these students? Then the teacher thinks through the range and level of materials that will be needed in moving the group forward. Again, major problems and issues, more than specific topics or textbooks, lend themselves to this kind of planning.

The good organizing center for learning has capacity for movement — intellectual, social, geographic or chronological. The class must be able to move somewhere with what confronts it. Such a capacity is almost always present in certain favorite units of study. Consider for a moment the capacity for all the above kinds of movement in a study of the Pilgrims or of the American westward migration. Such studies have settings in time that facilitate the relation of one epoch to another. They almost always involve the search for human freedom and convey the persistence of this search everywhere. They move human beings across whole continents and open boundless vistas to the inquiring intellect. By contrast, units on the Indians usually are disappointingly sterile. Time and place are difficult to establish and the social movement involved is invariably downward, away from freedom. Such difficulties are overcome with adults and could be overcome with children through a radical overhaul of content using sociological and anthropological approaches. The capacity for movement is thus recreated and these studies once more can provide human appeal. Teachers often keep diaries of their teaching that describe not only what went on but how satisfied they felt about each activity. In all probability, their greatest satisfactions would be shown to arise when the organizing center used offered almost boundless opportunity for movement in time and space.

Principles of the sort presented above provide a reasoned basis for working out constructive multiple alternatives for classroom activity. Without such thinking the teacher has no sound basis for accepting or avoiding what may prove to be fickle, passing and nonproductive student interests or for clinging to the rigid prescriptions of the textbook. Put into practice, they go far toward determining the teaching style or variety of styles that will characterize teacher behavior.

Summary: The Key Ideas

The right decision at the right moment is the essence of good teaching. Right decisions are those that time learning perfectly for the individual student. A series of such decisions moves the student forward at an optimum pace. Obviously, such timing and pacing are no more accidental than is the perfect catch by the professional out-fielder. They are, indeed, complex but they can also be acquired. They are attainable only through the dedicated application of a reasonable amount of intelligence, especially in planning. Acquisition of teaching lore is no guarantee of good timing and pacing in teaching, but good teaching is not possible without it.

Quality learning occurs in an optimum habitat. Central to such a habitat is a succession of stimuli to intellectual inquiry. For the most part, these stimuli are the result of diligent, informed teacher planning. The teacher encompasses in his span of control those factors that affect learning. He anticipates those more elusive factors that could as readily block as aid in learning if left to chance operation. He plans alternative organizing centers for learning, each satisfying multiple criteria of usefulness. The total process proceeds somewhat as follows:

1. The teacher brings within his span of control those factors most influencing the learning-teaching act. This involves not only identifying the most pertinent factors but also collating significant data relative to them. The factors are these:

    a. Selfunderstanding
    b. A sense of direction
    c. Insight into learners
    d. Insight into learning processes
    e. Understanding of content
    f. Time, space, and materials

2. The teacher anticipates the possible intrusion of influences or variables not central to teaching but often inadvertently carried into the learning-teaching act by students and teachers. He makes provision for screening out as many negative influences as possible and for turning others into positive agents. Examples of variables that obscure teaching alternatives are the following:

    a. Conflicting goal perceptions
    b. Inadequate perceptions of the curriculum
    c. Certain prevailing perceptions of coverage
    d. Certain prevailing perceptions of standards
    e. Inadequate and distorted perceptions of the learning process

3. The teacher, in the light of the "givens" and the "variables" as he sees them, poses certain teaching alternatives. In essence, he plans a variety of organizing centers for learning that:

    a. Encourage student practice of the behavior sought
    b. Are economical of time
    c. Encompass ability floors and ceilings of the group
    d. Build on what has gone before and prepare for what is to come
    e. Buttress and support other learnings
    f. Have educational significance in their own right
    g. Are comprehensive
    h. Have organizing capacity
    i. Have capacity for movement

4. The teacher now introduces learning tasks.

5. Individual student learning processes are stimulated and changes in behavior occur.

If teaching is to grow as a profession, its decisions must be made on the basis of professional lore. Pertinent lore is amassing at an accelerating rate. We can ignore it and still teach. We cannot ignore it and teach well.

REFERENCES

1. JOHN R. GINTHER. *An Evaluation of the Atlanta Area Teacher Education Service.* Georgia: Atlanta Area Teacher Education Service, 1955.
2. HORACE W. STURGIS. "The Relationship of the Student's Background to the Effectiveness of Teaching." Unpublished Ph.D. dissertation. New York: New York University, 1958.
3. For a report of several appropriate studies, see ERNEST A. HAGGARD. "Socialization, Personality, and Academic Achievement in Gifted Children," *School Review 65,* 1957, pp. 338–414.
4. For further elaboration, see JOHN I. GOODLAD. "Three Dimensions in Organizing the Curriculum for Learning and Teaching," *Frontiers of Elementary Education III,* Vincent J. Glennon, ed. New York: Syracuse University Press, 1956, pp. 11–22.
5. For a report of this work, see JOHN I. GOODLAD. "Illustrative Programs and Procedures in Elementary Schools," *The Integration of Educational Experiences.* National Society for the Study of Education, Fifty-Seventh Yearbook, Part III. Chicago: University of Chicago Press, 1958, pp. 172–193.
6. Unpublished Stanford Achievement Test results. Florida: Englewood Elementary School, 1957.

CURRICULUM DESIGN: THE END PRODUCT OF CURRICULUM DECISIONS

More than thirty years ago Alfred North Whitehead wrote, "Let the main ideas which are introduced into a child's education be few and important, and let them be thrown into every combination possible." These wise words are gradually becoming more than pious ideals for education.

SOURCE: Edmund S. Hoffmaster, James W. Latham, Jr., and Elizabeth D. Wilson, "Design for Science," *The Science Teacher,* 31 (November 1964), pp. 15–17. Reprinted by permission of the authors and the publisher.

Particularly has this been true within the last decade in science education as teams of scientists and teachers, spurred on by national and private grants and by professional backing from various associations, have struggled to improve the quality of science offerings in the public schools through treatment in depth of the basic elements of scientific content and process. The resulting courses of study, units of work, and materials of instruction, built around Whitehead's concept of "live ideas" are becoming increasingly available to schools at both the elementary and secondary levels.

As this quiet revolution in science offerings has been taking place, more knowledge has also been accumulating about the development of the cognitive and creative powers of school children. Psychologists are now suggesting that youngsters can be helped to "learn how to learn." Such experts, moreover, are pushing the teaching profession to specify educational objectives in behavioral terms on the assumption that children learn the behaviors they practice.

Both the curricular reform movement in science and the general ground swell relating to "learning how to learn" are forcing school districts to reexamine traditional science offerings from kindergarten through the senior high school. Such reexamination is making necessary a more rational definition of scope and sequence than has been the case heretofore. In other words, if the elementary and secondary students of the future are to derive maximum benefit from current reforms, their science programs need to tie together the pieces of new science curriculum in a continum which is logically and psychologically sound. Therefore, school districts are searching for overall criteria which will help them evaluate local offerings objectively and which can serve as a basis for choice among the several good new curricula being developed at science centers throughout the nation.

The public school system of Montgomery County, Maryland, has been addressing itself to this problem. Indeed, it has been trying to develop working models of curriculum designs in all subjects on a kindergarten through grade 12 (K-12) basis. John I. Goodlad of the University of California, Los Angeles, has served as a continuing consultant in this curricular effort and has guided us, both in the development of curriculum theory and in the translation of that theory into viable operational terms. During these years classroom teachers, teacher specialists, science supervisors, school administrators, and education generalists have all been involved in one fashion or another. In the spring of 1964, however, the science design for K-12 pushed ahead of the designs in other subjects. A small group of science teacher specialists and supervisors, working intensively in the Office of Curriculum Development, produced not only a rather sophisticated verbal design for science, but also managed to translate this verbal design into a three-dimensional working model. This paper and accompanying picture and diagrams are intended to describe the science design and model and to suggest some ways in which it may be

| (Side) | (Front) |
| FIGURE 7.1 BEHAVIORAL ELEMENTS | SUBSTANTIVE ELEMENTS |

First Section: Grades K-2; Second Section: Grades 3–5; Third Section: Grades 6-8; Fourth Section: Grades 9-12.

tested and used. The reader will be introduced first to the model as a whole and then to the separate sections or pieces from which it is built.

Figure 7.1 shows the physical model which we have developed. Note that there are four vertical cross sections of boxes, moving from the front to the back of the model. Each of these sections or "faces" represents a gross age or grade level in the K-12 continuum. The four faces are thus big steps in the time dimension. The first section outlines the dimensions of a science curriculum for the youngest children (K-grade 2); the second section is the framework for science in the upper elementary grades (3 to 5); the third section encompasses grades 6 to 8; and the fourth section, the senior high school or grades 9 to 12. Each section is composed of the same number of blocks and the same basic organizing elements.

We have assumed that a curriculum design at any one of these four age levels must deal with both content and process — with both substance and behavior. The basic organizing elements of this design, therefore, are of two kinds. One we have called the substantive elements and the other the behavioral elements. We believe that curriculum design becomes operative only when the curriculum planner describes both the behavior which the students should practice and the large area of subject matter within which the behavior occurs. Thus, if we specify that the student should observe events (behavioral element) we must also specify *what manner of events* he is to observe, such as events having to do with the nature and structure of matter or events relating to the nature of energy (substantive elements). (See Figure 7.2.)

Furthermore, we think that interaction of behavior and substance is important whether the particular curriculum being built is for a kindergartner or for a twelfth-grader. In each of the four sections of the model the substantive elements of the design are placed on a horizontal axis and the behavioral elements on a vertical axis, an arrangement which defines a series of what we have called "instructional intersections" within each section. (See Figure 7.3.)

Substantive Elements

The selection of a manageable number of substantive and behavioral elements to form what has become known locally as a *Goodlad Grid* was not a simple matter. We needed a high enough level of abstraction to permit great differences in sophistication and complexity along the continuum and at the same time enough definition to hold the entire scope and sequence together in a reasonably solid fashion. Thus, for the horizontal axis which describes the nature of the field of science we wanted a summary of the substance of science with enough closure to suggest direction and enough openness to accommodate change. After a review of new curriculum developments across the country, study of other attempts at science designs, and a careful look at a series of generalizations from the field of science developed here in the County, we selected five large areas of content to serve as the major substantive organizing elements of our design:

1. The nature and structure of matter
2. The nature of energy
3. Physical interactions
4. Biological processes and interdependencies
5. Cultural, social, and technological implications of science

These five substantive elements permit us to use some relatively simple generalizations about the field of science, such as "energy exists in many forms," to serve as the substantive direction finders for very young children. We can then proceed up the time continuum through two other sections to a complex generalization about energy like "properties of a substance are related to the energy of the atoms, molecules, and crystals of the substance." In other words, a large category like the nature of energy has many facets and can be described by a series of simple generalizations at the primary school level and also by three other sets of more and more complex generalizations at ascending levels of difficulty. In such a manner we have been trying to make operational the following statement by Jerome Bruner:

> . . . the basic ideas that lie at the heart of all science and mathematics . . . are as simple as they are powerful. . . . A curriculum as it develops should revisit these ideas repeatedly, building upon them until the student has grasped the full formal apparatus that goes with them. . . .

Behavioral Elements

But science as a field is not only a series of concepts and generalizations which organize discrete factual knowledge. It is also a process, a mode of inquiry, a point of view which many believe to be more basic than the categories of knowledge. Equally important for the design then was the selection of major behavioral elements. The raw material from which the major behavioral elements were abstracted included not only descriptions of the scientific process and the way in which a scientist works, but also descriptions of the developmental levels of children's maturity according to the observations of master teachers and such experts as Piaget and Havighurst, and the taxonomies of cognitive, affective, and psychomotor behavior suggested by Benjamin Bloom and his associates. From such materials five behavioral elements were selected as follows:

1. Observing events and using symbolic forms
2. Relating and developing event meanings
3. Investigating meaning and relationship
4. Restructuring events
5. Acquiring attitudes and values

Again, just as the substantive elements are further defined at each of the four time levels, so also are the behavioral elements specified in some detail at each level of complexity. For example, "observing events and using symbolic forms" is a large behavioral category for all levels. For primary children it is further defined thus:

He observes objects and events through many direct sensory experiences.
He translates his impressions into symbolic form.
He expresses his ideas in appropriate science language and symbolic forms.
He listens to the ideas of others.

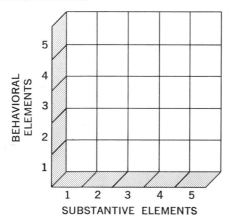

FIGURE 7.2   Gross grade section.

At the senior high school level, the large category is described thus:

He observes situations and occurrences in his environment and describes them in an analytical way.
He reports questions, observations, alternatives, results, and conclusions with instrumental objectivity, noting all variables.
He acquires the terminology for dealing with understanding in the areas of science.

When the five substantive and five behavioral elements are arranged on a grid, the same numbers of intersections for each of the four levels are defined.

Furthermore, the organizing elements are arranged so that those which are the least complex appear as first entries on the coordinate axes of the grid. For example, "observing events" is considered a simpler behavior than "restructuring events," and the "nature and structure of matter" is less complex than "biological processes and interdependencies." Thus an ordering of increasing complexity (a hypothesis to be tested) exists on each axis. The pattern of interactions where students practice behavior in relation to big categories of substance becomes more and more sophisticated as the students advance through the model.

This ordering of the two sets of elements is further defined by the use of the color spectrum in the model. The bottom layer of each cross section is red, the next layer orange, the next yellow, and so on. The white boxes at the top are summary boxes. Each of these colors represents a behavioral element in the design. Thus the red behavioral element "observing events

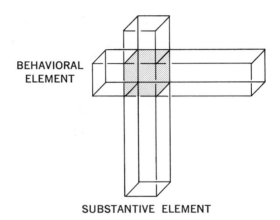

BEHAVIORAL
ELEMENT

SUBSTANTIVE ELEMENT

FIGURE 7.3   Instructional Intersection

and using symbolic forms" is believed to require less psychic energy than the yellow element "investigating meanings and relationships." Indeed, as we refine and use the model, we hope to shade the colors to represent a flow of science learning from simple beginnings at the kindergarten level toward more and more sophistication at the senior high school level.

Now, if we return to the model as a whole, we can see that a horizontal row of cubes represents intersections of one large behavioral element with each large substantive element, whereas a vertical row of cubes represents one substantive element intersecting with each behavioral element. Gross grade levels are symbolized by vertical cross sections of the whole. Four such sections make up the total science design model. Each subsection makes use of the same behavioral and substantive organizing elements, but each subsection differs in its operational definitions of behavior and substance. In addition, color is used for further differentiation of the elements from simple to complex.

So much then for a description of the model and its interlocking parts. Obviously, it must be tested and used. We believe it can help us reexamine our old curriculum and make more sensible choices from among the new materials which will be increasingly on the market. We realize, however, that what we now have is merely the skeleton of a science curriculum. The task will be complete only as we are able to put some flesh on these bones — to outline realistically and concretely the variety of illustrative units of work which can fill up the boxes. An important next step is further definition of each instructional intersection so that these "organizing centers" come to life for everyday classroom use. The more we study the design the more possibilities for research and development open up.

Therefore, although the tasks ahead are formidable, the model gives a sense of direction we have never had before. We can proceed now to build a science curriculum based not on random, disconnected, and sometimes incoherent science "topics," but rather on a logical, rational, and coherent design. And as we set about reorganizing our science curriculum in the years ahead, we hope the design will force us, both in our overall County planning and in everyday classroom operation, to give equal weight to the nature of the learner and the nature of science.

PART IV $\qquad$ *Tomorrow*

Part IV looks into the future with respect to the deployment of teachers, the preparation of teachers, the modification of existing schools, and the design of new schools. Many educational practices persist simply because they have become venerable through long use. Nothing should be immune from searching inquiry. But criticism is not enough.

The four concluding papers of this volume (Chapters 8 and 9) present alternatives for certain traditional ways of utilizing teachers, educating teachers, organizing school and classroom, and organizing the curriculum. Tomorrow's school — to be created by innovative teachers and administrators — will place unique demands on tomorrow's educators. Tomorrow's teachers will be educational diagnosticians prescribing tailor-made programs from a well-stocked pharmacy of tested alternatives.

Tomorrow's Teachers

THE INCREASING CONCERN FOR EFFECTIVE TEACHER UTILIZATION

Using teachers more effectively is but one of several proposals for assuring that our students will be well guided in their learning. Virtually all these proposals are predicated upon the assumption that the demand for qualified teachers will far outstrip the supply unless those available are used more imaginatively than they are at present. Several of these proposals are enjoying such acclaim that, however closely they may approximate their potentialities, the results will be disappointing. Quietly and little heeded, meanwhile, a soft voice in the background keeps persistently reminding us that the utilization of teachers or even of teaching talent is not the first question. The central problem is learners learning and not teachers teaching.

The Need to Establish Priorities

It is most improbable that we shall ever conclude that teachers are unnecessary. But the generally accepted conclusion that teachers are necessary in their own right has led frequently to the further conclusion that teachers should be utilized in line with factors derived from studying teachers and what they do and, ultimately, to the conclusion that the proper study of education is teachers. The danger in this line of thinking

SOURCE: *The High School in a New Era.* Francis S. Chase and Harold A. Anderson, eds. (Chicago: University of Chicago Press, 1958), pp. 133–145. Reprinted by permission of the publisher.

is an ultimate equation of teaching with the educative process. If the educative process cannot yet be described as a unitary phenomenon, at least some ordering of the relative factors must be attempted. Our central concern thus becomes the learning of students. Only by viewing learners learning can we come to see the appropriate roles of teachers in the educative process.

It is abundantly apparent that such appropriate priorities are not clearly established in the minds of some educational practitioners. For example, recently a group of high-school teachers engaged seriously in the planning of a curriculum for a new school. They gave attention to the purposes of this school, to the kinds of activities that should go on in it, to the way the program should be organized, and to like significant questions. They agreed, after extensive analysis of the social studies and the language arts, that some combinations of these fields would be in the best interest of the learners. They then turned to the planning of daily schedules, and the order of priorities suddenly shifted. Teachers are most comfortable teaching in a single subject of specialization, some said. Teacher time is used most effectively, said others, when each uses the same lesson preparation as frequently as possible. Thus a teacher should teach both a single grade level and a single subject area. Clearly we have now moved down from the question of advancing learning to that of advancing the comfort of teachers. We are now on the road to deciding that twenty-five young people are enough for any teacher to handle. By relating these conclusions, we describe the classroom setting within which American education is largely being conducted: a single teacher working very much on his own with a group of from twenty-five to forty adolescents in a single subject at the secondary level and with all or most subjects at the elementary-school level.

Crystallization of such a setting for instruction set in very quickly after the Quincy Grammar School in Boston — a graded school and a landmark in the emergence of lock-step in school organization — opened the doors of its new, specially designed school building in 1848. By the end of the century the curriculum was a chopped salad, prepared by cutting content vertically into grades and horizontally into subjects. Textbooks prepackaged these curricular goods, presumably for easier pupil consumption, and teachers prepared themselves with a keen eye to grade level, subject field, and prescribed textbooks.

However, the interlocking pieces in the graded school were only beginning to settle comfortably into place when thoughtful educators were observing that overemphasis on order was hobbling creativity. Consequently for several decades, spanning the old age of one century and the childhood of another, experiments like the Gary Plan, Pueblo Plan, Winnetka Plan, and others chipped away, with some temporary success, at the tightly meshed machinery that grew steadily more ponderous. But educators grew increasingly reluctant, apparently, to tamper with any part of the machinery for fear of stripping the gears. Since the thirties, when advocates of the core curriculum stirred up a little excitement, we have contented ourselves with shifting our eyes elsewhere or with applying a little oil here and adjusting a valve there, perhaps in the fond hope that, unseen and unheard, the monster would just shuffle off on synchronized treads.

Ghosts of past failure stand guard over our mechanized legacy. The various experiments of several decades ago are now but dimly understood. It is easy to say that they did not get at the heart of the educational problem, that they were but manipulative devices seeking to get more wear out of buildings and teachers. In part, such criticisms are valid, but most of the explorations having at least temporary influence went much deeper. They made some attempt to analyze the learning process. The Winnetka Plan, for example, recognized different types of learning, even if superficially when judged from today's analyses. Too often, unfortunately, it was the form that spread, and innovations became increasingly mechanistic in proportion to the number of models separating each new version from the original.

It is now so easy and, sometimes, so convenient to equate the insights of new proposals with the forms of the old and to predict dismally, "These things too shall pass away." The suggestion that teams of teachers work for various purposes with groups of varying sizes is casually dismissed as an attempt to revive the monitorial system. While previously inadequate approaches to old problems are not likely to be successful if merely dressed in modern garb, at least we must be willing to study the past dispassionately in recognition of the possibility that previous timing may have been poor or previous analyses imperfect.

Pressures Requiring Consideration of Effective Utilization of Teachers

We can ill afford to be chilled into immobility by ghosts rising up from the past. Tangible dangers threaten us. Hordes of pupils rampaging through our elementary schools come clambering at the doors of our high schools. We could cheerfully say that the situation is temporary. But it is not. Children already born, nearly 25,000,000 of them not yet in school, will tax our schools for twenty years to come, and the birthrate, although stabilizing, shows little sign of slackening significantly. We cannot truthfully say either that the school has found a solution for greater pupil absorption or that it is coming through its ordeal unscathed. It has merely sought to adjust. For example, the plan of action of the Association for Childhood Education International calling for elementary-school classes of twenty-five pupils appears anachronistic in an educational environment where enrollments up to 100 per cent higher still occur.

The elementary school entered into its period of crisis under certain favorable circumstances. The Bachelor's degree as a minimum credential and equal pay with high-school teachers were in the process of establishment for its personnel. The wholehearted embracing of in-service programs focusing upon the child and his learning created a gratifying *esprit de corps* among some schools in every state. Critics boring in on inadequacies, real and imagined, came away licking wounds inflicted by irate parents who believed in their schools and who then intensified their efforts to make the schools better.

The American secondary school faces grave ideological, as well as crushing physical, burdens. From above and below and from all sides it is being caught in a squeeze.

From below come millions of youngsters educated in a school unit espousing a philosophy of taking children from where they are and doing with them the best it can. Elementary-school policies of acceleration, retardation, or both do not materially reduce the increasing variability in pupil achievement with which teachers must deal. Consequently the secondary school either must anticipate great variability and plan accordingly or must set minimum standards that will doom a considerable portion of our population to six, seven, or eight years in the high school. From above, in these times of increasing college enrollments, comes the cry that the high schools are not adequately preparing their graduates for college. From "Take them from where they are" to "Bring them up to rigorous standards" lies a mighty gulf! But from the elementary school to college extends a brief span of years for bridging it.

From all sides is heard a clamor of voices. We are losing our technological race with Russia; prepare our young people in the sciences. Men cannot live by bread alone; teach them the meaning of life. Cultivate the gifted; develop remedial programs for the laggards. Education is for those who can profit from it; weed out those who cannot. Determine pupil potentialities early; set up academic programs for the college-bound and vocational programs for the remainder. Most assuredly, the American people are not giving today's secondary school clear-cut directives as to function.

Meanwhile, toward this school the hordes advance. To predict for it an unchanged future would, indeed, be unrealistic. We look at the statistics and conclude that one out of every two or three college graduates, rather than the present one in every four or five must be attracted into teaching if current pupil-teacher ratios are to be maintained. Realizing that there is little likelihood of such a marked shift, we conclude that teachers must be utilized more effectively. But again we hear the soft voice reminding us of first questions, and we ask: Utilizing teachers more effectively for what? A hierarchy of questions now spins out before us:

Who shall be educated in the high school and for what?

What is the nature of the process in which these learners shall engage and how shall the school be organized for carrying out the process?

Who and what shall assist in this process and how shall these teaching resources be used most effectively?

How shall the human recources be prepared for, and inducted into, these various tasks?

When the tumult and the shouting shall have faded into the somewhat softer sounds of a social institution doing well what it knows how to do, an important reaffirmation will have been made: A vigorous, self-appraising society demands an educated citizenry. Furthermore, the American people will be much closer to conceiving an educated citizenry as one that devotes serious thought both to its central problems and to the directions that intelligent social action should take. Education, in large measure through the secondary school, must serve both to extend the view of reality held in common by larger and larger numbers of people and to expose for analysis those views that markedly differ. We must not be deluded into the beguiling notion that a significant portion of our people shall be excluded from such an education simply because they appear to lack the appetite or the capacity for it.

The definition of common kinds of behaviors for our educated citizenry and the identification of a range of possible educational experiences conducive to their attainment does not mean that the school shall endorse, willy-nilly, participation in whatever strikes the learner's fancy. Each specific educational activity indorsed must be seen as both pertinent to envisioned goals and more pertinent than other alternatives. Nor does this mean that prescribed blocks of content are to be "covered" by all in uniformly prescribed periods of time. Learning, as we shall define it, cannot be equated with covering anything. Nor does it mean that learners of widely varying abilities shall proceed over any given route at the same time. Such a proposition is inane.

Broad Bases for Teacher Utilization

Several broad bases for using teaching resources now move into position. While resources will be committed to at least a common core of ends, they will not necessarily be committed to common means. Furthermore, while diversity in learner interests and abilities will be the prime determinant of diversity in means, unique approaches will be designed also to provide excitingly fresh ways of viewing the same phenomenon or of developing the same skills in alternative settings. Dewey turned the energies of his pupils toward the school shop, for example, not because he wished to substitute vocational for intellectual ends, but because new materials offered a fresh challenge to the processes of inquiry he deemed paramount.

The foregoing paragraphs suggest, also, that creative utilization of resources will facilitate widely varying levels of insight or skill as outcomes of the learning process even though a given group of learners may be engaged in an outwardly common learning experience. (By definition of "experience," of course, there exists no truly common learning experience.)

Finally and more important, development of an educated citizenry will demand utilization and organization of teaching resources in such a fashion that differing cultural groups will share the associations essential to greater cultural unification. The "blue-stocking" child, the labor child, and all the others learn to communicate with their own kind whether or not they learn to read and write. But they will not readily acquire the communication systems of other than their own kind — and hence membership in the widest possible range of groups — unless they associate some of the time with other than their own kind. When education is viewed as serving only to foster and refine tool skills such as reading and writing, preparing teachers for instructing learners grouped for long periods of time on criteria of likeness seems quite appropriate. But such a practice runs counter to the broader view of education indorsed here. Regrettably, there are, in our society, persons who advocate various kinds of long-term educational segregation because they hold a narrow view of education, and there are also persons who recognize only too well such a practice will safeguard the advantages which they acquired automatically through initial membership in a favored, sealed-off group.

We must recognize that the final roosting place of all learnings — and the only place where they can be properly understood — is in the lonely self of just one individual, standing alone and trying to live with his aloneness as best he can. There is nothing sacred, then, about the group or any particular size of group for learning in general. There may be, however, something extremely significant about both the size and the character of a group for a particular learning. For example, if a considerable portion of a school population has relatively little insight into the fact that where and when one lives profoundly influence the character of human living, then grouping these young people to view a skillfully prepared film of persons living in other times and other places may be quite appropriate for at least introducing them to the concepts involved. If, on the other hand, the purpose is to explore the relation of social, political, and economic factors in England to the development of social institutions in America, then an appropriate group may perhaps include only twenty learners whose time and space concepts are well advanced. But, within this small group, a few students will be motivated to dig deeply into the relationship between cultural transmission and communication systems. These few will require access to books, pictures, tapes, and records, perhaps to specialized human talent, and to peers who are exploring related phenomena. Some learning is in no way hindered even when a given stimulus is placed before hundreds of learners simultaneously. Other learning proceeds best in a small group carefully constituted on a basis of specific criteria. And learning sometimes is blocked when the group is larger than one person.

Any stimulus for learning (and, therefore, the structure for conveying that stimulus) must take into account the present attainment floor and attainment ceiling of the group for whom the stimulus is intended. Gross data such as intelligence-test scores, for example, constitute inadequate bases for establishing groups for a variety of learning. Furthermore, the distance between attainment floor and attainment ceiling to be spanned by a single stimulus probably can be greater in one area (language arts) than in another (mathematics). Consequently, in contemplating expanded group size — for economical reasons, say — we must be cognizant of the extent to which such expansion threatens to destroy the capacity of appropriate stimuli for spanning any increased distance between attainment floors and attainment ceilings.

But individual and group readiness for certain learning involves much more than either general ability or specific attainment. Increasingly, we are seeing that anxiety-producing situations in school or elsewhere inhibit learning, even when the student's general ability level and certain specific attainment levels are high. A generalized state of anxiety, not causally related to the present learning situation, may block the experience hoped for although the stimulus appears to be well suited to other aspects of pupil readiness. Perhaps, then, each secondary-school student should spend a portion of the day with a group of his peers and a teacher skilled in group-guidance procedures. This might well be the group, constituted on criteria of diversity rather than similarity, in which the important culture-unifying processes would be refined. Research must tell us how large such groups should be, how frequently and for how long they should meet, and what kind of diversity in membership is best suited to the functions to be served.

Suggestions for Effective Teacher Utilization

Even the brief analysis of learning presented here challenges the desirability of promoting all learnings through a group of thirty learners assigned to a single teacher for a given subject, at a given grade level, and for an arbitrary time period. Present group, grade, and subject patterns may have come into being on the basis of at least some conception of learners learning, but they have been perpetuated, apparently, for reasons of a quite different sort.

So far, I have implied suggestions for identifying and utilizing teaching resources but have not attempted to make them explicit. The film picturing other times and other places need not be prepared by teachers or with the objectives of secondary education in mind. But an educator must decide its appropriateness for a particular segment of high school youth. The large-group stimulus might as readily be a distinguished philosopher, poet, or humanitarian appearing on closed-circuit television. Again, however, someone close to the particular learners involved must determine the timing of the specific stimulus. Similarly, the variety of small-group situations requires a variety of resources — human and otherwise. The group seeking to deepen a given mathematical concept often requires the clear exposition of a person who sees the concept in all its ramifications. It may be possible to observe the initial presentation on film and to test its application through textbook problems; but direct human help, probably providing talents differing from those of the film demonstrator, frequently will be important to the learner as he struggles with his successes and failures.

In view of the variety of learnings to be carried on and of the situations and resources appropriate for their pursuit, it becomes clear that the variety of teaching talents desired cannot be found in one person. Nor is there any good reason for seeking this variety of teaching talents only among those now classified as teachers. Communications experts, under the guidance of curriculum specialists, appear to be the logical persons both for developing educational films, filmstrips, tapes, and recordings and for planning the uses of television. Artists, scientists, engineers, and specialists of endless variety constitute a source of talent we have not yet learned to channel effectively. Many well-educated mothers who feel that a full-time teaching load would seriously endanger the conduct of their home responsibilities would be thrilled at the opportunity to come into the school on a part-time basis. Future teachers, frequently far from the scene of high school activity until they engage in student teaching, would profit from participation as student aides throughout their preparation programs.

The central problem in utilizing this diverse array of potential teaching talent is, of course, an organizational problem, and it is viewed here as belonging in the hands of professional career teachers and administrators. This does not mean, however, that all career teachers would assume a kind of entrepreneur role, managing the enterprise as one manages a business. Let us instead visualize a team operation, which brings together a number of individuals representing talents appropriate to the tasks in which a designated group of learners probably would engage. A given team, perhaps organized with social-studies instruction in mind (although there is nothing inviolable about subjects as a basis for team organization), might include two experienced and highly qualified career teachers. The particular talent of one might be skill in presenting and clarifying central concepts; that of the other, identifying and moving toward the solution of group problems. Both would have a sound understanding of school function, learning, curriculum development, and other educational lore. Only part of their day, instead of the entire day as in conventional practice, would be spent in direct association with children. A significant portion of daily time would be devoted to curriculum planning — that essential but frequently neglected aspect of the educational enterprise. The remaining time would go to diverse aspects of team leadership. Other members of the team would be anything but robots. The team would include technically qualified but inexperienced teachers preparing for team leadership. Part-time lay persons, employed on a continuing relationship, would assist individuals and groups of learners, and highly specialized "guest teachers" would contribute in line with their talents and the requests made of them. All of these, with the possible exception of persons in the guest category, would meet regularly for the purpose of developing a reasonably common view of the over-all program, of the diversity of learning activities going on at given times, and of the potential contribution of each team member.

This description certainly does not exhaust team possibilities. Nor does it reveal the potential cross-team enterprises and the school-wide planning of the entire professional staff functioning as the very heart of the school organism. But it does suggest using teaching resources to further learning without doing violence to, or even slightly damaging, teacher selfhood.

The team concept in teaching already is under attack on the ground that it creates several classes of teacher-citizens. Different classes of citizens are, indeed, created when membership in a given class is restricted to present membership or when affiliation is denied on the basis of personal characteristics unrelated to group purpose. In the arrangement described, however, not only do the avenues to advancement remain open to all, but a greater number of avenues is created. Furthermore, the mother and part-time team member, who currently is under pressure to survive as a full-time teacher or not teach at all, simply because no other alternative is open, may elect to add some teaching to home responsibilities without harm to either set of obligations or to self.

The present lot of teachers promises to be materially improved through the identification of diverse teaching opportunities and the creation of teams directly related to the learning tasks to be promoted. At present, teaching frequently fails to attract and hold certain talented persons who could contribute to a team but who simply cannot see themselves indefinitely carrying on the demanding range of activities now required of teaching. The team-leadership role offers both continued challenge in teaching and the possibility of increasing remuneration, whereas top salaries are now available only through moving from teaching to administration. Currently, developing one's unique talents frequently leads to no increased opportunity to exercise those talents, let alone to being materially rewarded for them. It is difficult to see how a structure that creates greater opportunity for upward movement on the basis of professional competence, and broadens task selection on the basis of unique talents, is detrimental to a profession or its membership.

Attack on existing patterns of utilizing teacher talent is not likely to be productive (for education, for learners, or, in the long run, for professional teachers) until we are clear about who are to be educated and for what. Then the potential resources for teaching and the patterns for utilizing these resources effectively begin to move into view in almost endless variety. Obviously, then, the team concept suggested here and elsewhere is only one of the exciting new possibilities that more and more will become established in practice.

THE PROFESSIONAL CURRICULUM
OF TEACHERS

Professional performance rests on ideas, on insight and understanding. The surgeon, for example, must know not only how to cut but also whether to cut and, if so, when and where. The final performance is a synthesis of many pertinent understandings acquired through long prep-

SOURCE: *Journal of Teacher Education*, XL (December 1960), pp. 454–459. Reprinted by permission of the publisher.

aration, much of it rigorously prescribed.* The "practice" part of the surgeon's preparation is that part where understandings are applied and where techniques are refined. Practice may motivate study, but it is through the study that understandings are, for the most part, acquired and deepened. If practice alone were all the surgeon needed, surgery would not be a profession. If practice alone were all the teacher needed, teaching likewise would not be a profession.

To find out what education a teacher requires over and above whatever he should have as a generally educated person, it is necessary to analyze teaching. It is necessary, also, to assume some desirable level of performance in the same way that we assume surgery to be something other than butchery. Teaching demands that the teacher make value judgments of many kinds that lead to employing the most promising techniques for stimulating and guiding learning.

Teaching: A Synthesis

The identification, description, and classification of knowledge pertinent to teaching provide a science of teaching. Bringing this knowledge effectively to bear in teaching is a technology — the technology of teaching. At times, the synthesis of knowledge is effected with such sensitive understanding of the scientific components that it is akin to art — the art of teaching. Teaching, then — a professional behavior — involves science, technology, and, at times, art. Teacher education, in turn, involves preparation for all of these.

Teacher education curricula as usually constituted have three divisions: studies in one or more organized teaching fields, studies in the field of education, and practice. The first of these divisions commonly is referred to as "specialized subject matter"; the second and third are lumped together as "professional education."

The several errors involved in viewing professional education in this way are of such magnitude that the following lamentable circumstances can be largely attributed to them:

1. Education as a field of study and professional education usually are conceived to be one and the same.

2. The various teaching fields, labeled "special," not "professional," slip out of the realm of professional education. Thus, the subject-field of the high school teacher, for example, is not scrutinized to determine what is relevant for the professional curriculum.

* The term "synthesis" is used throughout this paper in referring to the highly personal relating of ideas to action that occurs in teaching. The teacher education curriculum cannot effect the synthesis, but it can at least encourage the process by deliberately accounting for the elements thought to comprise the teaching act.

3. Instruction in the various "special fields" studied by teachers proceeds largely without reference to the uses to be made of these fields by the future teacher.

4. The various divisions of the future teacher's curriculum are so segmented and walled off from one another within the structure of institutions of higher learning that the possibility — indeed, even the idea — of the needed synthesis taking place within the teacher is effectively denied.

5. All too commonly, curriculum development in teacher education is a haphazard process, guided largely through debate, in which arbitrarily selected pieces of undetermined value are shuffled into kaleidoscopic patterns. The personal synthesis desired in professional behavior occurs by chance, if at all, simply because not all of the components essential to this synthesis are first brought into the curriculum design.

Education as a Field of Study

Education is a field of study. As such, it is not synonymous with professional education. There is considerable inconsequential debate over whether education is a field of study in its own right or merely a composite of several fields. Certainly, education draws from economics, political science, sociology, and other fields of knowledge, but so do these fields draw from and overlap one another. The geographer never quite knows whether he is a physical or social scientist; usually he is something of both. The fields of study are man-made, after all, and as such have untidy edges.

Education as a field has a definable body of subject matter in that education has long been a phenomenon conducted and examined by human beings and affecting them. It now has a considerable body of lore. Because of the nature of its lore and of its methods, education is classified as a social science in the structure of human knowledge and, usually, of higher education. The field has a certain kinship to other divisions of study, however, certainly to the humanities and the biological sciences.

Education as a field of knowledge seeks to describe a realm of human thought and experience. Its findings and conclusions are available to all who would use them. These findings and conclusions are available to guide professional behavior such as teaching. But these findings have relevance in and of themselves, whether or not there are teachers and whether or not teachers use them. If there were no teachers in the conventional sense but there were, nonetheless, human processes of education, the field of education would still have legimate and identifiable subject matter.

To repeat, education is a field of study. As such, it is not identical with teaching, but some of its subject matter is pertinent to teaching. Content from the field of education is combined with content from other fields in the act of teaching. All content drawn upon in the act of teaching must be considered "professional" content, regardless of its category among the classifications of human knowledge.

The Teaching Field

The high school teacher of, for example, mathematics, employs subject matter from this field in the teaching act. He may gain insights about the nature of the teaching act from many fields, but there is no escaping certain demands which the discipline of mathematics places upon teaching — even if the teacher is not fully conscious of these demands or cognizant of their nature. To understand the nature of these demands is to be more knowledgeable about the science of teaching and is to increase the possibility of being more rational about the practical decisions that make up the technology of teaching. These two conditions in turn tend to free the teacher to be more creative, more artistic, in teaching. The assumption here is that, as humans become better educated, their behavior becomes less primitive in those areas to which their education is transferable and is transferred.

The example of a high school teacher of a given field is used here simply because it lends greater simplicity to this discussion of professional education for teachers. Were the various theses being developed to be applied to the preparation programs of elementary-school teachers, curricula considerably different from those commonly planned would result.

Returning to the example of mathematics teaching, it is apparent that this field — like other teaching fields — must be rigorously examined in order to determine its contribution to and demands upon teaching. What are its methods, its basic assumptions about truth and knowledge? What elements constitute its character and hold it together as a field of human inquiry? In what way do these elements — concepts of time, number, quantity, and space, for example — discipline and limit the kinds and order of learning opportunities to be provided? How does the very nature of the field give direction to practical classroom operations, such as grouping pupils for most effective instruction, using films and tape recorders, employing teaching machines appropriately, and so on?

These are questions not usually raised in the mathematics curriculum of higher education. But such questions must be raised in the professional curriculum of teachers. Solutions to them demand a knowledge of mathematics as well as of learners and learning. The nature of learners and of learning constitutes part of the subject matter of fields other than mathematics.

It becomes apparent that questions revealed through analysis of teaching demand for their solution knowledge drawn from many fields. It follows that the teaching act demands the synthesis of knowledge from many fields. The character of the teaching field — its assumptions, propositions and organization — profoundly influences the kind of teaching syntheses that can and should be effected. The teaching field must be examined, then, for its potential contribution to the *professional* education of teachers, and accounted for accordingly in the curriculum.

Practice

The student planning to teach should perceive rather clearly the nature of the tasks for which he is preparing. In fact, he as well as his instructors should be able to formulate the questions posed by teaching acts. Student observation of practice becomes an essential part of the professional curriculum.

In the past, the observation of practice has presented some very real difficulties to the faculty members who would use such observation as one basis for organizing the professional curriculum. Arranging classroom visits for a large group of prospective teachers demands more time than the anticipated benefits appear to warrant. The particular observation opportunity needed at a given moment usually is not available. And, in a large group, few students observe the same classroom incidents; common reference points for discussion are thus lacking.

There is no need today for such obstacles to obstruct the inclusion of observation in the professional curriculum of teacher education. Closed-circuit television now makes it possible even for very large groups to observe practice together and to identify the questions central to teaching. Extensive use of videotape is coming with the achievement of less costly means of preparation and production. Through such devices, students readily may become familiar with the demands of teaching and, under guidance from the faculty, begin to apply understandings previously acquired and to study familiar fields with new purposes in view.

In moving from observation to practice, the prospective teacher undergoes a crucial metamorphosis. He progresses from analysis to synthesis, from student to teacher. If he is a good teacher, he will always be a student, too, but a student who sees through a teacher's eyes.

Actual practice, then, is the test of professional behavior. It should be closely guided by teachers who have mastered the science of teaching in considerable depth and who have perfected the technology of teaching at the level of artistry. Practice should provide for protected innovation. Never again, in all probability, will the neophyte enjoy such a unique opportunity for "trying out" under conditions that permit drawing back before it is too late. In the practice of teaching, professional synthesis is perfected.

Implications and Conclusions

The foregoing pages present at least a partial rationale for developing the teacher education curriculum. To the extent that this rationale is sound, it is a guide to practical decisions concerning organization of the scientific foundations of teaching in the total teacher education curriculum, provision for technological application in the professional curriculum, and allocation and utilization of faculty.

An understanding of the fields of education and, for example, mathematics is necessary to application of knowledge from these fields at the level of teaching. There is no point in arguing *how much* prior study of both is desirable — obviously, as much as possible. The quantitative question has been answered in the past and is likely to be answered in the future on the basis of how much the traffic will bear and how much the college or university will allow. The professors of education and of mathematics undoubtedly will continue to lobby in the academic market place for their respective roads to the good life. Should they change their character, the world would be poorer — and much less interesting!

Two central curricular questions are likely to go unanswered in any strictly quantitative upward push toward five- and six-year preparation programs containing more and more of both education and the teaching field. First, what adaptations must be effected in these foundation fields if they are to be made most useful for the professional curriculum? Second, what specific arrangements of content and personnel will be most conducive to synthesis of pertinent understandings by the student? The preceding rationale suggests one kind of solution to these questions. There are conflicting viewpoints and the practices stemming from them are clearly evident in some existing teacher education programs.

One notion — a rather popular one, judging from practice — is that little can or should be done to assure personal synthesis through deliberately planning a curriculum to promote it. The student completes a major in mathematics, a required collection of courses in education and student teaching, discovering the inter-relationships where he finds them. This lack of any curricular planning for synthesis leaves far too much to the student.

Courses in the field of education carry similar titles from institution to institution, but the content differs radically. The introductory course is historical, philosophical, sociological, or a combination of all three, or is a group guidance course on teaching and its demands. The course in methods usually is a general one which, because of the miscellaneous array of students in it, can do little more than present techniques of class-room management. When "special" methods courses are taught, only rarely does the instructor possess the unique combination of preparation and experience that might be hoped for in the person fulfilling such a de-manding role.

Most of the content suggested above is entirely legitimate subject mat-ter for the field of education. However, the great divergence in what is included in preservice teacher education suggests that we have not yet identified those ideas from the field of education that are most pertinent to teaching. Failure to bring together at some point in the curriculum the components essential to teaching suggests that we do not yet know much about the teaching act or, for that matter, the bearing of various fields upon it. Are we, then, asking students to act on the basis of inter-relation-ships perceived only dimly by their teachers? To affirm that the teaching synthesis is individual and unique and, therefore, that it cannot be in-duced through planning the curriculum is to indulge in escapism.

An extreme alternative to encouraging personal synthesis through cur-ricular planning is elaborate care in planning the specific ways in which subject matter from education and from the teaching field might be fused in performing teaching acts. The subject matter of professional education thus becomes a field of its own, put together and laid out for student con-sumption. This cook-book approach is as prescriptive and restrictive as its opposite is chaotic.

This paper does not suggest the creation of a new field for teachers; but neither does it propose that the teaching synthesis be left to chance. In-stead, it implies that the following steps be taken in improving the pro-fessional education of teachers:

1. *That university faculty members in each of the teaching fields perti-nent to high school teaching examine their subject matter with a view to determining how it conditions, in fact disciplines, various decisions that teachers must make.* Thus, in time, they would extract certain concepts over and above the concepts of mathematics *per se,* concepts which are pertinent to teaching and, therefore, to the professional education of teachers. These concepts would then be organized and brought to bear upon the problems and practices observed by prospective teachers in the practice part of their professional education. The mathematics studied by

these students prior to this time is mathematics *per se* — the mathematics basic to the education of engineers, accountants, physicists, and, for that matter, mathematicians.

2. *That university faculty members in the field of education examine their field critically to identify those concepts that appear most pertinent to teaching.* Thus, in time, they would extract concepts common to most teaching, whatever the teaching field might be. These concepts would not differ from those often dealt with in education courses. But they would have been culled rigorously from the field because of their supposed bearing upon teaching acts and would be taught in relation to those teaching acts for which they appear to have significance. We cannot afford the luxury of having future teachers select at leisure and at will from the present offerings in education as though all of them were equally pertinent to teaching.

3. *That representatives from the several appropriate fields join in seeking to apply to teaching what their respective studies suggest as significant.* During the past decade professors of education and of the various teaching fields have come far in accepting one another and in recognizing mutual responsibility for teacher education. In the next decade, they must both clarify their separate contributions and implement the mutual contributions necessary to the effective professional education of teachers.

The separate responsibilities and contributions already have been suggested. The mutual responsibility is in team planning and teaching. Needed in the team is a professor of the teaching field, a professor of education, and a first-rate practicing high school teacher. The focal points for analysis and discussion are the teaching acts themselves, as observed by the group and laid out as for autopsy on the conference table.

Perhaps in the process, professor and student alike will come to understand the nature of professional teaching syntheses and the contributions of the respective fields to them. Perhaps in the process, too, the student will catch a vision of the creative teaching acts he might hope some day to effect.

He will not effect the acts examined in his professional curriculum, however. Nor should his instructors require him to. They will say, no doubt, "Go, thou, and do likewise." But he will not. Instead, when he comes to teach, he will say of models once dissected, "Get thee behind me, Satan," and will create anew.

▶9

Tomorrow's Schools

THE SCHOOL OF THE FUTURE

It is assumed that several individuals projecting the school of the future would agree on desiring good schools. Differences in what they envision would depend on fundamental differences in what they view as "good." It seems useful, therefore, to identify criteria for the good school that specify the values of the writer. These criteria then become standards for judging the status of a school within the particular value framework posed.

This paper applies one man's perception of what is good to a series of persistent educational questions. The results describe the "character" of education desired. Faculties of individual schools are urged to exercise caution in using as guides to action the results of comparing their own answers to these questions (as expressed in school practice) with the answers posed in this paper. Should these answers appear to agree in kind, it may be suspected that the writer and the faculty group fundamentally agree in viewpoint. Acceptance of the specific proposals of this paper as goals for faculty action would make some sense. But should these answers basically disagree in kind, then these proposals become focal points for reexamining values, not goals for action. The reader should consider himself forewarned.

What Purpose or Aim?

Some years ago, the problem of slow-learners in school was brought to the attention of an influential citizen. To the query, "What should be done with them?" he replied, "Kick 'em out. That's what we did at West Point."

At another time and place, essentially the same question was addressed

SOURCE: *Education in Transition,* Frederick C. Gruber, ed. (Philadelphia: University of Pennsylvania, 1960), pp. 99–109. Reprinted by permission of the publisher.

to Sir Richard Livingstone, then visiting Emory University in Atlanta, Georgia. Greek scholar and philosopher, Sir Richard gazed reflectively toward the window and replied, "I think I should try to interest them in building a bird's nest, or something like that."

These two quite different answers to a single query are useful in examining the question of what schools are for. There seem to be, currently, two major positions, not neatly separated in practice but interwoven in such a way that it is extremely difficult if not impossible to sort out schools clearly representing one or the other viewpoint.

The first position views schooling as a set body of learnings to be mastered. When these learnings are mastered, one has acquired, presumably, "an elementary or secondary education." From this position certain school practices follow. There are prescribed tasks that mark a beginning and an ending as well as specific steps along the way. It is consistent to keep some children out of school until they are "ready" and to retain others in school if they appear not to have accomplished the learnings specified for various stages.

The second position views education as a means of enriching living for young people during a specified period in their lives. A reasonable interpretation of this position views schooling as helping children live more effectively now but in such a way that they will be more effective, also, in meeting the personal and social demands of later periods. Such schooling takes its cues from the development period of the learner and the demands thus placed upon young people, not from a prescribed series of tasks to be mastered.

In my judgment, the second position will emerge dominant for the school of the future. We must come to realize that time has marched on — right past the period in our history when a little reading, writing and arithmetic were *both* primary *and* terminal education. It was appropriate, once upon a time in America, to lay out a little stuff (call it an elementary education) to be mastered. Often, those enrolled in the elementary schools for the learning of it were young adults. Increasingly today, the educational needs of adults — even when the meeting of these needs calls for learning to read and write — are met through adult, not elementary, education. Implementation of the first position — and this position enjoys considerable current support — to the point of the mastery implied would retain some persons in the elementary schools until their beards draped in the inkwells.

The good school has as its aim, then, the education of children rather than the provision of something fixed called education. One thinks of this education initially as *childhood education* in the same way that one thinks of adult education as education for adults.

A number of specific practices now fall into place. The entrance age for beginning school is defined by years and not estimates of "readiness" for prescribed learnings. Consequently, in the future, children who reach a given entrance age by a date set uniformly nationwide will automatically be admitted wherever they happen to reside. Children requiring specialized attention of various kinds will attend school in the same building with their peers except in those relatively few cases of amentia, dementia or physical disability where the welfare of others is seriously endangered. In fact, the range of special developmental problems provided for by the school will be such that it will become well-nigh impossible to differentiate between those children receiving "special" and those receiving "regular" education.

In brief summary, to assure an intelligent, self-governing, future citizenry of the sort implied in the term "democracy," our young people must be encompassed by education designed to develop to the full the potentialities of *all* of them.

What Responsibilities and Objectives?

The school is only one of several institutions contributing to childhood education. The good school constantly reexamines its responsibilities in relation to the responsibilities of other institutions in order to assure clear-cut priorities.

School people are and have been "takers-on." Admittedly, our society has demanded more and more of its schools. But the good mother hen that is the school has been quite willing to become foster parent for ducklings and goslings as well as its own chicks.

Over the years ahead, teachers and principals will become less involved in activities involving medical and dental care, feeding and transportation. The amount of time spent on these activities, especially by principals, constitutes a sad commentary on appropriate use of professional talent. In slipping away from direct control of teachers and principals, however, these activities will assume greater significance as instructional interest centers to be used meaningfully in the educational program.

The school's objectives will narrow to those involving cognition, high-level psychomotor skills and values and attitudes essential to living with many different groups and peoples around the world. These will be defined in behavioral terms of sufficient precision to permit ready differentiation between appropriate and inappropriate means to their attainment.

In a very real sense, the school of the future will emphasize its own dispensability. It will come to be recognized as merely a device attendant on childhood through which the child comes to say about learning, "I can and I will," and in so saying embarks on a process of life-long but largely school-free education.

What Kind of Curriculum?

Sometime in the near future, the "sacred cow" concept of the school curriculum will perish. Its demise will be in keeping with the aim of education endorsed earlier.

A few years ago, the physicist, Robert Oppenheimer, pointed out that most of what is worth knowing was not in the textbooks when today's adults were in elementary schools. Others commenting on the expansion of knowledge point out that more knowledge has been accumulated in the last 60 years than in all previous human history. And of all the scientists ever born, 95 per cent are still alive.

The problem of selecting for the curriculum of the elementary school a little knowledge of most worth is akin to selecting the best handful of straw from a thousand silos filled with straw. The task defies human powers of discrimination. In many curricular practices, however, we continue to act as though this task already had been accomplished and that what is of most worth not only can be identified but already is laid out for pupil consumption.

The "sacred cow" approach to the curriculum creates a formidable dilemma for the teacher. No matter how carefully curriculum guides state that topics are merely suggestive, traditional grade mindedness fosters pressure to cover: so much by Halloween, so much more by Thanksgiving, half the year's work by Christmas. Soon, admonitions to use the interest of the children and persistent problems of living as organizing centers for learning become mere slogans. How does one *cover* the work perceived to be prescribed *and* use opportunities for learning and teaching that arise in class?

In the good school, processes of inquiry are developed through organizing instruction around relatively constant threads or elements: concepts, skills or values. The behaviors sought and elements defined suggest the range of learning opportunities to be offered. They do not prescribe specific topics "to be covered" by all. Thus, in the social studies, a teacher will be relatively untroubled about whether to teach Egypt, Switzerland or neither in the fifth grade. Instead, he will be very concerned about whether a selected procedure and topic offer opportunity for students to develop insight into the differences in problems of human living encountered where and when one lives. The specific means employed to develop such insight will vary from teacher to teacher and school to school according to the needs, interests and abilities of the children involved. But the kinds of understanding deemed worthy of development in education will be reasonably similar from place to place.

The organizing *elements* or threads around which instruction is to be woven will remain relatively constant. After all, basic geographic principles are not changed by the creation of new capital cities or the revision of boundary lines separating countries. Our understanding of patterns of acculturation and of historical method change relatively slowly, in spite of the rapid expansion of knowledge. The organizing *centers* used in developing these threads will vary according to the creativity of the individual in working with his class.

A curriculum consisting of relatively constant organizing threads and relatively variable organizing centers for instruction is virtually opposite from the situation currently prevailing. Such a concept of curriculum development must emerge, however, if teachers are not to be completely overwhelmed by the explosive accumulation of new knowledge.

What Kind of Habitat for Learning?

No Artificial Rewards ▪ Some of the most sweeping changes of the future are to come about in the classroom habitat for learning. The good school eliminates all rewards external to the learning process, extolling as central reward the satisfaction that comes from learning itself.

The superlative product of any educational enterprise is the intrinsically motivated student. The self-motivated student needs no gold stars, no candy bars, no flattery. He is challenged by the task and rewarded by the satisfactions that come from grappling successfully with it. It becomes apparent that the habitat for learning must provide challenge for all. The provision of stimuli adequately differentiated for the wide range in degree and kind of talent in the school still remains our most formidable educational challenge.

So many of the early efforts of young humans are inappropriately rewarded by bribe and adult approval that some children fail to have adequate experience with true success. Not having tasted the genuine fruits of accomplishment, they have little appetite for learning. Teachers who hand out prizes for classroom behavior cheat their pupils by depriving them from learning what intellectual inquiry is all about.

Reduction of Anxiety ▪ The good school reduces anxiety in learners by deliberately screening out many of the pressures seeking to intrude from the outside world. We have tended to make too much of the virtues of education that is lifelike. For many students, schooling should be anything but like their life outside of school.

School should not be a constant reminder of the squalid, fear-ridden existence many young people experience outside of school. Instead, school should help the child catch a glimpse of personal potentialities not previously perceived, personal potentialities that often defy identification in the home environment.

School must not perpetuate the inequalities of society represented in the home [1]. Instead it must provide the opportunity for a fresh start. For some children, this fresh start must be provided each day until they come to realize that the behavior demanded of them out of school is not to be held against them in school. And, in time, under proper guidance, the behavior acquired in school will come to guide more and more of their behavior out of school. If education must be forever lifelike, our schools will never do more than mirror life around them, the best undifferentiated from the worst.

Schools must serve to counter-balance much of society in providing for the most as well as the least gifted learners. Many of our intellectually gifted children fail to perform at levels anticipated for them. Some educators and psychologists fear that the lives of children are so cluttered with activity after activity that their energies are frittered away. They have no time to think, no energy for creativity [2]. Many such children become anxious over failure to come up to their expectations for themselves.

Instead of pressuring these young people into more and more effort, higher and higher accomplishment, perhaps the school should provide a change of pace. There should be time for reflection, encouragement to envision a new approach, and virtually unlimited opportunity to pursue special interests. We seem to assume that high level learning, like a straight line, is the shortest distance between two points. Very often true learning is the winding, twisting, meandering route to the other side of the problem where it can be viewed afresh. Anxious, troubled children who are reminded by school of the things that trouble them are not likely to take the creative route.

Interest Centers, Electronic Aids and Self-Propelled Learning ▪ The good school provides an assortment of "interest centers" inside and outside the classroom, arranged in such a way that they do not satisfy children's interest but cause them, rather, to ask "why" about many things that may not have concerned them previously. To an increasing degree, these interest centers will be found outside of the classroom as industries and community agencies assume responsibility for challenging the inquiring minds of young people. In addition, however, intellectual challenge will be brought into the classroom through itinerant art displays, television programs and a host of electronic devices.

Among electronic devices, teaching machines and tapes will offer opportunity for individual exploration. Teaching machines make it possible for young people to practice skill and concept development without the need for teacher supervision and without the danger of repeating errors to the point where considerable unlearning of incorrect responses is required. Tapes on a variety of topics provide opportunity for children to follow personal interests quite apart from the progress of classmates.

Increased use of electronic aids poses the need for a new kind of classroom divided not into a single rectangle of perhaps one thousand square feet but subdivided, rather, into a number of cubicles and small conference rooms [3]. The partitions separating these cubicles will be collapsible and movable so that rooms of various sizes may be created at will. Is it not exciting to visualize the classroom of tomorrow separated into perhaps a half-dozen or so smaller units each containing a pupil or small group of students busily pursuing their respective learning interests? The teacher in such a situation assumes the role of coordinator and resource person, busily anticipating learning demands and providing for them through many media.

In the school of tomorrow, children will be largely self-directing, following individually and in small groups a variety of significant educational ends.

What Patterns of School and Classroom Organization?

The teacher-per-class-per-grade concept of classroom organization we now know will disappear. The good school is uninterrupted in its vertical organization by the lock-step of grade levels. In my judgment, the differentiated rates of progress called for in meeting the individual differences encompassed by the school can be achieved adequately only in a nongraded school. In such a school, the words "promotion" and "nonpromotion" disappear simply because there is no longer any practice to which to apply them.

Increasingly, in the future, we will come to see that certain principles underlying the self-contained classroom are applicable in a learning environment where children have contact with several teachers rather than one. There is no research to tell us how long learners should remain with a single teacher in order to achieve the security deemed desirable by educators and psychologists. Youngsters manage to live quite successfully with two adults — a mother and a father — from the time they are born.

There is no good reason for assuming that they can't live equally success-fully with two or more adults in the school environment as well. There-fore, in the future, teachers often will work in small teams representing the minimum range of special competencies needed for guiding the learn-ing of much larger families of children than now make up our self-con-tained elementary-school classrooms. But for these larger families to re-ceive instruction together as a unit will be the exception rather than the rule. They will be divided into a number of subgroups as suggested above, each group drawing upon appropriate resources that include one or more teachers. Teaching teams will include student teachers, teacher aides, and secretarial assistants to a degree not possible under our present system of classroom organization.

Very often, students in the school of the future will be grouped accord-ing to a process of self-selection, with groups forming after rather than before determination of the tasks to be accomplished. They most certainly will not be grouped according to any single criterion (such as I.Q.) ap-plied to *all* children.

The school of the future, then, will be organized so as to provide con-tinuous, individual, vertical progress for each pupil. And it will be organ-ized horizontally so as to break down class-to-class barriers in gaining in-structional resources beyond anything that can be provided by a single teacher working in an isolated cell.

How Educate Our Teachers?

The good teacher education program is conducted as a cooperative venture of the highest order embracing many departments of the college or university and the profession itself, as represented by participating schools. The department of education becomes only one of several con-tributing to the prospective teacher's education.

Increasingly in the future, prospective teachers will become involved with learners and their learning almost from the moment of entry into the teacher preparing program. The primary responsibility of the teacher edu-cation institution will be to assist the teachers-to-be in making a prelimi-nary synthesis of those understandings basic to professional decision-making.

The preservice program will be regarded by all concerned merely as a beginning, not a completion of teacher education. The beginning teacher will engage in a residency period on-the-job, ultimately three years in length. There will be some college supervision of this work but direction will be primarily the responsibility of competent teachers in the cooperat-ing schools. These teachers will be responsible for doing everything possible to assure success for the neophyte. At the end of the three-year period, the successful "resident" will be ceremoniously inducted into the profession with all the "rights, privileges and responsibilities thereto appertaining." Normally, too, he will be granted the Master of Arts in Teaching degree indicating that he has now effected in practice a synthesis of knowledge and skills essential to teaching. He will now qualify, too, for a salary equivalent to ten years of service today in our better communities.

The teacher education program described here offers some promise that the vast majority of educational decisions ultimately will be based on scientific facts and principles — a body of professional lore. Only then will we have a true profession of teaching.

In Conclusion

Many persons looking ahead sound a note of despair over the apparent decline of the family as an educative agency. I take a quite different view. In my judgment, the home and family will rise in educational influence.

Most of us live phrenetic lives in a fast-moving age. Our homes, be they suburban split-levels or urban apartments, increasingly offer sanctuary. Into them can come, with little judgment on our part, the richest cultural offerings of listening and seeing the world has ever known. Into them, too, could come and will come, via electronics, lessons for all so programed that opportunity for continuous study of the world's rapidly accumulating knowledge will be as close as a teaching machine. Such machines, like television and hi-fi sets, will be inexpensively accessible to all.

The aim of public education, as initially stated in this paper, increasingly will be to teach young people to learn; that is to develop the learning skills and attitudes essential to self-propelled education. It is conceivable that virtually all young people could learn these skills and acquire these attitudes during the period of instruction termed childhood education. But then, everyone — children and parents alike — will have the identical problem of keeping reasonably up to date in a world of exploding knowledge. Is it not conceivable, then, that entire families might devote several hours a day in the sanctuary of their homes, enjoying the best of man's cultural products and grappling with man's newest inventions and discoveries? It seems reasonable to expect, too, that they might discuss together their adventures of the mind, testing perceptions and weighing conclusions.

Yes, it is not fantastic to conceive of families being drawn together in a common endeavor long ago conceived by philosophers to be a rightful aim for man: the worthy use of leisure through cultivation of the mind.

REFERENCES

1. Bruno Bettelheim. "Segregation: New Style," *School Review* (Autumn 1958, pp. 251–272.
2. Ernest A. Haggard. "Socialization, Personality, and Academic Achievement in Gifted Children," *School Review*, vol. 65 (Winter 1957), pp. 388–414.
3. Francis S. Chase. "The Schools I Hope to See," *NEA Journal*, vol. 46, No. 3 (March 1957), pp. 167–168.

MEETING CHILDREN WHERE THEY ARE

The University Elementary School of the University of California, Los Angeles, is a nongraded school. Children normally enter before the age of four and move upward through their twelfth year without encountering the grade levels so characteristic of our educational system. They are not promoted from grade to grade; nor do they repeat grades. There are no grades.

This school stands with a small but growing company of schools now abandoning the grade labels — grades one, four, seven, or eleven — in favor of what educators call a continuous progress plan. Nobody knows for sure how many of our 85,000 public elementary schools and 24,000 public secondary schools are nongraded. Most school systems have at least considered the idea for their elementary schools, but actual implementation in more than 5 per cent probably is a generous estimate. And the few high schools claiming nongrading are conspicuous because of their rarity.

These nongraded schools are not alike, any more than graded schools are alike. The educators responsible for them are not agreed on what nongrading is or could be. But these schools all have one feature in common: the grade labels have been removed from a substantial portion of the school. University Elementary School at UCLA is a completely gradeless school.

There is no magic in the removal of grade labels. If this is all that takes place, we have the same old school under a new name and a fraud has

source: *Saturday Review* (March 20, 1965), pp. 57–59, 72–74. Reprinted by permission of the publisher.

been perpetrated. There are fads in education as in everything else. Not to be caught up nowadays in nongrading, team teaching, programed instruction, or educational television is to be regarded in some educational circles as to be woefully out of touch. Consequently, there are those administrators who have merely removed the labels and then declared a nongraded school to be in existence. Others have replaced three or four grade levels with twelve or more rigidly arbitrary achievement levels. Fortunately, some schools are being redesigned in a much more fundamental way.

There is ample evidence to suggest that elements of nongrading appeared in nineteenth-century European and American schooling. In fact, any tutor-to-pupil teaching relationship devoid of grade norms and grade standards has a certain kinship with nongrading. The one-room school has been erroneously proclaimed as the prototype of the modern nongraded school. Actually, such schools more often than not were rigidly graded, the promoted child moving into a new row of seats and the nonpromoted one staying where he had been the previous year — even when child and seat no longer fit! And orders came down from on high to rank the children by grade on a normal curve. Try that one on five children in the first grade, three in the second, two in the third, four in the fourth, and so on up to ten in the eighth, as the writer was expected to do a quarter of a century ago.

The one-room, strictly graded school may very well have sharpened the need for something different. It certainly did for me. Insistence on fifty-six periods of instruction (based on an average of seven subjects for eight grades) was the height of graded folly, especially when a fourth grader's eager but unsolicited contribution to the eighth graders' geography discussion frequently was the most insightful of the lesson. Nonpromotion, promotion, and grade-skipping appeared to this neophyte teacher to be tardy treatment for a very sick system. Just how the system should be changed or what kind of new one should be designed was not at all clear to me. Elsewhere, a conception of nongrading was having its organizational beginnings, using the terms "ungraded" or "primary unit plan."

Interest faded during World War II and its aftermath but reappeared vigorously in the 1950's. The decade from 1955 to 1965 saw the firm establishment of nongrading in schools from Pacific to Atlantic oceans and from Canadian to Mexican borders, and serious discussion of the concept by educators throughout the world.

Until recently, nongrading was thought of as an organizational device for permitting youngsters to move through a common body of material at somewhat differing rates of speed, according to their individual readiness to proceed. Most thinking and most nongraded schools are geared to this conception. It is the conception with which the writer began and about which he has most written. Certainly, it represents progress from the Procrustean inflexibility and crippling consequences of fitting the child to the system. But differentiated progress through what are still essentially graded assignments represents, at best, only significant tampering with a concept of education that has been seriously questioned by educational reformers from Rousseau to Bruno Bettelheim and A. S. Neill.

Nongrading, as used and defined in the balance of this paper, is both a concept and a plan within a larger view of education embracing a few simple but nonetheless compelling principles of child development, learning, school function, and pedagogical practice.

First, children are different, much more different than we have up to now recognized. We have been shamefully remiss in taking these differences into account in our educational planning and teaching.

Second, an essential in seeking to provide intelligently for these differences is educational diagnosis of and prescription for the individual. Mass techniques and common expectations for all are inimical to these highly sensitive human processes.

Third, there must be alternatives from which to fill the prescription. A monolithic school structure providing only pass or fail as the alternatives in regulating pupil progress simply does not square with the range of alternatives necessary to coping imaginatively with human variability.

Fourth, the proper question to ask in starting a child off on his school career is not, "Is this child ready for school?" but, "What is this child ready for?" This is the most pregnant idea and is, indeed, at the heart of nongrading.

Fifth, criterion standards replace norm-based standards as the measure of pupil progress. Norm-based standards are sloppy standards geared to group performance. They tend to result in unjustified rewards for high but inadequate performance on the part of the able and relentless, punishing failure for the slow and deprived. It has been estimated that 25 per cent of children in school receive 75 per cent of the failing grades based on group standards. These children ultimately come to regard themselves as failures — not just in school but in life itself. Most of this loss to mankind could have been prevented by asking and carefully answering the question, "What is this child ready for?"

Criterion standards seek to arrange a sequence of difficulty or a meaningful progression in work assignments. Instead of pronouncing the child to be at the fourth-grade level, which tells us very little and most of that misleading, these standards seek to provide a profile of where the child is now functioning with respect to the skills and concepts comprising the sequence of learning. These are really tougher standards, each child pitting himself against the rigor of the material rather than the uncertainties of group competence and variability. Unfortunately, we are still at a relatively primitive stage in the development of these criterion measures but rapid progress is being made in projects designed to change the curricula of America's schools.

Sixth, sound learning is meaningfully cumulative. That is, the child's progression does not suffer from what psychologists call retroactive and proactive interference. A percentage problem for the child who has no conception of parts and wholes, let alone the number base on which per cent depends, contaminates his present mathematical knowledge and interferes with what follows. Such is the unhappy, cumulative product of several "bare passes" in a graded system.

The graded school was brought into being at a time when we knew little about individual differences in learning. The assumption then, in the middle of the nineteenth century, was that the content of instruction could be divided into roughly equal packages and mastered, a year at a time, by children of the same age. Soon, there came to be graded content, graded textbooks, graded children, graded teachers, and graded expectations for schooling. Graded tests and graded norms came later. The entire graded machinery was efficient in classifying the hordes of children pouring into our schools in increasing numbers throughout the balance of the nineteenth century and into the twentieth.

But the children didn't fit. Some simply could not master the work of a grade in a year; others romped through it. Good teaching raised the level throughout; poor teaching lowered it. A formidable gap between the swift and the slow remained.

Nonpromotion (grade failure) and double promotion (grade skipping) were used — and still are used — to narrow the gap within any one grade. Neither has proved effective. The nonpromoted child, repeating the grade, rarely is stimulated anew. Studies reveal that nonpromoted children generally do worse than children of like ability and past performance who are promoted to the next grade. In fact, some nonpromoted children fail to equal their own performance of the previous year on the second time around.

The answer, however, is not simply to promote the slow-learning child. Inadequate or faulty comprehension, if not checked, leads to an accumulation and compounding of inadequacy. Promotion and nonpromotion are the ineffective adjustment mechanisms of the graded system. The answer appears to be to transform or replace the system.

The nongraded school is one replacement for the graded system. It is not simply a corrective mechanism. The component parts of grading and nongrading are not interchangeable. The two systems are built on differing assumptions, arouse differing expectations, and demand differing teacher behavior. They require differing language for their description and interpretation but, unfortunately, a language of nongrading has not yet developed. We are forced to think and talk about nongrading using the terms characteristic of grading and, as a consequence, we never quite escape gradedness.

Let us not abandon the graded school out of hand. There is little danger in our time! Let us, instead, create alternatives. There can be no meaningful comparisons of what we now have without alternatives. Let us not create alternatives capriciously, however. Let us instead build alternatives which can be argued vigorously from supporting data.

The facts of individual differences among learners support the nongraded alternative. Children coming into the first grade at the age of six differ by as much as four years in the mental maturity factor considered so essential to their success in today's schools. This spread increases as they move upward through the third, sixth, and tenth grades.

See how easy it is to communicate with this word, "grade." We all know what it means. But do we, really? The members of a fourth-grade class are physically *in* the fourth grade. But resemblance between the children and our expectancies for the fourth grade virtually ends there. Our error lies in trying to squeeze varying learners into this graded expectancy.

The usual fourth-grade class contains children achieving at second, third, fourth, fifth, and sixth grades in some aspects of their school work — and even occasionally above and below these levels. The average spread in achievement is four years. In a fifth-grade class it is five; in a sixth, six years in tested achievement, and so on. These are not fourth or fifth or sixth grades except in name. They are composites of many grades, each graded class overlapping graded classes above and below. In a field like reading, the picture is even more startling. Children in a fifth-grade class commonly range in reading from the second or third to the ninth or tenth.

The commonsense protest here is that, given ideal school conditions, these slow pupils could be pulled up substantially. True, but given equally ideal conditions for the able, they too would move up beyond these performances.

A commonsense solution to managing this vast range of attainments, frequently posed by lay critics of the schools, is to group those of like achievement in a single class. (The term used often but incorrectly for this achievement grouping is ability grouping.) But some additional evidence gives us pause. The variability in attainments within one child sometimes parallels the variability in an entire class. A child, like a class, is not a second, fourth, or sixth grader. Johnny can be in the fifth grade for arithmetic computation, the sixth for arithmetic reasoning, the seventh for spelling, the eighth for word meaning, the ninth for paragraph meaning, and the tenth for language — and yet be officially registered in the sixth grade. In the same class is Jean, whose scores range from low third to high seventh; Bill, from high second to high fifth; and Pat, from fourth to tenth. (These figures, incidentally, are taken from actual class roles.) Children are downright ornery. They refuse to grow up all of a piece.

Under a plan of grouping for likeness in achievement, Johnny, Jean, Bill, and Pat would join a new group for each subject and rarely would be together in the same groups. Their class groups, to be closely homogeneous (that is, comparable in attainment), would be composed of children from throughout the building, brought together because of their assumed readiness for identical learnings. A monstrous scheduling problem is involved. This can readily be managed through modern computer techniques.

The main problem is not logistics. Three other matters come in for attention: the composition of the class groups brought together in this fashion, the degree of homogeneity actually produced, and the accomplishments of students in such groups.

Strange partners often come together. Is a class made up of pupils ranging from seven to twelve years of age but alike in reading attainment a teachable reading group? Are the same materials for all likely to be appropriate? The answer to both questions, of course, is no. A new and at least equally perplexing problem of dealing with individual differences has been created. This is a caricature, admittedly, but it serves to sharpen the fact that grouping children for likeness in one trait creates groups of vast differences in most other traits.

Still another problem arises from the fact that students grouped for likeness on a trait are not alike on subelements of that trait. When two things look alike, this usually means that the viewer is not looking deeply or carefully enough. Children grouped for likeness in reading achievement, for example, usually have comparable test scores representing a combination of paragraph meaning and word recognition. But when one examines these children for six or eight separate factors involved in reading, he discovers that these "homogeneously" grouped youngsters are really very different in each of them. The grouping pattern performs a disservice because it lulls the teachers into proceeding as though the group were one when in reality it is markedly diverse on the components which must be provided for in the productive teaching of reading. Patterns of school organization should reveal not hide human variability.

Presumably, students of like ability are brought together to enhance their learning. The evidence is not convincing. Studies in England, Sweden, and the United States show no significant advantages in achievement for homogeneous groups over mixed or heterogeneous groups. The findings in any given study are either inconclusive or, if statistically significant, are offset by another study concluding the exact opposite. Grouping of any kind is productive only when designed to serve a specific purpose and when accompanied by special provisions of an intimate and highly individualized sort.

The potentiality of complex grouping patterns fades and the crucial significance of individualizing instruction looms large. An important clue for redesigning American education falls out. Needed is a system of such flexibility and responsiveness that it is scarcely a system at all. Such a system must reveal individuality, not disguise or obscure it. Once revealed, human variability most assuredly will demand alternatives.

Grades obscure individuality. To strip away the grades hiding individuality is to create a promising opportunity to deal with that individuality. To go beyond the removal of grades to diagnosis and prescription for the fostering of human variability and potentiality and then to the filling of prescriptions from a wide range of viable alternatives is, among other things, to bring into being a nongraded school. The nongraded school is but a part, albeit a significant one, of the total educational system needed for the identification and proper nurturing of precious, individual, human talent.

It is more meaningful now to talk specifically about one nongraded school than to talk in general about the alternatives in content, grouping, pedagogy, and expectations for children available through nongrading. In 1960, UCLA's University Elementary School consisted of seventeen graded rooms: three nursery school, two kindergarten, and two of each subsequent grade through the sixth. Each was largely self-contained; that is, teachers worked alone in providing the daily diet of reading, arithmetic, language arts, social studies, and science but called upon help as desired for art, music, health, and physical education.

Five years later, University Elementary School consisted of nine nongraded clusters of children and teachers, each cluster ranging in size from as few as 25 to as many as 75 children, each child assigned to one of these clusters and, subsequently, to subclusters within these larger ones, on the basis of diagnosis and prescription. Instead of the alternatives being pass or fail, the alternatives are several in number, no one of which is grade repetition or skipping. The clusters were different in number and organization last year; they will be different again next year. The school evolves as the staff clarifies beliefs and subjects them to test.

Most clusters are staffed by teams of full-time and part-time teachers. This team teaching has facilitated the inclusion of part-time personnel, some of them students in the University, in a way that was not possible five years ago. Although the budget is only slightly larger, because of normal salary increases, fifty per cent more people are on the payroll. Not all teachers are in teams. Some maintain about the same pattern of self-sufficiency that existed throughout the school five years ago. Teachers, too, are individuals and deserve alternatives.

Team teaching is not essential to nongrading. There are nongraded schools with self-contained classrooms and team-taught schools with grade levels. But team teaching as a way of clustering children and teachers fits nicely with nongrading as a way of guiding students upward through the school. They are compatible, flexible patterns of school and classroom organization which provide a useful array of alternatives for dealing with pupil variability. Since University Elementary School developed both at about the same time, the two are almost indistinguishably interwoven in practice and, consequently, in this description.

Let no one think that change comes naturally to a laboratory school, especially if its primary function has been demonstration. Such a school is in the public eye. To change what has long been demonstrated and from which have come success and recognition is to suggest that the practices being replaced were never good when, in reality, they may have been first-rate for their time. Further, time for planning change is hard to come by. In a laboratory school, the work load of teaching children, advising future teachers, assisting many University faculty members in the conduct of their research, demonstrating various procedures, and interpreting programs to endless streams of visitors is almost unbelievably demanding. To effect basic changes while keeping the ship afloat is an unsettling experience.

The route from yesterday to today was often a tortuous one. It included changing the function of this laboratory school from demonstration to inquiry, innovation, experimentation, and research in schooling. It began with two aspects of teacher dissatisfaction which were traced to a common source. First, class membership remained rather constant from year to year, as is typical in a graded school. Consequently, children were always the oldest or youngest and rather consistently followers or leaders. They had little opportunity to shift roles and explore new relationships. Second, certain learning ills persisted for some children into the upper elementary years. The problem was less pronounced than in most schools, but it was particularly frustrating for these teachers because the school was highly regarded for its instruction, and rightfully so. Teachers did everything possible within the graded organization characteristic of schools generally but often were unable to overcome what appeared to be unfortunate but irrevocable pupil placements. The placement adjustment for inadequate learning appeared to be retention and grade repetition, a solution which these teachers regarded as disagreeable and noncorrective.

They were boxed in by the graded system, a system which they had often stretched to the near-breaking point but always was retained. It is unwise to break away from long-established practice when no reasonably clear alternative is in sight.

The search for an acceptable alternative led to better understanding of what was hidden by the graded structure, the fact that the seventeen classrooms were graded in name but not in pupils' attainment. The graded structure now looked less sacred and inviolable than it had before. Some teachers who had read or otherwise learned about nongrading wanted to abolish the graded system then and there. This decision was not to come for another year.

By collapsing the next three years, we come to the present. The school is now viewed as having three broad levels of function and expectations, each successive level overlapping the previous one both in function and expectations and in the age of children assigned to it.

The early childhood level enrolls children from under four to over six. The primary function is to develop a sturdy, wholesome self-concept. Children are expected to interact productively and satisfyingly with the children, adults, and things of their daily environment. Teachers are there to assist them in working at these relationships. Concern for this wholesome self-concept carries over into the lower elementary level where diagnosis and prescription for needs in this area continue. But now the central function becomes progressive development in the fundamental skills of self-directed learning, especially reading. The age spread is now from six to eight or nine, but age is not a primary factor in placement. The upper elementary level of function normally embraces children from eight or nine to eleven or twelve years of age. Again, attention to wholesome self-development continues, particularly as it relates to inadequate learning skills demanding special attention. The central goal now, however, is to develop the ability to understand and use man's approaches to studying social and natural phenomena. Hopefully, children will leave the school with a desire to continue learning and considerable self-directing proficiency in it.

These three levels of function are not organizational units of the school, although at one point in the school's recent evolution they were. The nine broad clusters of children are not evenly distributed among them. One cluster, for example, enrolling 65 children from age seven to age eleven, obviously cuts across both lower and upper elementary levels, reaching toward the bottom of the former, and well up in the latter. The three-levels concept of function underlying University Elementary School simply emphasizes that the function of elementary education is not unitary throughout but, rather, shifts in emphasis from the early childhood to the early adolescent years.

Each cluster of children, whether large or small, whether team-taught or self-contained, has a wide spread in age. For example, a cluster entirely within the lower elementary level might contain children of age six, seven, and eight. Another conceived to be entirely within this same lower elementary level of function might contain children from seven to nine. One cutting across lower and upper elementary conceptions of function might spread from age seven to twelve.

This system of school organization virtually forces teachers to recognize and provide for individual differences. Several ages together serve as a blinking light reminding teachers that the students are not all alike. A single age group could lull them into forgetting the wide range of differences actually residing in it. With a little care, a mixed age group can be put together so that the overall individual differences are little or no greater than in a single age group. But experience suggests that the revelation of one kind of difference — namely, in age — creates pressure to deal with differences generally.

The learning environment in a cluster of children provides a wide range of activities appropriate to the functions involved. A cluster of forty children from age four though six, for example, shares two rooms which formerly were separate classrooms but which have now been merged by knocking out part of an intervening wall. It is not unusual for them to share other indoor spaces with neighboring clusters and the simultaneous sharing of outdoor spaces is standard practice. The skilled observer would see a certain rhythm to the daily activities. At a given moment, a subgroup is talking about a walk from which the children has just returned; another is busily engaged in a variety of jumping and balancing activities; another is sitting at a table with reading materials; and little clusters of two and three are deeply involved in still other tasks. What one child is doing now, another will be doing an hour from now. The range and variety are in part possible because, in expanding total cluster size, additional personnel also are added.

Each of the tasks mentioned above is believed to be a prelude to or part of reading. Each child is working at a point thought to be appropriate for him and, most of the time, selected by him. Progression through such tasks is far from ordered, partly because some of them are parallel rather than sequential and partly because research has not yet defined the most productive sequences. Further, a productive sequence for one child usually only partly overlaps a productive sequence for another. Individual diagnosis and prescription are essential. The child is not incapable of self-diagnosis and prescription, especially if the range of alternatives is broad, visible, and attractive and he is helped to see what these alternatives are designed to accomplish.

Progress through any sequence is only very loosely related to age. The number of years a human being has lived is a poor yardstick for determining what he is ready to learn. Each of the subgroups above contained fours, fives, and sixes, for whom the task at hand was appropriate. The subgroups assembled for the next tasks of the day also would contain this age distribution but the children comprising the group would not be entirely the same. Here we see sharply revealed a key difference between grading and nongrading. The graded school is geared rather closely to age and to arbitrary provision of what children of that age (and grade) are to learn. The nongraded school is geared to readiness to learn which, in turn, is determined from continuing diagnosis.

Another key difference is flexibility in expectations for children. The graded school presents a series of graded expectations. Contrary to much popular opinion, these are not rigorous expectations for all. But they are unfair. As pointed out earlier, they punish the weak and fail to challenge the strong.

University Elementary School provides a broad range of expectations — broad enough to reach from the floor to the ceiling of individual attainment — within each level of function. A child is not expected to reach a set level of reading by the age of six. Nor is he retained in an early childhood cluster of children until he does. But he will have engaged in activities considered basic to reading — many of which, unfortunately, are not seen by the layman as designed to prepare the child to read — as well as in many other kinds of learnings. On moving to join older clusters of children, where these children will now be the youngest rather than the oldest, some will be among the most proficient readers in the new environment, some among the slowest. New groupings for reading will occur to take these individual differences into account. Staff and resources are now geared to make special provision for reading, with a range of expectations far in excess of those normally assumed under the label, "grade."

A child does not just grow into readiness for learning. Nor does he profit much from being indiscriminantly watered and cultivated. A child is a human being, not a tree, and, capable, therefore, of making choices. The developing person, in contrast to one merely growing older, is a person learning to choose wisely from a steadily enlarging smorgasbord of alternatives. In time, he becomes known as an educated man. Regrettably, the much-schooled man is not always an educated man.

A child in University Elementary School seldom remains less than a year or more than three years with a cluster of children and teachers, depending on the size of that cluster, the age spread in it, and the diagnosis of that child. In principle, a child is moved whenever placement in another cluster appears to be desirable. In practice, however, every effort is made to keep a child in a cluster of children for at least a year, on the assumption that this continuity contributes to his sense of identity in a world of increasing anonymity. A child in a cluster for three years will have seen children come and go each year, will have a long-term continuing relationship with some of these children and with several teachers, and will have enjoyed the experience of being at first one of the youngest and then one of the oldest members of the group.

Placement for each subsequent year grows out of a series of meetings taking place in the spring of each year. There are total faculty meetings in which general policies are reiterated and refined. There are single cluster meetings in which teachers who have been closely associated with these children, sometimes for as long as three years, pool data and observations concerning each child. There are cross-cluster conferences in which children likely to be assigned to one of several possible alternative clusters are discussed in relation to the teachers and to the expectations of each cluster. The data come from many sources but particularly from children's present teachers, from parents, from the school principal, and from the children themselves.

At no time is there a squaring of each child's performance with a predetermined set of common expectancies for all four-year-olds or all nine-year-olds. Criteria are derived from the functions of the level of schooling; adequacy from a study of the child's performance over a long period of time. These are decisions for teachers to make, teachers who are close to the data. The principal participates as a member of the team, not as a final arbiter "passing" on each decision.

When the decision is to move a child from his present placement to a new one, the question is, "Which alternative?" In a carefully organized nongraded school, there should be a minimum of three alternatives from which to choose. Each of these alternatives will differ in several strategic ways, the most significant of which is the differences among the teachers. It is the responsibility of the total staff, with the principal's guidance, to determine just how these alternatives will differ: in anticipated learning activities, in the teachers to be in charge, in group size, and in actual group membership. All of these can be and should be manipulated in seeking to set up productive clusters of teachers and children for each subsequent year. Consequently, at University Elementary School, final placements of children are held up until the composition of each tentative cluster has been carefully examined. Frequently, on the basis of this examination, clusters initially proposed are modified through reassigning children.

Teachers find this process to be excruciatingly difficult at first. They must consider much more than the relatively simple alternatives of to promote or not to promote. They need to know a great deal about the children with whom they have been working — parental expectations and their effects, peer group associations, feelings of success and failure, ability to tolerate restrictions or permissiveness, and so on — and about their colleagues. They are uncertain about the criteria to use, largely because, as a total staff or as subgroups of that staff, they have not previously discussed the matter. And, to their surprise and frustration, they usually discover that they possess far too little useful information about the children with whom they have been working. In brief, they are confronted with a new and highly challenging professional task and, understandably, can be somewhat unnerved by it.

Supported and encouraged, however, most teachers learn the behavior required and practice it with growing satisfaction. At University Elementary School, the second round of spring meetings was a marked improvement over the first. Teachers came armed with data and hammered out the criteria in the process of making pupil placements. The third round was strikingly professional. But now a new kind of frustration emerged. The teachers wanted data going beyond their own observations, sensitive test data in all areas of child development — data derived from criterion measures, not norm-based data general to group and graded standards. Such data are conspicuously absent in education. To create a demand for them is to speed their coming. Nongraded schools, of the type conceived here, create this demand.

Needed in a nongraded school is a person knowledgeable in both education and the information sciences. He might well be the guidance counselor. His job is to set up a system for the collection, organization, storage, and retrieval of data designed to assist teachers in their vital decisions of diagnosis and prescription. He must join the teachers in these processes, learning more about them, bringing data to bear, and refining the information processing system as needed. The necessity for collecting masses of data, for maintaining them over long periods of time, for assembling them in many different ways, and for quick retrieval suggests the potentiality of a computer serving several schools or school systems simultaneously. Computers are now being used experimentally for similar purposes in research projects scattered across the country.

Complex? Yes, at first, simply because these are not familiar modes of thought to most people. It is not easy to escape more than a century of gradedness. The early phases of comprehending nongradedness are something like a first experience with English money. One is forever trying to translate pence, shillings, and pounds into cents, quarters, and dollars (and those half-crowns are maddening!). Or, perhaps better, it is comparable to the way most of us struggle initially and awkwardly with a foreign language. We sought to translate French literally into English rather than to think and to communicate in French. What a revelation it was when the intervening translation disappeared and we found ourselves thinking, reading, and speaking French!

Similarly, we must come to think in nongraded terms before the potentialities of this redefined and redesigned school open up. To translate nongrading into graded nomenclature is to stay within the limited possibilities of yesterday's schools. Until fully functioning nongraded models have been carefully developed, meaningful discourse about and comparisons of nongrading and grading will be impossible. But even with models of both standing side by side, experimental comparison will be difficult and, for persons holding differing conceptions of education, probably impossible. For grading and nongrading are fundamentally differing expressions of schooling, based on fundamentally differing conceptions of what schools are for and of how learners should progress in them. Ask not if this child is ready for school but what this child is ready for.

University Elementary School is still becoming. The promise of the future far outstrips the accomplishments of the past. Several years have now elapsed since the faculty committed itself to nongrading and jokingly promised to fine its members for each use of the word, "graded." The school is not yet fully nongraded; it never will be. For, as quickly as one goal is attained, others come into view. As former Chancellor Lawrence Kimpton once said about the University of Chicago over which he presided, "This probably isn't a very good place for the pursuit of happiness, but it's a wonderful place to find happiness in pursuit."

C D E F G H I J 7 0 6 9 8

THIS BOOK WAS SET IN
CALEDONIA AND BULMER TYPEFACES
BY THE PLIMPTON PRESS.
IT WAS DESIGNED BY THE STAFF OF
BLAISDELL PUBLISHING COMPANY.

LB2806 .G58   010101 000

Goodlad, John I.

School, curriculum, and the in

0 2002 0067195 2

YORK COLLEGE OF PENNSYLVANIA 17403

69750

LB
2806   GOODLAD
.G58   SCHOOL, CURRICULUM,
          AND THE INDIVIDUAL

DISCARDED

27